FACULTY WRITING SUPPORT: EMERGING RESEARCH FROM RHETORIC AND COMPOSITION STUDIES

PERSPECTIVES ON WRITING
Series Editors: Rich Rice and J. Michael Rifenburg
Consulting Editor: Susan H. McLeod
Associate Editors: Johanna Phelps, Jonathan M. Marine, and Qingyang Sun

The Perspectives on Writing series addresses writing studies in a broad sense. Consistent with the wide ranging approaches characteristic of teaching and scholarship in writing across the curriculum, the series presents works that take divergent perspectives on working as a writer, teaching writing, administering writing programs, and studying writing in its various forms.

The WAC Clearinghouse and University Press of Colorado are collaborating so that these books will be widely available through free digital distribution and low-cost print editions. The publishers and the series editors are committed to the principle that knowledge should freely circulate and have embraced the use of technology to support open access to scholarly work.

Recent Books in the Series

Jenn Fishman, Romeo García, and Lauren Rosenberg (Eds.), *Community Listening: Stories, Hauntings, Possibilities* (2025)

Steven J. Corbett (Ed.), *If at First You Don't Succeed? Writing, Rhetoric, and the Question of Failure* (2024)

Ryan J. Dippre and Talinn Phillips (Eds.), *Improvisations: Methods and Methodologies in Lifespan Writing Research* (2024)

Ashley J. Holmes and Elise Verzosa Hurley (Eds.), *Learning from the Mess: Method/ological Praxis in Rhetoric and Writing Studies* (2024)

Diane Kelly-Riley, Ti Macklin, and Carl Whithaus (Eds.), *Considering Students, Teachers, and Writing Assessment: Volumes 1 and 2* (2024)

Amy Cicchino and Troy Hicks (Eds.), *Better Practices: Exploring the Teaching of Writing in Online and Hybrid Spaces* (2024)

Genesea M. Carter and Aurora Matzke (Eds.), *Systems Shift: Creating and Navigating Change in Rhetoric and Composition Administration* (2023)

Michael J. Michaud, *A Writer Reforms (the Teaching of) Writing: Donald Murray and the Writing Process Movement, 1963–1987* (2023)

Michelle LaFrance and Melissa Nicolas (Eds.), *Institutional Ethnography as Writing Studies Practice* (2023)

Phoebe Jackson and Christopher Weaver (Eds.), *Rethinking Peer Review: Critical Reflections on a Pedagogical Practice* (2023)

FACULTY WRITING SUPPORT: EMERGING RESEARCH FROM RHETORIC AND COMPOSITION STUDIES

Edited by Jaclyn Wells, Lars Söderlund, and Christine Tulley

The WAC Clearinghouse
wac.colostate.edu
Fort Collins, Colorado

University Press of Colorado
upcolorado.com
Denver, Colorado

The WAC Clearinghouse, Fort Collins, Colorado 80524

University Press of Colorado, Denver, Colorado 80203

© 2025 by Jaclyn Wells, Lars Söderlund, and Christine Tulley. This work is licensed under a Creative Commons Attribution-NonCommercial-NoDerivatives 4.0 International license.

ISBN 978-1-64215-255-5 (PDF) 978-1-64215-256-2 (ePub) 978-1-64642-770-3 (pbk.)

DOI 10.37514/PER-B.2025.2555

Produced in the United States of America

Library of Congress Cataloging-in-Publication Data

Names: Wells, Jaclyn M. editor | Söderlund, Lars, 1984– editor | Tulley, Christine editor
Title: Faculty writing support : emerging research from rhetoric and composition studies / edited by Jaclyn Wells, Lars Söderlund, and Christine Tulley
Description: Fort Collins, Colorado : The WAC Clearinghouse, 2025. | Series: Perspectives on writing | Includes bibliographical references.
Identifiers: LCCN 2025016641 (print) | LCCN 2025016642 (ebook) | ISBN 9781646427703 paperback | ISBN 9781642152555 adobe pdf | ISBN 9781642152562 epub
Subjects: LCSH: Academic writing—Study and teaching (Higher) | English language—Rhetoric—Study and teaching (Higher) | LCGFT: Essays
Classification: LCC P301.5.A27 F33 2025 (print) | LCC P301.5.A27 (ebook)
LC record available at https://lccn.loc.gov/2025016641
LC ebook record available at https://lccn.loc.gov/2025016642

Copyeditor: Mike Palmquist
Designer: Mike Palmquist
Cover Photo: RawPixel Image 15631298. Licensed.
Series Editors: Rich Rice and J. Michael Rifenburg
Consulting Editor: Susan H. McLeod
Associate Editors: Johanna Phelps, Jonathan M. Marine, and Qingyang Sun

The WAC Clearinghouse supports teachers of writing across the disciplines. Hosted by Colorado State University, it brings together scholarly journals and book series as well as resources for teachers who use writing in their courses. This book is available in digital formats for free download at wac.colostate.edu.

Founded in 1965, the University Press of Colorado is a nonprofit cooperative publishing enterprise supported, in part, by Adams State University, Colorado School of Mines, Colorado State University, Fort Lewis College, Metropolitan State University of Denver, University of Alaska Fairbanks, University of Colorado, University of Denver, University of Northern Colorado, University of Wyoming, Utah State University, and Western Colorado University. For more information, visit upcolorado.com.

Citation Information: Wells, Jaclyn, Lars Söderlund & Christine Tulley (Eds.). (2025). *Faculty Writing Support: Emerging Research from Rhetoric and Composition Studies.* The WAC Clearinghouse; University Press of Colorado. https://doi.org/1010.37514/PER-B.2025.2555

Land Acknowledgment. The Colorado State University Land Acknowledgment can be found at landacknowledgment.colostate.edu.

CONTENTS

Acknowledgments vii

Introduction. 3
    Christine Tulley

PART 1. HOW FACULTY WRITE 15

Chapter 1. Planning, Tinkering, and Writing to Learn: A Model of Planning and Discovery as Composing Styles for Professional Academic Writers. 17
    Dana Lynn Driscoll

Chapter 2. Faculty Presence, Influence, and Authority in Interdisciplinary, Multi-Level Writing Groups. 43
    Aileen R. Taft and Rebecca Day Babcock and Maximillien Vis

Chapter 3. Faculty Writers as Proximal Writers: Why Faculty Write Near Other Writers 63
    Jackie Grutsch McKinney

Chapter 4. People Keep Knocking (or, I Have Answered 50 Emails Today): Balancing Work and Research as a WPA 81
    Lars Söderlund and Jaclyn Wells

Chapter 5. Complicating Techno-Afterglow: Pursuing Compositional Equity and Making Labor Visible in Digital Scholarly Production 105
    Paul Muhlhauser and Jenna Sheffield

PART 2. HOW TO SUPPORT FACULTY WRITERS 137

Chapter 6. Writing Support for Faculty of Color 139
    Laura R. Micciche and Batsheva Guy

Chapter 7. What Professional Academic Writers Want from Writing Coaching 163
    Beth L. Hewett

Chapter 8. Intentional Institutional Support for Future Faculty: A Focus on Grant and Professional Writing 197
    Charmian Lam

Contents

Chapter 9. Moving Beyond "A Basket of Skills and a Bunch of Publications": Developing a Writerly Identity through Facilitating Faculty Writing Groups 219
    Kristin Messuri and Elizabeth Sharp

Chapter 10. Leading Faculty Writing Academies: A Case Study of Writerly Identity. 239
    J. Michael Rifenburg and Rebecca Johnston

Chapter 11. Faculty Who Write with Their Graduate Students: A Study of Non-Peer Writing Collaborations. 255
    Kristina Quynn and Carol Wilusz

Afterword. Researching and Restructuring the "Scene(s)" of Faculty Writing. 275
    Kristine Blair

Contributors 283

ACKNOWLEDGMENTS

This collection is the product of many scholars' contributions, some of whom wrote chapters and some of whom helped construct, edit, and otherwise prepare the book.

Jaci and Lars wish to thank Christine for her perseverance with the book, staying on the project during exceptionally grueling times and giving the project a shot in the arm when it was really needed. Christine wishes to thank Jaci and Lars for the organizational work and productive discussions about faculty writing over the past several years.

We editors thank all our authors: Dana Lynn Driscoll, Aileen R. Taft, Rebecca Day Babcock, Maximillien Vis, Jackie Grutsch McKinney, Paul Muhlhauser, Jenna Sheffield, Laura R. Micciche, Batsheva Guy, Beth L. Hewett, Charmian Lam, Kristin Messuri, Elizabeth Sharp, J. Michael Rifenburg, Rebecca Johnston, Kristina Quynn, and Carol Wilusz. Thank you for staying committed to the book.

We thank our editors at WAC Clearinghouse and the Perspectives on Writing book series Heather Falconer, Rich Rice, J. Michael Rifenburg (who recused himself from the book's initial consideration), Johanna Phelps, Jonathan M. Marine, and Qingyang Sun.

We thank Jim Purdy for the rounds of editing he did on the book, especially in adjusting the book for the house style at WAC Clearinghouse. Jim and the rest of the staff at Defend, Publish, and Lead were instrumental in getting the book ready to submit to WAC Clearinghouse and editing it after it was accepted.

We thank Mike Palmquist for his work designing and copy editing the book on the publishing house side.

Special thanks go to Kristine Blair who has been a supporter of the project since early times, chairing the conference session where Jaci, Lars, and Christine finally met and writing the fantastic Afterword of this book.

Jaci wishes to thank Jeff, Vivi, and Travis for all their love and support. She also wishes to acknowledge her late mom and dad, Jim and Bonnie Wells, for encouraging her interest in writing.

Christine wishes to thank her father, Hugh Sauer, for taking an interest in and supporting her faculty writing career and The University of Findlay faculty writing group for productive discussions about faculty writing needs.

Lars wishes to thank his wife Laurel Söderlund for her support during the editing of the book. He also thanks Western Oregon University for employing him during most of the book's genesis. Finally, he thanks his son Lloyd for arriving in 2022 and putting dad's work in perspective.

FACULTY WRITING SUPPORT: EMERGING RESEARCH FROM RHETORIC AND COMPOSITION STUDIES

INTRODUCTION

Christine Tulley
The University of Findlay

I first became acquainted with Jaci and Lars and their research on faculty writing practices at the annual Conference on College Composition and Communication. I was attending to present research on a forthcoming book on disciplinary writing (*How Writing Faculty Write*, 2018) and, when looking in the program for conference sessions to attend, my heart sank when I saw the title of a presentation by Jaci and Lars. Both of our nearly identically titled sessions focused specifically on interview research with faculty writers. I confided to my colleague (Kristine Blair, author of the Afterword) that I planned to check out their session and see if I had been scooped. I remember feeling intensely frustrated that someone else discovered faculty writing as a disciplinary subfield, which up until then had only attracted a very small handful of rhetoric and composition researchers. Faculty writing was an unexplored corner. At the presentation, I realized that not only did we both do early-stage interview research, but we also worked in two totally different spaces. I studied the writing practices of "rock stars" of rhetoric and composition, while Jaci and Lars surveyed authors at various levels of seniority in disciplinary publications. Due to our shared interest, we discovered that these projects prompted more questions about faculty writing. *Faculty Writing Support: Emerging Research from Rhetoric and Composition Studies* is a result of those conversations about faculty writing that the three of us have had for the past several years.

In the process of planning this collection, we realized we remain fascinated by questions about writing that historically have remained elusive: Do writing studies-trained faculty use disciplinary knowledge to support their own writing processes? Do we teach other faculty (and future faculty) writers these techniques? What small- and large-scale efforts could we use at our own universities to support graduate student writers to develop into faculty writers? What about faculty writers in other disciplines? How could we argue for these efforts using emerging disciplinary research? What methodologies are most useful for studying graduate student and faculty writing? In short, just as Jaci, Lars, and I relied on our early projects to uncover what strategies lead to success in rhetoric and composition publications, we also wanted to find out how writing studies research interventions could impact graduate student and faculty writing productivity.

DOI: https://doi.org/10.37514/PER-B.2025.2555.1.3

As a developing subdiscipline of writing studies, faculty writing has only generated sporadic interest from rhetoric and composition researchers over the years. One early look at faculty writing through the lens of writing studies that prompted my study in faculty writing was Maxine Hairston's 1986 piece in *Rhetoric Review* titled "When Writing Teachers Don't Write: Speculations about Probable Causes and Possible Cures." Drawing on personal experience as a faculty writer, Hairston describes her own reasons for not writing:

> I was convinced that I would never be able to write the book, that I would have to admit that I was a fraud and return the publisher's money. I pulled out of that spell only when I had completed the first chapter by forcing myself to stay at the typewriter every day until I had written five pages. (p. 65)

Hairston uses her personal experience to offer advice that has since been enshrined in higher education faculty development guidebooks, such as the importance of entry points and collaboration in faculty writing. I still assign this article in graduate writing courses for advice like "[procrastination] lulls are necessary for incubation or reflection" (a principle I describe in *How Writing Faculty Write*) and "writing just takes a long time" (emphasizing that developed writing is recursive and has many stages) (p. 65).

Hairston's (1986) advice is echoed frequently through popular, more recent academic writing advice guides, such as Paul Silvia's (2017) *How to Write a Lot* and Wendy Belcher's (2009) *Writing Your Journal Article in 12 Weeks*. As academic lore, these frequently reinforced faculty writing techniques serve as collective "experience that has been expressed, circulated, imitated, sustained and confirmed by repetition, achieving canonical status as 'common sense' through its range of cultural distribution and its staying power" (Phelps, 1991, p. 869). For faculty writers and those who support them, lore is often reassuring and often useful. At the same time, as Johnson (2017) notes, guidebooks and composition scholarship built on lore provide "a temptingly clear vision of the scholarly writing game" (p. 63) but a limited and often conflicting picture of faculty writing processes because they often rely on single narratives of individual faculty writers as evidence.

As our title suggests, we seek to expand development of the subfield of faculty writing by offering a first look at disciplinary grounded research interventions with faculty and advanced graduate student writers. Many calls to study faculty writing from inside writing studies exist (Johnson, 2017; Tulley, 2018; Wells & Söderlund, 2018) and a given tenet in rhetoric and composition is that writing teachers should be writers (for just a few, see Gebhardt, 1977; Hairston, 1986; Murray, 1968; Reid, 2009). Yet it's somewhat surprising that although we have used a variety of methods, including those with an empirical framework, to study student writing from a movement stemming 60 years ago (Schriver, 1989), we haven't given our own faculty writing processes the same attention from this standpoint, with a smattering of exceptions (Geller & Eodice, 2013; Tulley, 2018; Wells & Söderlund, 2018). To date, one of the most cited faculty writing research studies comes from outside the discipline—psychologist Robert Boice's 1990 *Professors as Writers*, where he advocates using a daily writing practice to avoid writing blocks, based on interventions with faculty writers.

Acknowledging both the value of the individual faculty writer experience and culture of lore around faculty writing, we solicited chapters for the collection with a tacit understanding that using advice guide lore or relying on individual writers' narratives as data points offers valuable contributions to understand what other research methods might generate. Faculty and graduate student research interventions such as Micciche and Guy's chapter on "Writing Support for Faculty of Color" and Lam's "Intentional Institutional Support for Future Faculty: A Focus on Grant and Professional Materials" build a more complete picture of how we develop, support, and research faculty writers through the lens of writing studies research. Mark Dressman, Sarah McCarthey, and Paul Prior, drawing on the work of Gieryn (1999) pointed out in a 2009 editors' introduction in *Research in the Teaching of English* that "English studies at large [including rhetoric and composition] benefits from blurred boundaries and ongoing negotiations between scholarship vs. creative writing; quantitative vs. qualitative research . . . and, of course, that most basic border of Disciplinarity—disciplinary knowledge vs. everyday belief and culture" (Dressman, McCarthey & Prior, 2009, p. 133). *Faculty Writing Support: Emerging Research from Rhetoric and Composition Studies* operates within this space of border negotiation related to how we study faculty writing within the discipline. Rather than serving in opposition to circulated lore on faculty writing across higher education, *Faculty Writing Support: Emerging Research from Rhetoric and Composition Studies* offers a way to further develop our inquiry into the emerging disciplinary subfield of faculty writing studies by recognizing the wide range of methodologies, both inside and outside writing studies, used to construct knowledge about graduate student and faculty writers from rhetoric and writing studies scholars and beyond. We ask that readers absorb the collection as a first constellation of approaches that move beyond lore-based approaches to faculty and graduate student writing research interventions. Because faculty writing studies is still in its infancy as a subdiscipline within rhetoric and composition, chapters should be conceived as "first looks" at the various spaces where faculty writing is taught, shared, supported, and circulated: graduate school, faculty writing groups and persons who teach others about faculty writing, writing program administrators, center for teaching excellence directors, dissertation chairs, and writing coaches.

"Interventions" here might be defined as actions taken to understand faculty writing processes and to improve a faculty writer's experience during the writing process, as they identify as a faculty writer (versus a teacher or researcher), or as they undertake new writing tasks and the academic decision-making process while writing. Methods to "verify" the effectiveness of actions range from the survey research of Muhlhauser and Sheffield that examines the invisible labor of writing for born-digital journals in rhetoric and composition to Driscoll's case studies of faculty writers as "Discoverers" and "Planners," bridging the gap between single narratives about faculty writing and empirical study. In her landmark essay "Theory Building in Rhetoric and Composition: The Role of Empirical Scholarship," Schriver (1989) points out that within writing studies, empirical research is dialectical in nature and complements and enriches disciplinary study, noting, "As with other kinds of knowledge-making, empirical knowledge is a product of a dialectic which takes place among a speaker, an interpretive community or social group in which the speaker is trying to contribute, and the historical, political, material, ideological, and situational context in which the speaker is working" (p. 272). As such, Schriver suggests that though we rely on a variety of methods to capture verifiable truth, rhetoric and writing studies scholars understand better than most that "empirical work is a complex rhetorical act in that we use evidence to convince each other of the plausibility of assertions about experience" (p. 273).

As editors of the collection, we understand that faculty writers are individuals and exist in all types of social and gendered spaces with socioeconomic challenges within the context of higher education, making human writing notoriously difficult to study. The chapters within this collection represent the difficulty in capturing faculty writing success. Does success equal publication? More time spent writing? Faculty satisfaction with writing? Ease in transition from graduate student writer to faculty writer? If empirical data is evidence-backed data, we broadly define interventions in this collection as empirical using Schriver's (1989) disciplinary description. Through the methods of interviews, surveys, observations of audio recording of writing groups, and random sampling of questionnaires, research featured in this collection contributes to a broad scope of data points suggesting how we might understand faculty writing and how interventions with future faculty and faculty writers affect how faculty writing operates within higher education. *Faculty Writing Support: Emerging Research from Rhetoric and Composition Studies* provides some initial answers to (a) how we might go about studying faculty (and future faculty writing); (b) what support writers need to write; (c) what successful writing looks like for the writers themselves in the context of a specific intervention; and (d) what disciplinary factors improve, complicate, or hinder writing production. This collection, we hope, is just one of the first about how writing studies scholars research faculty writing. As Dressman, McCarthy, and Prior (2009) suggest, "an expansive, complex, and diverse field offers the greatest possibility of progress of improving our ability to understand and shape the expansive, complex, and diverse literate work of [faculty] people" (p. 135, insertion mine). Empirical research, even when perhaps more broadly defined within the discipline of rhetoric and composition, enriches our understanding of faculty writing and offers a more nuanced discussion of how writing studies specialists can help ourselves and our colleagues with scholarly writing.

Beyond its contribution to the scope of research conducted with future faculty and faculty writers, we encourage readers to consider this collection as a call to turn our disciplinary attention to faculty writing within higher education. The importance of taking ownership of faculty writing practices as rhetoric and composition scholars cannot be overstated for our future position as a discipline within the university. Though rhetoric and composition has made some headway in developing graduate programs and undergraduate writing majors, the majority of the students we teach are in first-year and service writing courses. Studying faculty writing and engaging in data-driven study offers us another avenue to remake our role as writing scholars providing support within a university. More practically, faculty writing support offers a strategic support opportunity that first-year writing does not. Like many of the authors here, I've used my own interest in faculty writing to strategically improve my position and that of my discipline within the university. Offering to run technical support for tenure and promotion for a course release led me to make a case for offering faculty writing groups to support scholarship efforts. I tied data on faculty writing groups to faculty retention rates, showing the cost savings of investing in another course release—for me, a semester spent on this effort was more than worth it. The more faculty who earned tenure under my guidance about scholarly publication, the more I set myself up as the expert on faculty writing in my university. This expertise led to permission for me to design and develop the Master of Arts in Rhetoric and Writing program at my university, with the explicit goals of developing future faculty members as writers and sending graduates with strong academic writing foundations to doctoral programs. Other colleagues I know have similarly tied a focus on faculty writing to the financial interests of the university—for example, getting a course release to assist grant writers and improving grant acceptance rates, improving tenure track placement of doctoral candidates through writing workshops, or running workshops for scientists to publish results from expensive labs. Research from this collection can be used to make a similar case for support efforts for specific populations of faculty writers, argue for faculty writing centers, design graduate mentoring and programs to support future faculty, and enhance tools we already widely use, such as faculty writing groups and retreats.

Examining developing research on graduate student and faculty writers also benefits faculty writers within rhetoric and composition. The field of rhetoric and composition is multi-disciplinary and multi-modal, and faculty writers within it are unlike faculty writers in any other discipline. While productivity in faculty writing is crucial in most disciplines to extend knowledge and attain tenure, promotion, grant dollars, and career mobility, it is crucial in the discipline of rhetoric and composition, where our scholarship is tied to administration and the teaching of writing and often unrecognized in tenure decisions (Tulley, 2018). Producing scholarship remains crucial despite heavy teaching and administrative loads. At the same time, our faculty writing processes extend beyond print scholarly articles as we recognize audio, video, and image as texts, and make scholarly arguments using these mediums in journals such as *Kairos* and *Computers and Composition*. We often call upon other disciplines such as psychology, literature, and digital humanities to make arguments. And of course, we study writing and teach others to write. All of these unique disciplinary markers complicate how faculty writing is understood and valued within our own discipline. Goggin (2000) points out that publishing scholarship is a hallmark of rhetoric and composition as a discipline. Connecting our disciplinary grounding in writing studies with the types of writing we do and the genres we value as writing studies continues to develop is essential. Finally, and perhaps most importantly, published research of faculty writing practices by disciplinary specialists contributes to a culture where faculty writing isn't hidden behind a closed office door. Unlike other disciplines such as nursing that actively study their own faculty writing habits (Woodward & Hirsch, 2023), most composition faculty know more about first-year students with us for one semester than we do about the writing habits of our faculty colleagues whom we've worked with for years. As overlapping racial tensions (Settles et al., 2021) and the COVID-19 pandemic (*Chronicle of Higher Education*, 2020) have illustrated, faculty writers, particularly those who do not fit the traditional faculty writing model, are struggling and need support. *Faculty Writing Support: Emerging Research from Rhetoric and Composition Studies* offers a starting point for additional research and data-driven arguments for faculty writing support, and a look at current faculty writing culture within higher education.

Jaci, Lars, and I have been fortunate to be counted among early explorers of faculty writing practices. Yet it should be noted that exploring this area is a privilege that we are keenly aware of. We are all white, abled, middle-class faculty with stable tenured positions. We have job security and decent incomes that permit us to have the luxury to spend time conducting research. We've all served as writing program or center administrators where we are often in positions to make decisions about some of the most vulnerable populations in our universities: contingent faculty, non-native speakers of English, first-generation college students. At the same time, all three of us experience pressures of academic parenthood, where caregiving collides with teaching responsibilities, year-round administrative work (often poorly compensated in release time), eldercare, and—most importantly for this collection—time to write. All of us took academic positions that have brought us stability in the academy but also have presented logistical and financial challenges for childcare, even with supportive partners, because like many academics we moved far from family support. As faculty writers composing this collection, we've experienced a variety of personal circumstances that slowed down our completion of this collection including illness, new children, death of close family members, job changes, and sending children to college. Thus, we've experienced firsthand the writing challenges faced by graduate students and faculty described within the chapters of *Faculty Writing Support: Emerging Research from Rhetoric and Composition Studies*. We are faculty writers who can benefit from the strategies within these pages to support our own writing processes.

We also recognize the term *faculty* itself is privileged. This collection offers specific examples of research-based interventions with future faculty and faculty writers primarily in doctoral, tenure-track, and tenured spaces, because the penalties of not producing scholarship are highest for those seeking tenure-track jobs, those pursuing tenure and promotion, and those searching for career mobility and leadership roles. Yet the collection also serves as an invitation for other writing scholars not only to develop additional research into faculty writing support but also to diversify the population of researchers able to conduct it. Researchers using this collection might consider collaborating with co-authors from various backgrounds and studying other faculty writers within the academy, including non-tenure track lecturers, faculty with primarily administrative loads, faculty writers in libraries or centers, faculty with heavy teaching loads, contingent faculty, community college faculty, postdoctoral researchers, struggling ABD ("all but dissertation") students, and writers from a range of diverse identities. We look forward to future opportunities for extending Micciche and Guy's research from this collection.

This volume is organized by juxtaposing two corresponding sides to faculty writing support: research examining faculty writing practices in a variety of contexts to understand *how* faculty write and research on *how to support* faculty writing practice across career advancement tasks such as writing for publication, cover letters for new opportunities, and arguments for funding. In *Part I: How Faculty Write*, we open with a collection of studies of faculty writing that examine composing processes, participation in writing groups, and decision-making in selecting outlets for publication. *Part II: How to Support Faculty Writers* turns from research on faculty writing habits, processes, motivations, and decision-making to rhetoric and writing based interventions both inside and outside the university structure that seek to support faculty in these areas. Current dean, former department chair, and experienced journal editor Kristine Blair synthesizes both sides of faculty writing study in the Afterword, where she suggests future directions and the role of rhetoric and composition in emerging research.

HOW TO USE FACULTY WRITING SUPPORT: EMERGING RESEARCH FROM RHETORIC AND COMPOSITION STUDIES

This overview offers a variety of interventions illustrated by emerging writing studies research. As a developing field, we offer several ways readers might use the various essays in this collection as researchers of faculty (and future faculty) writing practice, as writing program or center professionals, as faculty developers, and as faculty writers ourselves.

Researchers of Graduate Student and Faculty Writing Practice

Those seeking to study doctoral student or faculty writing practices will find that essays in the collection offer methodological models and calls for action. Finding explicit methodologies to study faculty writers is a challenging task, and one I describe in *How Writing Faculty Write* (2018), where I discuss how I modified *Paris Review* style interviews with literary writers to ask established rhetoric and composition disciplinary leaders about their writing practices. Researchers might look to Driscoll's mixed methods of studying "expert writers" using direct observation of the writing process, participant writing journals, and regular interviews with participants, as well as writing analytics through the use of Google Documents and Google Draftback and Lam's codes for analysis in Chapter 8.

Writing Program Administrators, Writing Center Directors, and Writing Across the Curriculum Professionals

As both a writing program administrator and writing center director, I had the opportunity to support faculty writers in various ways. While most administrative practices focus on supporting undergraduate student writing in first-year writing courses, undergraduate writing majors, and writing intensive courses outside of English, there is a rich body of literature from rhetoric and composition scholars on supporting the teachers of those courses in the teaching of writing (see Geller and Eodice's 2013 *Working with Faculty Writers* for several examples). The essays by Wells and Söderlund and Muhlhauser and Sheffield featured in this collection offer a look at how to support those teachers of writing as writers themselves in time management and journal selection for scholarly output. Quynn and Willuz's chapter on faculty writers as collaborators offers a useful model for administrators seeking to enact other models of faculty writing support beyond a pedagogical framework.

Faculty Developers

Because faculty writing support is developing as a viable administrative area for rhetoric and composition faculty due our "uniquely valuable preparation for faculty development" with training in supporting teaching assistants, writing curriculum, and designing faculty training (Artze-Vega et al., 2013, p. 164), several chapters in this collection illustrate how writing studies practices can be taken to the broader faculty and graduate student population. For example, Hewett's chapter on faculty writing needs that go unmet in the university structure is useful for identifying where specific interventions might be most productive. Grutsch McKinney's chapter describes a practice of proximal writing that might be useful for designing writing spaces that foster this connection. These models can also be used to make arguments for faculty writing support by showing a successful pattern of intervention. Blair's Afterword offers suggestions about the role of research-based practice in supporting faculty and offers some avenues for study by faculty developers.

Struggling Faculty/Future Faculty Writers in Rhetoric and Composition . . . and Beyond

Through dual lenses of faculty writing practices and interventions in faculty writing, this collection offers clear techniques to address an overarching question: What gets faculty writers to write? Graduate students might use these essays as studies into some of the challenges that come with being a faculty writer in rhetoric and composition and how to preemptively combat these challenges. The interventions offer more tools in the future faculty writer's toolbox—the ability to write resiliently through larger class sizes, more administrative work, etc.—all features of tenure-track positions in rhetoric and composition studies. For struggling faculty writers, research-based rationales for participation in a faculty writing group presented by Rifenburg and Johnson; Taft, Babcock, and Vis; and Messuri and Sharp offer multiple imaginings of what faculty writing group participation might look like. Muhlhauser and Sheffield illustrate the decision-making process behind choosing a journal for publication within rhetoric and composition while Wells and Söderlund look at time pressures on writing for writing professionals. Driscoll's study of different avenues to write as a "Planner" or "Discoverer" (or a "Hybrid") provides a helpful framework for identifying a writing identity and working with existing writing preferences.

I close with a final word to those who support faculty writers outside of writing studies: our close colleagues in psychology studying writing behaviors, productivity specialists in business looking at efficiency, librarians who collaborate with faculty writers, scholarly publishers who support faculty writers through the editorial process, and more. Though rhetoric and composition faculty increasingly have taken on faculty development positions due to our intertwined interests of faculty and graduate student support, writing studies research, and the disciplinary link between the teaching of writing and writing (Artze-Vega, 2013), faculty writing studies is, in essence, interdisciplinary. Consider how many interventions across disciplines it took me to write this introduction: conversations with Jaci and Lars as co-editors and disciplinary colleagues, a reading of this draft from a faculty developer outside writing studies in higher education, a chat over coffee with a psychologist about why some of the interventions worked (which led to me writing this very paragraph), editorial feedback received from the WAC Clearinghouse, and a research appointment with a librarian. While an emerging subfield in rhetoric and composition, faculty writing studies will naturally grow (and has grown) in other communities studying academic writers from other angles: behavioral scientists, scholarly publishers, even universities themselves. Our disciplinary contributions might overlap and borrow from these areas, but research from writing studies is essential to understanding best practices in supporting faculty writers in the writing process. We hope *Faculty Writing Support: Emerging Research from Rhetoric and Composition Studies* prompts new research in this area.

REFERENCES

Artze-Vega, I., Bowdon, M., Emmons, K., Eodice, M., Hess, S. K., Lamonica, C. C. & Nelms, G. (2013). Privileging pedagogy: Composition, rhetoric, and faculty development. *College Composition and Communication, 65*(1), 162–184. https://doi.org/10.2307/43490807.

Belcher, W. L. (2009). *Writing your journal article in 12 weeks: A guide to academic publishing success.* Sage. https://doi.org/10.4135/9781526402276.

Boice, R. (1990). *Professors as writers: A self-help guide to productive writing.* New Forums Press.

Chronicle of Higher Education. (2020). On the verge of burnout: Covid-19's impact on faculty well-being and career plans. *Chronicle Connect.* https://connect.chronicle.com/rs/931-EKA-218/images/Covid%26FacultyCareerPaths_Fidelity_Research Brief_v3%281%29.pdf%0d.

Dressman, M., McCarthey, S. & Prior, P. (2009). Editors' introduction: Literate practices: Theory, method, and disciplinary boundary work. *Research in the Teaching of English*, *44*(2), 133–135. https://doi.org/10.2307/27784354.

Gebhardt, R. C. (1977). Balancing theory with practice in the training of writing teachers. *College Composition and Communication*, *28*(2), 134–140. https://www.jstor.org/stable/pdf/356098.pdf.

Geller, A. E. & Eodice, M. (2013). *Working with faculty writers*. Utah State University Press.

Gieryn, T. F. (1999). *Cultural boundaries of science: Credibility on the line*. University of Chicago Press. https://doi.org/10.7208/chicago/9780226824420.

Goggin, M. (2000). *Authoring a discipline: Scholarly journals and the post-World War II Emergence of rhetoric and composition*. Routledge.

Hairston, M. (1986). When writing teachers don't write: Speculations about probable causes and possible cures. *Rhetoric Review*, *5*(1), 62–70. https://www.jstor.org/stable/pdf/466020.pdf.

Johnson, K. (2017). Writing by the book, writing beyond the book. *Composition Studies*, *45*(2), 55–72. https://www.jstor.org/stable/26402783.

Micciche, L. R. & Carr, A. D. (2011). Toward graduate-level writing instruction. *College Composition and Communication*, *62*(3), 477–501. http://www.jstor.org/stable/27917909.

Murray, D. M. (1968). *A writer teaches writing: A practical method of teaching composition*. Houghton Mifflin.

Phelps, L. W. (1991). Practical wisdom and the geography of knowledge in composition. *College English*, *53*(8), 863–885.

Reid, E. S. (2009). Teaching writing teachers writing: Difficulty, exploration, and critical reflection. *College Composition and Communication*, *61*(2), 376.

Schriver, K. A. (1989). Theory building in rhetoric and composition: The role of empirical scholarship. *Rhetoric Review*, *7*(2), 272–288. https://unwrite.org/rhet-readings/theory-building-in-rhetoric-and-composition-karen-a-schrivner/.

Settles, I. H., Jones, M. K., Buchanan, N. T. & Dotson, K. (2021). Epistemic exclusion: Scholar(ly) devaluation that marginalizes faculty of color. *Journal of Diversity in Higher Education*, *14*(4), 493507. https://doi.org/10.1037/dhe0000174.

Silvia, P. J. (2017). *How to write a lot: A practical guide to productive academic writing*. American Psychological Association. https://doi.org/10.1037/11537-000.

Tulley, C. E. (2018). *How writing faculty write: Strategies for process, product, and productivity*. Utah State University Press.

Wells, J. M. & Söderlund, L. (2018). Preparing graduate students for academic publishing: Results from a study of published rhetoric and composition scholars. *Pedagogy: Critical Approaches to Teaching Literature, Language, Composition, and Culture*, *18*(1), 131–156. https://doi.org/10.1215/15314200-4216994.

Woodward, K. F. & Hirsch, A. (2023). Discipline-specific writing support in graduate nursing. *The Journal of Nursing Education*, *62*(4), 253–256. https://doi.org/10.3928/01484834-20230104-01.

PART 1. HOW FACULTY WRITE

Part I examines current research on factors that encourage faculty writing. Factors studied in this section include composing styles of experienced faculty writers, the effects of writing near others and in support groups, and the impact of digital publishing on composing.

In Chapter 1, "Planning, Tinkering, and Writing to Learn: A Model of Planning and Discovery as Composing Styles for Professional Academic Writers," Dana Driscoll examines three distinct composing styles of expert writers engaged in writing for publication: "Discoverers" who embrace writing to learn and write their way into understanding, "Planners" whose composing process is more linear and planned, and "Hybrids" who use both planning and discovery in their writing process.

Driscoll's overview offers a useful look at other group interventions such as in Chapter 2, "Faculty Presence, Influence, and Authority in Interdisciplinary, Multi-Level Writing Groups." In their chapter, Aileen R. Taft, Rebecca Day Babcock, and Maximillien Vis III examine the experiences of faculty who participate in multi-level interdisciplinary writing groups and compare two iterations of such groups. From narrative research, they compare the interactions with the authority of the participants, outcome, stability, and effectiveness of the writing groups to understand how faculty writers experience participation and how presence in a group affects faculty writing.

Chapter 3, "Faculty Writers as Proximal Writers: Why Faculty Write Near Other Writers" develops this idea of social connection in writing further. Jackie Grutsch McKinney looks at self-reported faculty preference for social versus isolated writing. Drawing on data from a national survey of those with proximal writing experiences, Grutsch McKinney captures how and why some faculty writers report they use proximal writing.

In Chapter 4, "People Keep Knocking (or, I Have Answered 50 Emails Today): Balancing Work and Research as a WPA," Jaclyn Wells and Lars Söderlund dig deeper into a past dataset of 20 rhetoric and composition writers to isolate the role administration plays on disciplinary faculty writing practice. While earlier chapters focused on faculty in general, this chapter examines specific factors that make publishing difficult as a writing program professional and offers strategies for administrators as writers. Supporting faculty writers, as noted earlier in this introduction, often falls to rhetoric and composition faculty through extensions of administrative roles to help students, and this chapter offers a valuable contribution in considering how to support faculty writing administrators as writers.

Concluding Part I, Chapter 5, "Complicating the Techno-Afterglow: Pursuing Compositional Equity and Making Labor Visible in Digital Scholarly Production" by Paul Muhlhauser and Jenna Sheffield, turns to the invisible labor inherent in writing for born-digital disciplinary publications and how faculty writing practices differ when writing for hypertext publication. Muhlhauser and Sheffield explore scholars' decisions to participate in digital scholarship and the "resort to print" (i.e., traditional publishing) mentality that exists in the rhetoric and composition field stemming from unfair evaluations and appreciation of labor processes, ultimately arguing for compositional equity: an understanding and appreciation for the different labors that comprise digital and traditional scholarship.

CHAPTER 1.

PLANNING, TINKERING, AND WRITING TO LEARN: A MODEL OF PLANNING AND DISCOVERY AS COMPOSING STYLES FOR PROFESSIONAL ACADEMIC WRITERS

Dana Lynn Driscoll
Indiana University of Pennsylvania

Abstract: *This chapter explores three composing styles among expert academic writers: planners, discoverers, and hybrids. Planners outline extensively before writing, discoverers write to understand and discover their ideas, while hybrids combine both approaches. Using Google Draftback for detailed analytics, I conducted a longitudinal study with in-depth interviews, writing journals, and survey data from 198 scholars. The findings reveal that writing style preferences significantly influence initial engagement, drafting, and revisions. This study offers insights for supporting graduate students' development in academic writing, proposes new methodologies for studying writing processes in real time, and considers how these composing styles can inform mentoring practices.*

Over 50 years ago, Cowley (1958) theorized that successful writers had two different "writing styles." Based on famous musical composers, he identified "Beethovians" as writers that dove right into their writing and did not engage many invention strategies and identified "Mozartians" as writers who spent extensive amounts of time engaging in invention, which may include developing various kinds of outlines, lists, or other prewriting to help them draft (p. 8). A similar concept is known in the creative writing community: "planners" and "pantsers." Planners are those who meticulously outline their characters and plots in advance while some writers fly by the seat of their "pantsers" and leave the story to unfold as they write (Brooks, 2011). It was these two concepts—the Beethovians and the Mozartians—that motivated the present article. In designing a longitudinal, exploratory study of expert writers' composing processes, I was curious if these "writing styles" applied to those who were writing for publication in the field of composition studies. My study used a combination of direct observation of writing process and self-reported techniques to explore the writing processes of expert participants as they composed an article or book chapter for publication. Observations were done through a program called Google Draftback, which creates both videos of composing and writing analytics, while I employed writing journals and interviews to hear from participants firsthand. While I originally saw this question about Mozart and Beethoven as a fun "aside" to engage with my participants in our initial interview, multiple sources of data in the study showed that Cowley's initial insights had merit and demonstrated a fundamental distinction among expert processes. That is, even though all expert writers produced a publication, some writers align more with planning out their work in advance before and between composing, and others align more with discovery.

Thus, this article explores what I call planning, discovery, and hybrid composing styles through case studies of three expert writers and a larger-scale survey of those writing for publication, all within the field of composition. Through in-depth exploration of three writers' interviews, journals, and recorded textual data, I offer interviews, writing analytics, and direct evidence of planning, discovery, and hybrid styles. This article demonstrates that composing style is a key distinction that shapes much of writers' early engagement with texts, ideas, and invention, and it also directly shapes how their writing process unfolds on the page. After presenting this rich case study data, I present data from a large-scale survey of 198 members of the field of composition to describe the prevalence of these styles and demonstrate that composing styles largely are a matter of a writer's preference rather than tied to identity or institutional position. The chapter offers several key contributions and implications: First, it offers a model of operationalized definitions and features for the three composing styles, tying these with both recursive writing processes and writing to learn. Second, it offers a discussion about how understanding these styles may better support graduate students' entry into professional academic writing and includes a list of suggestions for those working with graduate students. Finally, the chapter offers a novel methodology using Google Draftback as a way to directly study writers' composing processes, opening up opportunities for future writing-process research.

BACKGROUND

Exploring the composing styles and writing processes of expert writers requires a consideration of three bodies of related work: the writing-to-learn movement within composition, the existing interdisciplinary literature on expert writers, and research on expert writing processes. Through this discussion, I argue that we will see that, while rich information exists on expert writers and self-reported discussions of writing processes, the field needs more direct observational studies of writing processes and explorations about how expert academic writers engage in discovery, invention, and the production of texts.

Cowley's (1958) "Beethoven" writers are essentially using what compositionists know as writing to learn. Fulwiler and Young (1982) differentiated between "writing to communicate" (transactional writing) and "writing to learn" (p. x), the latter being where individuals would use writing as a tool to deepen understanding and generate new ideas. These differences between writing to communicate and writing to learn were borne out by a wide body of early research in composition (Emig, 1977; Langer & Applebee, 1987) that confirmed that students of all ages and in diverse settings wrote their way into understanding. Writing to learn has a long history within composition, and unlike many other early theories of composition, it has had tremendous staying power because it appears to be a consistent truth across writers and contexts. Drawing upon this body of work, Bean (2011) argues that writing to learn should be at the center of writing instruction in higher education and across the disciplines. Recent studies continue to support writing to learn as an empirically validated construct, including writing's capacity to aid long-term memory (Silva & Limongi, 2019) and writing's ability to support learning content in a variety of fields (Henry & Baker, 2015; Klein & Unsworth, 2014). While ample evidence exists about the efficacy of writing to learn in secondary and undergraduate education across the disciplines, two questions arise: How might this concept function for expert writers engaging in writing for publication? In what ways do expert writers use writing to discover or deepen their purpose and thinking?

The literature on expert writers offers limited insights into how the writing-to-learn process may work with those engaged in writing for publication. Drawing upon the work of Flower and Hayes (1981) as well as his own experiments, Kellogg's (1994) work indicates that experts use a combination of planning (a range of invention strategies), translating (shifting ideas from the mind into prose), and reviewing (re-reading the text and making revisions and edits). Kellogg argues that these three activities are not linear; they are recursive. Thus, writers may cycle through rounds of prewriting, drafting, and revision as they engage with their text. Further, he notes that planning, translating, and reviewing can work together to help expert writers develop more sophisticated ideas and texts. Beyond these concepts, Kellogg's (2006) extensive overview of the research on professional writing expertise indicates that expert writers also manage a range of other considerations while composing: appropriate use of language, solving problems, managing the cognitive load, addressing specific domains (contexts and rhetorical situations), engaging with long-term memory, understanding audiences, and managing emotional challenges associated with writing (pp. 391–395). Further, Scardamalia and Bereiter (1991) recognized the importance of an expert writer deeply engaging in ongoing ways with both the content of the problem and the rhetorical situation in which they were writing. As we can see from this body of work, writing recursively and deepening purpose are possible aspects of expert writers' processes, although this body of work does not largely address how individual composing style preference may apply.

Another area tied to the present study is a recent body of work exploring the writing habits and writing experiences of faculty expert writers within the field of composition (Gallagher & DeVoss, 2019; Söderlund & Wells, 2019; Tulley, 2018; Wells & Söderlund, 2017). Wells and Söderlund (2017) interviewed 20 faculty who were successful in academic publishing within the field of composition and explored what habits supported their success. Again, the theme of recursivity emerged, this time focusing on feedback. Professional writers engaged in multiple rounds of revision based on feedback, both by trusted peers who would offer feedback prior to submission and then feedback based on blind peer reviewers and journal editors—this latter kind of feedback helped deeply shape drafts and lead to successful publication experiences (p. 148). Similarly, Tulley (2018) selected accomplished members of the field who had outstanding publication records and interviewed them about their process. One of Tulley's key findings was that faculty cultivate invention strategies that assist them with organizing their ideas and discovery and also recognize the importance of persisting through difficult parts of the writing process (p. 21). These studies offer yet another piece of compelling evidence that writing to learn strategies may be key for expert writers, although the field does not yet have a model of what those processes may look like. Further, while interview data forms an important contribution in our understanding of expert academic writers' processes, without systematic direct observation of expert writing processes, we have an incomplete picture of the nuanced writing processes that experts use to be successful.

METHODS

The study was designed to explore, define, and provide a model of composing styles that expert academic writers from the field of composition employ when writing articles. The data from this study comes from several data sources: a longitudinal, exploratory study of the expert writing processes of professional academic writers in composition and a survey of a broader range of members of the field of composition studies.

LONGITUDINAL PROCESS STUDY

After gaining IRB approval in Fall 2018, I put out a call for participants for a longitudinal writing process study. My call targeted those who considered themselves expert academic writers in the field of composition and who had considerable publication experience. Ten participants agreed to participate. A condition of participation was that participants would be starting a new work for the study and that they would compose their article or book chapter in Google Docs. They would keep a writing process journal that they would update each writing session, and they would be interviewed at least three times for 60 minutes each during their writing process. Key to this study was the combination of self-reported data (interviews and writing process journals) and direct observational data of their composing process through a Google Doc plugin called Google Draftback.

The Google Draftback plugin is an extraordinarily useful tool for writing process research. Google Docs already tracks each keystroke and change to a document that is made over time. The Google Draftback plugin renders these changes into a video that can be played back at a later date, allowing anyone with access to the document to directly observe how the text is shaped over time. The plugin also produces a range of useful analytics, including tracking when and how the document was modified, the changing size of the document, where in the document changes were made, hours spent writing, and visualization of the changes in the document.

Each participant in the study was interviewed three times via Zoom for 60 minutes. In the first interview, I asked them their preference of composing style using Crowley's (1953) terms. I also asked them to discuss their scholarly identity, research trajectory, typical writing process, and specifics of the book chapter or article they planned to write. The second interview occurred around the 70% drafting mark, where we discussed aspects from their writing journals, how the purpose of the document had shifted, and aspects of their composing process. The final interview happened after they had "finalized" the text and it was submitted for publication. In this interview, I offered them screenshots of the writing analytics from Google Draftback, we discussed more aspects of their writing journal and process, and we discussed the nature of writing expertise. Because I was engaging in analysis as the study continued, I presented initial findings to participants, which then we could discuss, and they could elaborate further.

Analysis of this rich set of data involved watching the process videos and taking detailed notes, comparing videos to the writing analytics and writing journals, coding interviews and writing process journals, and working to come to an understanding of how the direct observational data aligned or diverged from the self-reported interview data. Additionally, all three case-study participants had an opportunity to read and comment on this draft before submission, allowing for further member checking.

Due to the longitudinal nature of the study, at the time of writing, six of the participants—all in subfields of composition—had completed the study while the remaining four had completed either one or two interviews; some participants' writing processes were delayed due to the onset of COVID-19. I chose three case study participants from the six who had completed the study at the time of writing. Case study participants were selected on several criteria. First, they had completed the study at the time of drafting this article. Second, in initial interviews they indicated a preference for one composing style, and they enacted that style throughout their drafting. Additionally, all of these writers were working on book chapters that were using historical and textual data as their primary reference. Thus, they had a number of useful points of comparison. As a member check, all three case study participants read the draft of this article and were provided the opportunity to offer feedback on the representation of their writing process and their scholarly identity.

I will note here that it is possible that the metagenre (Carter, 2007) that the writer is working in may be a factor in how composing styles unfold. A participant who is working on an empirical, data-driven article may engage in more discovery during analysis than a participant working with textual or historical sources. Thus, selecting three participants working in a similar metagenre and drawing upon a similar body of evidence was important.

SURVEY

After engaging in two years of data collection for the ongoing longitudinal study, and after initial conversation with my case study participants on what I was now calling "planning" and "discovery" composing styles, I developed a large-scale survey to better understand the scope and prevalence of composing styles among members in the field of composition. After pre-testing and IRB approval, the online survey (hosted on Qualtrics.com) was distributed on three listervs: WPA-L, W-Center, and Next-Gen. Calls for participants were sent out in early October 2020 and then a follow-up call was sent two weeks later. The survey remained open for 30 days.

The survey was completed by 198 individuals associated with the field of composition who had either engaged in writing for publication or were starting to write for publication. This included 58 (29.3%) identifying as males, 128 (65.6%) as female, 3 (1.5%) as transgender, and 8 (4.0%) who preferred not to specify. Participants identified as Latinx or Hispanic (4, 2%), Native American

(3, 1.5%), Asian or Pacific Islander (10, 5.1%), African American (8, 4%), and white (173, 87.4%). Participants came from a range of statuses at the university, including graduate student (40, 20.2%), adjunct or part-time instructors (8, 4.0%), full-time non-tenured instructors (29, 14.6%), tenure-track faculty (33, 16.7%), tenured faculty (30, 15.2%), individuals in various administrative roles (44, 22.2%), upper administrators (10, 5.1%), and retired faculty (10, 5.1%). Participants had a wide range of teaching experiences, with many teaching full loads or having loads split between administration and teaching.

Submitted surveys were included in the analysis as long as the participant had answered at least half of the survey items. The survey was analyzed in SPSS; frequencies and descriptive statistics were calculated for demographic information and questions about expertise and composing styles. After ensuring the normality of the data, a Spearman's Rho correlation was calculated to understand what, if any, relationship there was between differences in demographic information, institutional affiliation, and expertise and composing style.

Positionality

My positionality as a researcher is someone who is curious about how different people compose, while recognizing my own nuances in composing due to being neurodiverse with dyslexia. As a writing center director who supports graduate writers, and as a faculty member teaching doctoral classes in dissertation writing and writing for publication, I grew curious about how to best support students' writing processes. Perhaps due to my own dyslexia, I've always allowed myself to be as messy and unstructured as I needed to be, and I do not stress about it because my brain works differently. But when I would talk to my graduate students, they were often distraught when they felt their writing processes were "messy" or "unstructured" and frustrated about not having a clean, linear writing process. In the end, it seemed that a variety of approaches yielded successful publications, so I wanted to better understand this phenomenon.

Limitations

Even with the technology of Google Docs and the interviews and writing journals, I am certain that there were aspects of the case study participants' writing processes that I could not capture—in particular, it was difficult to capture what happened between sessions beyond the limited information provided in journals and discussion during interviews. Due to the nature of writing processes over a period of years, I'm not sure that there would be a better way to capture this information at a distance, but this limitation is still worth noting. Further, my primary analysis of the longitudinal case studies is based on a small number of participants due to the size of the dataset provided by Google Draftback and the resulting intensity of the analysis. Further research is needed to understand the prevalence and features of these composing styles.

RESULTS: PLANNING, DISCOVERY, AND HYBRID CASE STUDIES

In initial interviews, I asked my 10 expert writers about Cowley's "Beethoven" and "Mozart" styles. All writers immediately grasped the difference and expressed preference in the direction of one of these two styles of composing. Five participants indicated a strong preference towards discovery, two participants towards planning, and three participants towards hybrid approaches (a similar breakdown in approach can be seen in the survey results, below). In what follows, I offer three case studies of successful academic writers who clearly demonstrate aspects of these composing styles: Alice offers a model of planning, Dan offers a model of discovery, and Ryan offers a hybrid discovery/planning process.

ALICE: STICKING TO THE PLAN

Alice[1] is a senior scholar who has widely published in the field of composition studies and whose impressive CV includes multiple books, well-cited articles, and editorships. Alice retired several years before the study began from her position as a full professor of writing and rhetoric at a public research university. In her retirement, she has continued to work on scholarly publishing projects, including writing articles, books, and editing a book series. I followed her through composing one chapter of her newest book, *Literacy Heroines*, which focuses on exploring historical female figures who sponsor or employ literacy in meaningful ways. The chapter I followed her through was titled "Ida Tarbell (1857–1944) and the Muckrakers" and specifically explored the work of a progressive era journalist who rode the wave of major technological developments and became both an exemplar and sponsor of literacy.

Alice described herself as an "orderly, organized writer" and noted that this did not change in retirement, although she now has more time to devote to writing. In fact, she said, she writes approximately three hours a day in a typical week. Throughout the interviews and reflected in her process, Alice demonstrated a strong preference for a planning composing style and emphasized how "the plan" defines what she writes and what order she writes it in. After our first

---

[1] Because this was a study of expertise, participants had a choice to be identified by name with real titles or pseudonym. All participants chose to be listed by their real name.

interview, she sent me an outline that described her plan further for each chapter. Alice's writing plan was supported by extensive pre-research, where she examines various historical sources to craft a narrative of each literacy heroine and then uses a board in her home office to capture important information needing to be written into her drafts—thus, she's engaged in an extensive invention beyond the page. In discussing how to manage the cognitive overload associated with advanced literacy, she said:

> I think this goes back to the business of having a plan. So, I'll be reading along in a biography and I come across some evidence. A lot of the people I'm looking at have written a lot and have had a lot written about them. . . . The deal was to extract all the stuff that I looked at. . . . So, how I deal with the cognitive overload is by having a plan and by staying pretty focused on the plan. I find as I find things as I do the research, as I encounter materials or talk to scholars. . . . But it's all tied in with the plan and the plan may or may not be explicit. It may or may not be—sometimes I do actually write out an outline. Often, it's very informal like 1, 2, 3, 4, 5, these are the things I'm going to discuss. But it's really about kind of sticking to the plan.

Alice further described how "the plan" manifests in her drafting process:

> I tend to jump in and start writing, because I have this plan. So, I will probably start this chapter by writing an introduction about just kind of a basic sense of why this person qualifies as a heroine. I'm looking at this list, I have a list of issues, historical issues, it's right up there in my bulletin board.

As we'll explore in the "writing process" section below, this commitment to planning results in a much more linear drafting process for Alice, where she often begins where she left off and writes in a linear fashion largely from beginning to end.

Dan: Discovery and Writing to Learn

At the time of the study, Dan was an associate professor of English and also serves as the writing center director at a public mid-sized university. He had published a number of articles, book chapters, and textbook materials; he also had been awarded several grants. His research focuses on writing centers, media studies, and cultural studies. Like the other case study participants, Dan was building his current book on a series of articles and projects that he had recently finished. I followed him as he drafted the introductory chapter for his book, tentatively titled *Writing Centers Beyond Writing*, which focuses on issues of ambience, embodiment, and affect in writing center settings. As he introduced his project, he noted:

> I don't know if this is one chapter or if I'm going to have to make two separate ones. This summer's project is an IRB and really just diving into the literature. My plan is that I'm going to start prewriting a bit in the summer as well and just trying to determine if this is one or two chapters.

Dan recognized that he needs to write to discover the nature of his chapters in the book manuscript. This demonstrates a strong alignment with a discovery mindset and accepting writing to learn as part of his process.

Dan's writing process for this project was similar to his previous works, where he had worked on multiple documents at once including one to two main text files and additional files with discarded-for-now-text, and comments to himself. He commented,

> Again, I had to laugh when you write Beethoven cause honestly I'll probably be writing sections of it just to help me think about it in the summer or just a little bits of commentary to myself. I usually have four Google Docs open for a project where one is a clipboard, one is one section, one is another section, one is a guide that I'll constantly use.

Dan described himself as a writer who composes his way into understanding through the use of these documents and uses writing simply to initially think through ideas; he pointed out that some of this will end up in his final publication, but some writing will not.

When asked about his composing style, Dan firmly indicated that he ascribes to the discovery (Beethoven) style:

> Yeah, I would say the Beethoven . . . some of these chapters have been—that I'm working on for this book—had been literal years in the making as I've been working on other stuff and just thinking about it. . . . As I've gotten further along my career and farther away from grad school and remembering anything that got me to this point, it's Beethoven in that well, I want to get writing so at least I have some sense of where I'm going and I'll do the research and I'll do the reading as I

go because it might let me see things a little differently. Honestly, having seen several friends in grad school get afflicted with that planning paralysis like waiting for that perfect moment reading everything but not generating anything. I'm a pragmatist in that regard.

Dan's discovery model differs from Alice's model of planning.

RYAN: "TINKERING" AND HYBRIDIZING PLANNING AND DISCOVERY

At the time of the study, Ryan was an associate professor of rhetoric and composition at a large public state institution. In addition to several edited collections and special journal issues, Ryan had also published numerous article manuscripts. His core work focuses on public rhetoric, both historical and contemporary, and, given the U.S. political climate during the Trump presidency, he's focused his recent work on Nazi and fascist rhetoric, demagoguery, and fake news. In addition to his academic scholarship, he has also written a variety of pieces on these areas for major news outlets. Like the other two case study writers, Ryan's current writing project stemmed from the project he was previously working on: a book chapter on fascism in the United States. Ryan started the project with what he called an "abstract proposal" and noted that:

> I don't know exactly what my thesis is yet but I have been working on and reading about and preparing to write this thing for the better part of a year and a half. By the time I sit down to write it I will have spent a fair amount of time in my own head working on it.

Ryan engaged in considerable reading and thinking outside of actually sitting down to write. He said:

> I do tend to sort of stew on things in my mind before I write things down. I've been collecting and reading articles for a long time. I have a whole folder, various things from popular press and from scholarly stuff. I jot notes all over the place. So, I just have random notes which are not ideal because oftentimes I don't remember what they refer to.

When asked about his composing style, Ryan indicated he uses both planning and discovery:

> I think it's sort of a combination. I spent extensive time planning, inventing, reflecting all of those things, and then I dive

right in and have multiple drafts and messiness. It's sort of the worst parts of both. All the preparation time and none of the focus.... I'm sort of smack in the middle of those things.

He noted that it depends, in part, on what he is composing, "I think that there are times that I have things that I very definitely planned to say and that come out really quickly and really easily."

However, in later interviews, Ryan and I returned to this issue of planning and discovery after seeing the progress of his own draft. He described a process he calls "tinkering," which he characterizes as:

> Sort of the way that I conceptualize it is like Mine Sweeper. I go and I click on one box and it will clear one thing and then I know that one's close to this and I click on that and then there's this whole big thing.... If I can just knock a little bit at a time then oftentimes big parts of things will clear up sort of out of the blue. But it happens mostly if I'm consistently doing the tinkering. But if I step away for too long or if I don't pay attention to it then often those big clarifying moments don't happen as quickly or as easily.

One of the aspects that is striking about Ryan's process is how he engages with the text frequently—sometimes five or ten different moments across the day, continually returning to his text and making small changes. He described this as a textual engagement technique: "It's better if I can just do a little bit every day and just to stay again involved and engaged." He noted that he uses more discovery early in the draft: "But the first 1,000 words or the first section up to the main argument for me is always the hardest part. It's always the part that takes the most tinkering to get to. It still works through all of these sections most of the time." Tinkering of the introduction in particular, which includes his purpose for writing, is critical for Ryan's process, which will also be reflected through his writing analytics, below.

WRITING TIMELINE, DOCUMENTS, AND WRITING SESSIONS

This section demonstrates how composing styles are not just self-reported preferences, but directly shape the drafting processes for Alice, Dan, and Ryan. Table 1 provides an overview of some key aspects of their composing gathered by the Google Draftback program. For this study, Alice worked in one document exclusively. Dan worked in three documents, including an early document that he worked on and compiled ideas in for 21 months (with the most extensive work during summers/breaks and into the first part of his sabbatical). When his sabbatical began, he started composing a second document and pasted large chunks from document 1, then extensively reworked them along with creating a third file that contains text he cut and pasted that he was not actively using. Finally, he cut and pasted the entire file into a "final" file, where he added references and engaged in light editing. Ryan worked in two documents, beginning with an initial draft where he composed the first 4,500 words. After a major shift in ideas, he transitioned to a second document where he completed the draft. The data in Table 1 compiles data from all documents each writer worked on during the study.

A "writing session" is defined by Google Draftback as any work on a document without more than a 10-minute gap. If a writer were to work on a document, then return to it 15 minutes later, or even pause to read a text for more than 10 minutes, that program would count that as a new writing session. Changes in a document (what Draftback defines as "revisions") indicate how many times the writer made additions, revisions, or deletions to the text.

Table 1.1. Time, Writing Sessions, Days, Changes, and Wordcount for Three Writers

Writer	Total Hours Logged in Google Docs	Total Writing Sessions	Total Changes in Document(s)*	Total Days when Writing Tool Place	Final Wordcount of Chapter
Alice (Planning)	21 hours 32 minutes	71	41,321	30	9,074
Dan (Discovery)	36 hours 41 minutes	146	117,516	48	12,182
Ryan (Hybrid)	51 hours 39 minutes	98	76,633	23	6,819

As Table 1.1 demonstrates, Alice worked on her text directly less than the other authors, both in terms of writing sessions and in terms of changes in her document. However, Alice's interviews and journal entries made it clear that she also devoted considerable time away from her draft reading, taking notes, and planning, none of which are accounted for in her total hours logged. On the other hand, Dan indicated that he had to write his way into understanding from the very beginning, and this was reflected in the amount of writing sessions and total changes he produced. Ryan's understanding of his purpose and goals shifted in significant ways several times, resulting in changes in his plan and shifting him into discovery mode. This shift is reflected in a moderate level of writing sessions and changes in the document.

Table 1.2 offers an overview of the average length of writing sessions and the average length of "writing days" for these three participants. As already described to some extent in the case study introductions above, the amount of time and frequency of writing depended on the material circumstances of each writer: Alice is retired and thus has regularly scheduled writing time throughout the week. Dan wrote primarily on his breaks and summers until his sabbatical, when he was able to dig in more deeply with regularly scheduled time. Ryan employed a writing strategy of frequently returning to his text to engage.

Table 1. 2. Session Length Recorded in Google Draftback

Participant	Shortest Recorded Session	Longest Recorded Session	Session Average
Alice (Planning)	48 seconds (4 changes)	1 hour 29 minutes (3605 changes)	18 minutes 12 seconds
Dan (Discovery)	13 seconds (25 changes)	1 hour 31 minutes (3725 changes)	15 minutes 0 seconds
Ryan (Hybrid)	26 seconds (15 changes)	1 hour 46 minutes (2360 changes)	25 minutes 24 seconds

Table 1.2 provides details about the length of the writers' writing sessions as recorded in the Google Draftback program. What is characteristic about the writers is that they may not have been "in" the draft the whole day, but they returned to it frequently (which Draftback registers as a separate writing session). The longest continuous writing for all three writers appears to be between 1 hour and 30 minutes to 1 hour and 46 minutes, although writers wrote up to three to five hours on average on a project in a long writing day, returning to the draft frequently, taking breaks, and engaging in other activities outside of the specific text.

WRITING PROCESS IN DOCUMENTS AND METRICS

What follows are writing analytic visualizations from Google Draftback that show both time (which you can read left to right across the graphics) and where in the document the writer worked (which you can read top to bottom). I have annotated the graphics further by indicating the primary activity that the author was engaging in during writing sessions in the graphics, which was ascertained from both the video playback in Google Draftback as well as writing journals each author kept. These phases include drafting, defined here as producing new text; revision, defined here as making higher-order or meaning-making changes to existing text; and copyediting, which is defined here as making small changes to existing text for the sake of clarity, precision, style, punctuation, or grammar. I offer these large phases with the caveat that these three phases are not mutually

Planning, Tinkering, and Writing to Learn

exclusive; all authors weaved between these three phases in various moments in their documents and for some, the different phases were melded together (and are thus indicated as such on the graphics). Thus, these broad labels offer a more generalized view about what they were doing in their document at various stages and can help readers better understand the analytic graphics.

Alice: Planning Composing Style

Alice's composing represented the most linear of the three styles in that she wrote on her draft from beginning to end. Reading Figure 1.1 from left to right, we see that Alice started her composing process at the top of her document, in the introduction, and worked her way methodically through the chapter. This linear composing is represented by the concentrated dots demonstrating that she stayed in the document largely where she was writing, and as she continued to compose paragraph after paragraph down the page. During her writing session on March 21st, she shifted to revision, which we can see by the dots appearing throughout the document and in several sections rather than in a linear fashion. She returned to linear writing on March 30th to complete the conclusion. After a break, she came back and began copyediting (represented by the long, thin lines showing she is moving from the beginning and down the document stopping at many points along the way), completing copyediting on April 9th.

What these solid lines represent is that Alice already has a clear plan for writing when she opens up her document and she is able to enact that plan in focused writing sessions where she completes sentence after sentence, paragraph after paragraph. Once most of the drafting is done, she turns her attention to revision, drafting the conclusion, and editing.

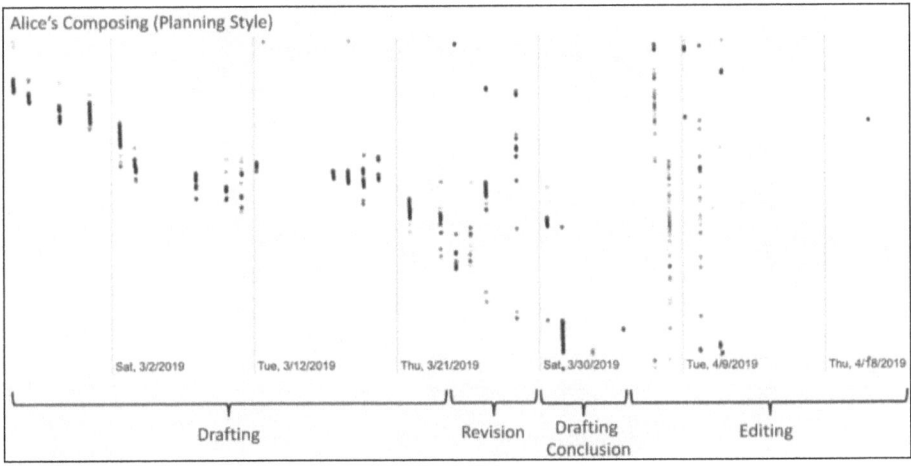

Figure 1.1. Alice's writing process

Dan: Discovery Composing Style

Figure 1.2 offers a visual of Dan's documents compiled from his multiple drafts. In comparing Alice's and Dan's images, we can immediately see differences in how the documents were shaped over time. Alice had clear "lines" where she was drafting ideas while Dan's moves around much more in his draft in each writing session and writing day. For example, in Dan's writing session on 9/6, many of the dots are spread out, indicating that he is making changes in many different parts of the document as he shapes his ideas. Evident in Document 1, Dan also returns frequently to the beginning of the document where he continues to refine his purpose for the chapter. The purpose evolves as his text evolves, which is why each time he opens Document 1, he first engages in the beginning of the document.

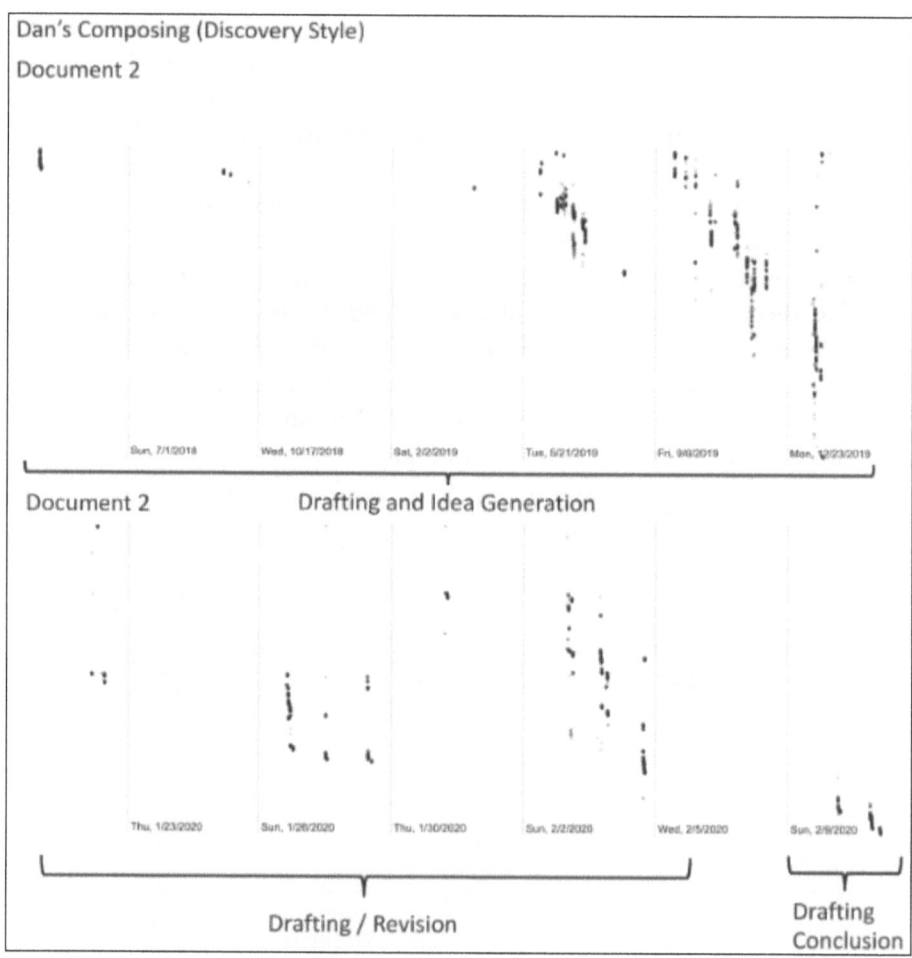

Figure 1.2, Dan's composing style

Planning, Tinkering, and Writing to Learn

Dan transitioned to Document 2 when he went on sabbatical, representing more focused writing time where he was able to complete his draft. Dan continues to generate and refine ideas in different places in the document, engaging in both drafting of new content and refining existing content. This is also when he creates the "notes" file where he cuts 2,400 words of text out of Document 2 and saves it in this file (as he indicates in his interview, for other parts of his book or for other later use).

The presence of engagement spread throughout the text is reflected in his interviews, the video playback of the text, and his writing journal. As Dan writes, he continues to refine his purpose over time, and often is returning to different sections of the document to refine, expand, or cut extraneous information and to figure out where material should be placed.

Ryan: Hybrid Planning/Discovery Composing Style

Ryan's process (Figure 1.3) represents a hybrid between the planning and discovery styles, which can also be reflected in how he engages with his text over time. Like Dan, Ryan frequently engages with the opening of his text and returns to it (in what he calls "tinkering") as he refines his purpose.

But, like Alice, Ryan also demonstrates more linear drafting, where he starts working on one section of a text and remains focused on that section for writing sessions. The major difference between Ryan and Alice is that Ryan "tinkers" with the earlier parts of the draft before coming to the next section and engaging in more focused composing, as he continues to refine his purpose. The revision/editing sections of Document 1 on October 29th and Document 2 on July 22nd represent Ryan reading through the text intensively and making both revisions to bring sections of the document in line with his evolved purpose as well as editing the document for clarity, precision, formatting, and punctuation.

While we see major distinctions in the drafting and revision portions of the writing process for the case study participants, the finalization of the manuscripts looks quite similar for all three writers. Once a writer's purpose is refined and the text is mostly drafted, all writers work on textual refinement and copyediting.

COMPOSING STYLES IN THE BROADER FIELD

Now that I've presented what the three composing styles are and how they function for writers as part of their process, I turn to examining how prevalent these styles are among professional academic writers in the field of composition, using self-reported survey data. The survey was completed by 198 individuals associated with the professional field of rhetoric and composition who had engaged in publication. Participants indicated a range of publication experience (from over

25 articles published to working on their first article). Participants reported a range of expertise in writing for publication, which was distributed fairly evenly among those considering themselves experts (27, 13.6%), advanced writers (52, 26.3%), intermediate writers (58, 24.7%), novice writers (49, 24.7%) or those not yet experienced (10, 5.1%).

Several multiple-choice questions asked participants to report their preference for planning or composing styles. I compiled the responses to these questions into composite responses indicating respondents' general composing style preference. Data show that Planners (strong or weak preference) comprised only 10.6 percent of the dataset; Discoverers (strong or weak preference) comprised 48.4 percent of the dataset. Hybrid Planner/Discoverers comprised 38.9 percent of the dataset; these numbers almost identically map onto the case study participant distribution. Thus, these statistics suggest that most writers employ discovery composing styles or use them in combination with planning, while only a small subset of writers rely more extensively on planning as a primary composing style.

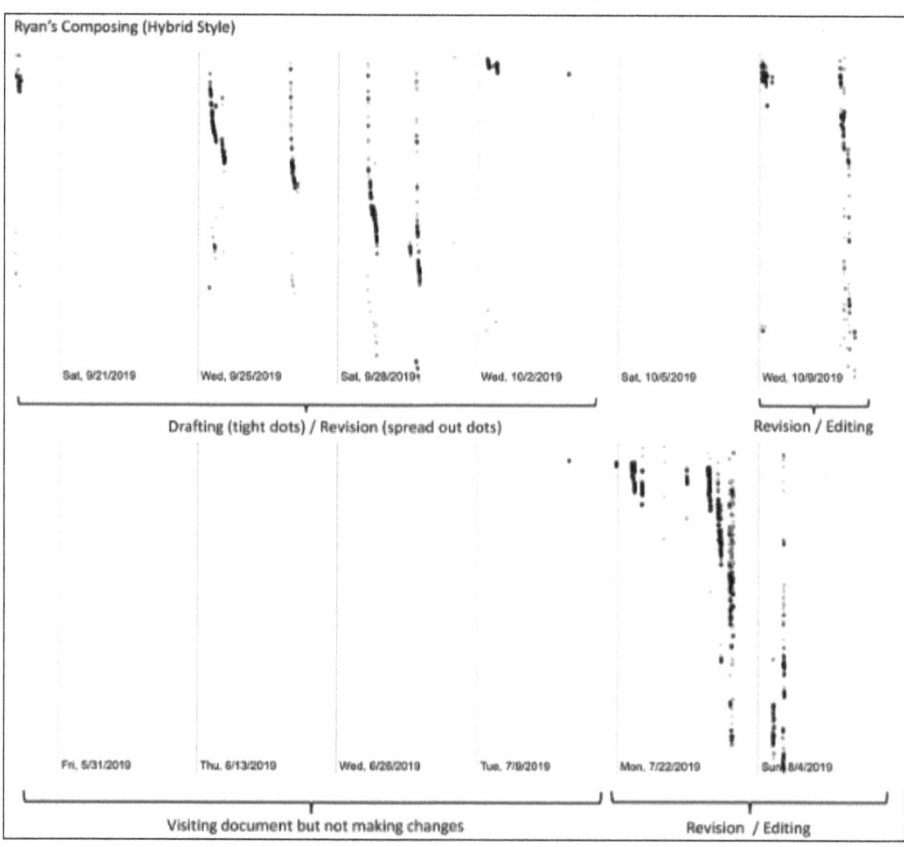

Figure 1.3. Ryan's process

Planning, Tinkering, and Writing to Learn

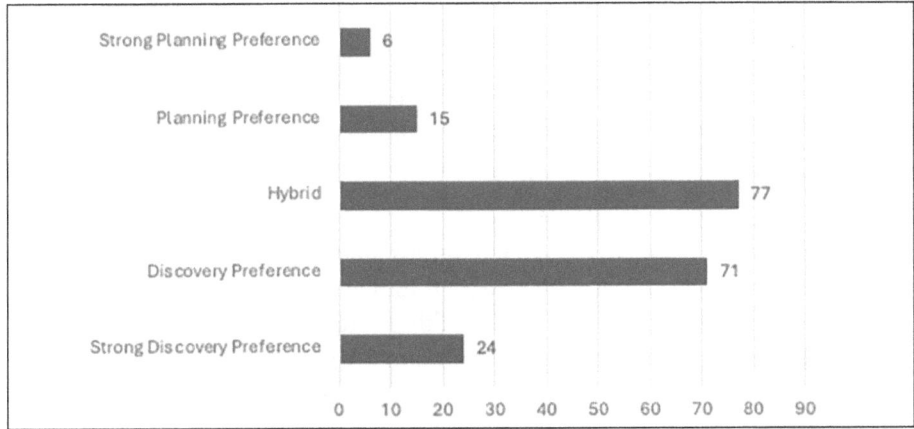

Figure 1.4. Composing styles among survey participants

I also asked whether composing style is correlated with the demographic or institutional factors. Composing style is not correlated with self-reported expertise, institutional status, teaching load, gender, ethnicity, or how many publications one has produced. However, composing style is significantly correlated with required publication (Pearson's correlation, two-tailed, bivariate, 0.142, p <0.048, n =194). That is, individuals who reported that publication was required as part of their job or studies were more likely to indicate a planning preference. Forty-eight percent (95) of participants indicated that writing for publication was a required part of their job, while five percent (10) indicated it was not.[2] But beyond this single correlation, composing style appears to be a matter of individual preference.

OPERATIONALIZING THE MODEL OF PLANNING, DISCOVERY, AND HYBRID COMPOSING STYLES

Based on the above, I offer the following definitions and model for the Planning, Discovery, and Hybrid composing styles, including features and developmental trajectories. For this model, one of the key differences between planners and discoverers is where the invention takes place: in the head or on the page. This, then, shapes the drafting and revision process for each writer.

---

2   Six percent of participants used the "other: please specify" category to outline myriad circumstances which mostly boiled down to "it's complicated but not required." Many noted their institutions "strongly encouraged" them to publish; others noted that while they were in adjunct or non-tenure lines, they wanted to publish to get a better position. Others, like graduate students, noted that while it wasn't a requirement, it was an expectation. These were coded as "not required" in the dataset.

35

Planners

Planners are writers who choose to employ extensive invention strategies to preplan their texts before they sit down to compose. The result of extensive planning allows them to achieve a more linear and direct writing process.

Features of Planning Composing Styles

- *Invention:* Planners engage in copious amounts of invention prior to sitting down to write. These activities may include outlining, making lists, organizing sources, and thinking through ideas. Planners may also create extensive outlines with target word counts, what the purpose of each section is, and the overall purpose for the piece.
- *Purpose:* Planners use their invention strategies to clearly define their purpose for the text prior to writing.
- *Drafting:* Planners engage in efficient drafting processes, writing directly to their purpose and generating a minimal amount of extra prose. Planners predetermine the order, length, and content of what they want to write, and their drafting proceeds from that plan.
- *Revision:* Revision often takes place after drafting, following a more classic writing process approach where the text is refined after the drafting is largely completed.
- *In between writing sessions:* Planners often have extensive "planning sessions" in between major writing sessions where they think through or outline the next phase of the draft. Thinking through these activities might be done during repetitive activity like exercising, walking, or cooking. Planners may make use of notebooks, boards, or other organizational aids as part of their process.
- *Process and order of ideas:* The writing process appears on the page as fairly linear; section after section is written in the planned order during drafting.

Discoverers

Discoverers use writing-to-learn as a way to generate new ideas, deeply explore concepts, and refine their purposes. Drafting is often messy, recursive, and may generate much more prose that is later discarded.

Features of Discovery Composing Styles

- *Invention:* Discoverers will jump right in to drafting with a very loose plan or purpose. While they have often thought about the ideas behind the text, this thinking process is often conceptual rather than driven directly towards producing an outline or writing plan. They recognize the power of writing to learn and depend on the act of writing itself to help them discover their purpose and write their way into understanding.

- *Purpose:* The purpose of the writing is refined and revised extensively during each composing session, although writers may wrestle with ideas in between sessions.
- *Drafting:* Discoverers frequently return to their overall goals and purpose to refine, scrap, or amend ideas. They may end up writing "multiple articles" and generating more prose than is needed for the text, sometimes on tangents that can later lead to future work. This can result in multiple versions of documents, cutting and pasting large chunks of texts that may be shaped into other publications, and writing in several potential directions before settling on one direction.
- *Revision:* Discoverers often engage in drafting and revision in the same writing session; writing done in previous sessions is revisited and refined throughout while the writer also drafts new material.
- *In between writing sessions:* Discoverers report engaging with ideas and concepts in between sessions, but not always towards crafting a distinct plan for writing.
- *Process and order of ideas:* The writer often jumps around considerably during the drafting process, and may work on small sections throughout the draft. These sections are not linear or sequential.

Hybrids

Hybrid Planner-Discoverers

Hybrids use a combination of planning and discovery, which may be either a personal preference or required due to the demands of the specific topic, their knowledge of the topic, and the genre they are writing in. Hybrid processes are a combination of the features above, but hybrid processes may manifest differently depending on the specific writer. Some writers have distinctive plans for certain parts of their draft, while recognizing that they need to engage in writing to learn (discovery) for other parts of their draft; thus, they employ both approaches simultaneously. Other writers may begin as planners with a clear and detailed plan, and then, once engaging in the writing process, quickly realize the original plan needs to be scrapped. This might be because their original idea wasn't nuanced or complex enough, their thinking or data had led them in another direction, or they encountered new information that shifted their thinking. Thus, while they started with a plan they thought was workable, they moved into discovery mode, where they worked to use the writing itself to develop a clear sense of purpose.

DISCUSSION

In the case of either planning or discovery, writers considerably engage with their subject matter, their sources, and their texts. The key difference that this study demonstrates is in both invention and drafting. For planners, writing is used primarily as a vehicle to convey their thoughts and purpose (returning to Fulwiler and Young's (1982) "writing to communicate"). For discoverers, writing is originally used to help refine and shape their ideas and to literally generate knowledge (or Fulwiler and Young's "writing to learn"). Discoverers later do shift to a "writing to communicate" approach as they enter the end of their revision and editing stages. Writers of both composing style preferences engage recursively with their texts (Kellogg, 1994)—planners simply do it in their heads and up front through notes and outlines, while discoverers find that the act of writing helps refine their purpose and thinking. Hybrids employ a range of these approaches depending on the rhetorical situation, their knowledge, and the genre.

One thing that is striking about the case studies is the way in which writers, when presented with the early planning-discovery composing style model, could both articulate their preference for the framework and offer a discussion of why that particular composing style worked for them. Expert writers offer deep understanding of their own nuanced writing processes and have learned, over time, to trust in the processes that they have developed. While these findings expand and deepen our understanding of writing process, they also closely align and support earlier works on expertise, both from the perspective of the psychology of writing (Kellogg, 1994; Kellogg, 2006), writing to learn (Bean, 2012), and faculty writing practices in the field (Wells & Söderlund, 2018; Tulley, 2018).

While the case studies in phase 1 of the study helped explore the nature of the planning, discovery, and hybrid composing styles, the survey offered broader insight into how these styles may manifest in members of the discipline and what factors, if any, correlate. Based on limited correlations in the survey and from my case study participants' clear articulation of their composing style, composing style appears to be a personal writing choice. That is, it does not appear to be impacted by one's expertise, number of previous publications, teaching load or administrative responsibilities, institutional status, experience, gender, or race. The one correlation this study found was that planning was weakly but significantly correlated with required publication, suggesting that individuals with the pressure to publish may engage in planning more out of necessity in a "publish or perish" situation. The choice of discovery was as likely to occur with those who identify as novice professional academic writers, including those new to publication, as it was for those who have published 25 or more books or articles.

The unequal distribution of those who express discovery or hybrid methods in the survey may also signal a deeper truth about the challenges of generating novel ideas and contributions that shape a discipline and ultimately contribute to human knowledge. Thus, it appears that for most writers, the act of writing itself is the best vehicle for this deep engagement with ideas to take place, through recursive processes (Kellogg, 1994) that allow deepening of thinking and purpose.

IMPLICATIONS: STRATEGIES FOR DEVELOPING EXPERT WRITING PROCESSES

One concern present in all of the case studies, both incomplete and featured here, was what appeared to be an implicit bias towards more orderly, linear, and planned processes. For example, one expert writer who in the longitudinal study indicated a Discovery composing style recognized that their "messy" discovery process produced high-quality publications, spoke of their process as a nightmare: "Again, I had to laugh when you write Beethoven [Discovery] . . . I usually have four Google Docs open for a project where one is a clipboard, one is one section, one is another section. . . . It's a nightmare." Another Discovery composing style participant said, "Yeah, I'm definitely a Beethoven (Discovery) and that's a nice way to put it because I've always thought of it as just a shitty first drafter or the opposite of the perfect drafter person." As these two quotes indicate, for some of those who engage in discovery-based processes, a negative view of a more "messy" process may impact their self-perception as writers.

I suspect this issue comes from at least two sources. First, despite the field's extensive research and theories concerning moving "beyond" the traditional linear process approach (Kent, 1999), much high school writing and first-year composition pedagogy is still taught with a linear view of writing, using the traditional writing process model. Second, the short deadlines required in many courses means there are simply fewer opportunities to engage in deep discovery—which for all case study writers took considerable amounts of time. Participants in my study wrestled with their texts for months and years before coming up with a manuscript that they were willing to submit for publication. Coursework seldom allows that to happen and creates perhaps a distorted view of the necessary writing processes for deep engagement.

In fact, in teaching doctoral-level writing for publication as well as supporting advanced graduate writing as the director of our university's writing center, I have frequently heard students express frustration over the messy nature of writing dissertations and articles. They come into a writing for publication course with an expectation that their writing should look somewhat linear and proceed in an orderly fashion and lament that there is something "wrong" with their writing when they end up having to engage in Discovery writing. During my analysis and early writing of this article, I shared my emerging results about composing styles with my writing for publication students. After experiencing the need to shift into discovery and abandon their plan, many students noted the relief that expert writers routinely experience these messy experiences and that they weren't "doing it wrong." Thus, one key implication of this work, I hope, is that we can use it to teach graduate students and novice writers that writing for publication is often messy, unstructured, and, ultimately, a process of discovery.

Given all of the above, I offer the following key points that can help the field broaden our understanding of expert writing processes and support novices seeking to write for publication:

- *Cultivating key habits of mind that support discovery-based and hybrid processes.* These habits of mind (Framework for Success in Postsecondary Writing, 2011) include (a) flexibility that allows writers to abandon previous plans in favor of novel directions and develop deeper purpose, focus, and goals through drafting; (b) openness to explore ideas originally not considered as part of a plan; and (c) creativity, which is critical to cultivate for the production of novel ideas. Central to these habits of mind is recognizing that when we enter new subject areas or write in new genres, we might have to write our way into understanding.
- *Understanding the ongoing and recursive nature of invention.* Invention for expert writers doesn't fit the typical linear process. Rather, invention is something that writers are always engaging in—as they plan, as they discover, as they refine their purpose and goals. Invention strategies may be internalized through a planning style or manifest on the page, through a discovery style.
- *Recognizing the value of purpose-driven drafting and recursive writing.* Key to both planning and discovery is defining and refining one's purpose for writing. As the writers' purpose was defined and refined, they shifted drafts, goals, and approaches.
- *Valuing the writing of extra prose.* Expert writers may write many more volumes of prose that ends up not being part of their final published products. It is useful not to see this extra prose as "wasted" but rather material that can be reshaped into future publications and projects.

CONCLUSION

Planning, discovery, and hybrid composing styles appear to be a key preference for expert writers that considerably shape their invention and drafting processes, and that seem to be a matter of personal preference. Understanding these composing styles can offer the field new ways both of exploring writing as a tool for communication and learning, and also in supporting graduate students and new scholars in developing successful approaches to writing. Further, this work opens up a potentially new line of writing process research. Some of the many questions future researchers might explore are: How do emerging professional writers' drafting processes for coursework versus publications differ? How might we best teach and study the efficacy of these practices? How do we cultivate the habits of mind necessary for flexible writing processes? I encourage teachers and researchers to continue to pursue these questions.

REFERENCES

Bean, J. C. (2011). *Engaging ideas: The professor's guide to integrating writing, critical thinking, and active learning in the classroom*. John Wiley & Sons. https://books.google.com/books/about/Engaging_Ideas.html?id=AnMsEAAAQBAJ.

Brooks, L. (2011). *Story engineering*. Penguin. https://www.penguinrandomhouse.ca/books/632707/story-engineering-by-larry-brooks/9781599632810.

Carter, M. (2007). Ways of knowing, doing, and writing in the disciplines. *College Composition and Communication, 58*(3), 385–418. https://www.jstor.org/stable/20456952.

Cowley, M. (Ed.). (1958). *Writers at work: The Paris Review interviews*. Vol 1. Viking Press.

Emig, J. (1977). Writing as a mode of learning. *College Composition and Communication, 28*(2), 122–128. https://doi.org/10.2307/356095.

Flower, L. & Hayes, J. R. (1981). A cognitive process theory of writing. *College Composition and Communication, 32*(4), 365–387. https://doi.org/10.2307/356600.

Fulwiler, T. & Young, A. (1982). *Language connections: Writing and reading across the curriculum*. National Council of Teachers of English.

Gallagher, J. R. & DeVoss, D. N. (Eds.). (2019). *Explanation points: Publishing in rhetoric and composition*. Utah State University Press. https://doi.org/10.7330/9781607328834.

Henry, J. & Baker, T. H. Õ. (2015). Writing to learn and learning to perform: Lessons from a writing intensive course in experimental theatre studio. *Across the Disciplines, 12*(4). https://doi.org/10.37514/ATD-J.2015.12.4.19.

Kellogg, R. T. (1994). *The psychology of writing*. Oxford University Press. https://doi.org/10.1093/acprof:oso/9780195098372.001.0001.

Kellogg, R. T. (2006). Professional writing expertise. In K. A. Ericsson, N. Charness, P. J. Feltovich & R. R. Hoffman (Eds.), *The Cambridge handbook of expertise and expert performance* (pp. 389–402). Cambridge University Press. https://doi.org/10.1017/CBO9780511816796.022.

Klein, P. D. & Unsworth, L. (2014). The logogenesis of writing to learn: A systemic functional perspective. *Linguistics and Education, 26*, 1–17. https://doi.org/10.1016/j.linged.2013.12.003.

Langer, J. A. & Applebee, A. N. (1987). *How writing shapes thinking: A study of teaching and learning.* The WAC Clearinghouse. https://wac.colostate.edu/books/landmarks/langer_applebee (Originally published in 1987 by National Council of Teachers of English).

Scardamalia, M. & Bereiter, C. (1991). Literate expertise. *Toward a general theory of expertise: Prospects and limits, 172*, 194. https://doi.org/10.1017/CBO9780511816796.011.

Silva, A. M. & Limongi, R. (2019). Writing to learn increases long-term memory consolidation: A mental-chronometry and computational modeling study of "Epistemic writing." *Journal of Writing Research, 11*(1), 211–243. https://doi.org/10.17239/jowr-2019.11.01.07.

Söderlund, L. & Wells, J. (2019). A study of the practices and responsibilities of scholarly peer review in rhetoric and composition. *College Composition and Communication, 71*(1), 117–144. https://www.jstor.org/stable/26821317.

Tarr, B., Launay, J. & Dunbar, R. I. (2016). Silent disco: dancing in synchrony leads to elevated pain thresholds and social closeness. *Evolution and Human, 37*(5), 343–349. https://doi.org/10.1016/j.evolhumbehav.2016.02.004.

Tulley, C. E. (2018). *How writing faculty write: Strategies for process, product, and productivity.* Utah State University Press.

Wells, J. M. & Söderlund, L. (2018). Preparing graduate students for academic publishing: Results from a study of published rhetoric and composition scholars. *Pedagogy, 18*(1), 131–156. https://doi.org/10.1215/15314200-4216994.

CHAPTER 2.

FACULTY PRESENCE, INFLUENCE, AND AUTHORITY IN INTERDISCIPLINARY, MULTI-LEVEL WRITING GROUPS

Aileen R. Taft
University of Missouri

Rebecca Day Babcock and Maximillien Vis
The University of Texas, Permian Basin

Abstract: *This chapter's research focuses on group dynamics, authority interactions, and group stability. The chapter outlines how faculty benefit from these groups by gaining mentorship, diverse perspectives, and sustained engagement in their writing practices. The authors highlight the advantages of mixed-level groups, particularly for contingent faculty and graduate students, and argue that writing studies could lead in promoting such groups for inclusive writing support across academia.*

The authors are members of a research team that has been looking at the social nature of writing since 2014. So far, we have done several conference presentations and produced several article manuscripts around this theme. Babcock's team comprises students (both graduate and undergraduate, including Aileen), adjunct, non-tenure track, and contingent faculty. The activities they are engaging in are writing fellowships, writing retreats (both online and in person), writing groups, and writing workshops. The reason for this is a workaround, as Babcock's home institution does not have a writing center in the traditional sense. This study looked at the experiences of faculty who participated in feedback-giving writing groups (as opposed to "just write" groups) that were multi-level and interdisciplinary. By "multi-level," we mean writing groups that included people from various disciplines and stages of career. Since we are affiliated with a medium-sized institution, such groups become a necessity as we sometimes do not have enough people to form a segregated group.

For instance, we tried recently to hold an online graduate writing retreat, but after not finding enough graduate students to participate, we opened it to both undergrads and faculty. We studied two iterations of one such group based out of a regional comprehensive university in the Southwest. Members of the groups were from the disciplines of English, Spanish, history, and psychology, both part-time university graduate teaching assistants and full-time community college faculty along with undergraduate students. We also presented narratives from faculty members who are in writing groups with non-faculty, both in the academic and non-academic context. A special focus will be on comparing the interactions with the authority of the participants, outcome, stability, and effectiveness of the writing groups.

Writing groups take many forms but primarily are broken down into feedback groups where writers share drafts and give each other feedback and "just write" types of groups where participants actually sit and write in supportive community settings either online or in person. Groups can be self-sponsored, or university- or workplace-sponsored. Wolfsberfer (2014) found that they can also occur in private, for-profit settings. Groups can focus on academic or creative writing, on a single discipline or level, or be mixed. Groups can be single gender or mixed gender. They can be online or in-person. In-person groups can meet in university settings, in public places such as coffee shops, people's homes, or outdoors. The combinations are endless, but the goal is the same: to develop as writers. Through participation in mixed level groups, faculty can benefit from viewing other perspectives, from having opportunities for mentoring, and for learning firsthand about various writing processes and practices.

LITERATURE REVIEW

Writing studies research has argued for the importance of writing support for a variety of faculty and students, including contingent faculty and graduate students from across the disciplines. However, writing studies scholars have not researched mixed-level groups, perhaps because these groups are still uncommon, despite the benefits these types of groups can offer all members such as peer mentoring, unconditional support, and a fresh perspective on ideas. Of course, various challenges are also involved, which our research will show. We draw from the higher education book *Writing Groups for Doctoral Education and Beyond: Innovations in Practice and Theory* (Aitchison, 2014), but we argue writing studies may be particularly well equipped to research mixed-level groups and that such groups may be especially helpful in providing the kind of writing support our field has called for, especially for graduate students and contingent faculty. Our chapter is a first step toward filling this gap.

One of the editors of this collection suggested we look at the edited collection *Speaking Up, Speaking Out* (Edwards et al., 2021) for potential mentions of writing groups. Interestingly enough, the collection does not mention writing groups at all, except for briefly and in passing. For instance, Mulally (2021) mentions other scholars talking about writing groups. One chapter mentions writing in a coffee shop (Gumm, 2021) yet rather than gathering to write, the two faculty who encounter each other at the coffee shop in this chapter actively avoided each other rather than engaging in community writing practices. Another article mentioned two faculty members writing together as a duo (Joseph & Ashe-McNalley, 2021). Perhaps the lack of attention to or mention of faculty participating in writing groups has to do with the high workload and lack of pressure to produce scholarship among non-tenure track faculty.

The collection *Working with Faculty Writers* edited by Geller and Eodice (2013) also mentioned faculty writing groups, including interdisciplinary faculty (Clark-Oates & Cahill, 2013) and graduate student groups (Garciaet al., 2013), but none of the groups mentioned in this collection were multi-level. Our group was not sponsored by a writing center; the lack of a writing center at our institution was one of the reasons why Babcock has arranged these groups. However, our group displayed many of the same dynamics as the writing center-sponsored group that Clark-Oates and Cahill described, such as "tensions" arising from "disciplinary differences," and groups having to "commit to co-constructing solutions to writing tensions by recognizing one another as fellow writers" (p. 114). As a multidisciplinary group, our group also displayed the positive effects noted by Garcia et al. (2013), such as witnessing ways of "thinking, researching and writing" other than what they "had grown accustomed to" (p. 267). We also reached the outcomes they mentioned of peer mentoring and learning about different writing processes and practices. Smith et al. (2013) found that in addition to professional development goals, writers also found a social outlet and support in their multidisciplinary faculty writing group.

Like many such groups, the make-up of the groups we studied was primarily women, which Bosanquet et al. (2014) noted in their literature review is very common. Bosanquet and her colleagues did not deliberately set out to form an all-women writing group, but it just turned out that way. Female faculty members in writing groups have indicated that their group "was able to informally provide writing supports, relationship supports, and a mechanism for understanding the culture of the . . . university" (Penney et al., 2015, p. 462). These groups can begin to construct an informal community of practice that extends beyond academia enabling "participants to reflect more meaningfully upon their own story and create a space for a collective understanding of experience and knowledge co-creation" (Penney et al., 2015, p. 463). The writing group assumed a role beyond critique where participants exchange similar experiences and challenges in their respective roles. While our groups were not exclusionary and were open to any gender, the group ended up as mostly female with only one consistent male student attendee and one or two other male attendees who visited for one meeting and did not return. All of the group's faculty members were female, not by choice but by coincidence.

Writing groups can offer early career academics a chance to find pleasure in academic writing (Dwyer et al., 2012). Other benefits of writing groups were "publishing acumen . . . collaborative collegiality . . . leadership" and enhanced affect, meaning over time, writing group members become "motivated, more confident, satisfied, pleased with the investment" (Galligan et al., 2003). Although the groups mentioned here in this chapter are not "just write" groups, as group members offered each other feedback on actual texts rather than just spending time writing together, the groups we reported here are for the most part interdisciplinary and multi-level. This allowed for flexible roles and for group members to act both as mentors and mentees (Mewburn et al., 2014).

When faculty were present in groups with undergraduates, graduate students, and even non-academics, roles were fluid and the "lines between 'master' and 'apprentice' [were] lightly drawn" (Maher, 2014, p. 91). Presence in the group by people at different points on the academic journey can be distinctly positive. Although faculty may hold the highest status within academia in relation to scholarship and student identity, a disparity exists between faculty and other individuals with assorted identities. Faculty often find themselves, as students well do, wearing multiple and variable hats. Faculty members not only serve students, but also may be graduate student teaching assistants serving their fellow peers, who may range from graduate students to post-graduate junior faculty to senior tenured faculty. Faculty status does not magically ensure independence but only further complicates the interdependence of faculty's multifaceted identity. Faculty in mixed-level writing groups working alongside graduate and undergraduate students can model what it looks like to be a productive writer and researcher. Maher (2014) noted that faculty presence in the *Write On!* writing group she studied was an inspiration to graduate students who could witness a model of productive writing and researching. These groups were not feedback groups but "just write" kinds of groups. Murray (2014) also noted the presence of "doctoral and post-doctoral writers" (p. 107) in the micro-writing groups she studied.

Scholarship on faculty identity in writing groups has been centered upon scholarly productivity. Whether that be doctoral studies within medicine or the liberal arts or science, scholarship centered around faculty focuses upon the discrepancy which exists in scholarship of post-graduates who serve as faculty in some regards and established and oftentimes tenured faculty. Chai et al. (2019) found that "Implementing a writing group focused upon junior faculty members that provides structured time for the discussion of academic advancement, while providing peer support in an equitable environment, can help to guide new faculty members" (p. 569). These transitional identities are seen to focus upon the scholarly responsibilities of faculty and downplay the intersectionality of teacher-as-student reality.

The writing group in its complex nature with regards to variable identity and scholarly or personal wants and needs establishes a microcosm of the expectations, practices, and standards of academia. Whereas interdisciplinary writing groups may or may not influence these scholarly social constructions, little has been done to elucidate how faculty benefit from being in writing groups with students. According to Haas (2014), whether a group is single- or multi-disciplinary or single- or multi-level does not influence the potential success of the group.

Multidisciplinary groups allow for cross-pollination and "fresh eyes" to look at writings as an educated outsider. Yet, the interdisciplinary aspect of academia seems to be a growing trend amongst post-graduate studies. Guerin et al. (2013) state that

> As traditional disciplinary boundaries blur and Ph.D. projects are increasingly focused on interdisciplinary investigations, the scholarly identities formed during the doctorate are also shifting. As disciplinary identities become progressively uncertain, so too do the proscribed communities of practice those identities seek to operate within. (p. 78)

The current trend of interdisciplinary scholarship increases the need for interdisciplinary writing groups as a writer may face multiple and various disciplinary connections through their research and writings. The more interconnected scholarly and scientific research becomes, the more there is a need for interdisciplinary feedback and peer review amidst academia. Multidisciplinary groups also run the risk of confusing people and making them feel the feedback is irrelevant. Faculty presence in writing groups whose participants include non-faculty members can initially cause the non-faculty members participation anxiety, as they are inclined to believe that their critiques are peripheral. However, the varied input from differing levels of academia as well as mixed disciplinary groups proves indispensable to the growth of writers, in particular, faculty participants who often lack professional academic interaction with student-level writers beyond the classroom (which can cause a messaging disconnect between entry-level audiences and academic audiences).

To investigate faculty presence and experience in writing groups, we decided to study the dynamics of two interdisciplinary, multi-level writing groups that contained both faculty and student members—including those (Graduate Teaching Assistants) in an in-between space. The first group we discuss was composed of three graduate students who met infrequently during a spring semester on Fridays for a writing "power hour." For some of their meetings, the three graduate students were joined by a faculty member of their acquaintance. For this group, we investigated the experiences of the faculty members present (and not present) in the group and how their authority was created and maintained (or not). We considered the intersectional nature of graduate teaching assistants for their perceived and interpreted faculty identity. We also speculated on people's motivations for participating in the group and what they took from it.

METHODS

We obtained IRB clearance to perform naturalistic observation through audio recordings of two iterations of a university-sponsored interdisciplinary, multi-level writing group. The nature of the group is to provide faculty members a community of practice through exposure of different viewpoints and methodologies and support as writers. Each group held semi-structured meetings in which participants met to discuss writing. These groups were not sponsored through a writing center or writing program, and two different master's students (graduate assistants) were assigned to facilitate such groups by their supervisor, Babcock, as part of their duties. Each graduate student was to meet with the group weekly and to solicit their participation in this study. Taft was a member of both writing groups, although she was more of a regular member of the first group and only an accidental member of the second. Researchers gained permission under IRB–003–2018 to conduct this research. Participants were not required to participate in the study to participate in the writing groups.

DATA

The data collected for this study consisted of Taft's and Vis's narrative recollections of the first and second groups and recordings and transcripts of the second group from three sessions in November 2023 (November 11, 18 and 25) during Writing Power Hours. Neither group was consistent with their documentation of the meetings due to technological and human errors. As a result, most of our data presented in this chapter consisted of Taft's and Vis's narratives and quotes from the recorded group. For a paper that analyzed the group talk itself, see Vis and Babcock (forthcoming).

Taft's Narrative of the First Writing Group

The first writing group began in the fall of 2018, the last semester of my graduate school experience. Tasked with co-founding a writing group by my department chairperson and supervisor, a fellow graduate teaching assistant (GTA) and I began a yearlong adventure into critiquing everything from freshman composition essays to adjunct faculty forays into psychological thrillers.

We met weekly in a classroom at the university. Attendance at the writing group varied, but after a month of meeting once a week, we established a reliable base group of writers. The group included Renee—my fellow GTA in the English department, Edwin—a freshman geology student, Kaitlyn—an adjunct professor in psychology, and me (all names are pseudonyms).

Given the varied academic background of each writer, the conversations surrounding the offered texts often sparked interesting dialogue and built a unique camaraderie among members. This was even clearer when a certain level of comfort was reached among the participants of the group. The intimidation of presenting writing to individuals who were still strangers caused some awkwardness, particularly to those in the group who were not used to critiquing or grading writing. To begin, Renee and I laid out some ground rules for our small group of aspiring and experienced writers. We would take turns presenting our writing to the group so that each person could receive help without any one person dominating the ability of the others to receive feedback. Renee first volunteered to share a term paper that she was writing for one of her graduate classes. Edwin and Kaitlyn were slow to offer input in the first meeting and would hesitate when giving an opinion or would second-guess themselves. They would make statements like, "I am sure you know the answer to this, but should there be a comma or a semicolon there?" and "I am a little unsure what you mean there, but I probably just missed something." These types of hesitant critiques were typical when either Renee or I would present our academic writings from the various classes we were attending. Kaitlyn was an experienced writer and did not want her voice to be the loudest in the room with writing feedback. Although Kaitlyn was the faculty member in the group, which may have warranted for a supervisory or expert role, her self-declared expertise was in psychology, not in writing. This caused Kaitlyn's faculty role in the group to fall into a unique position where she sought to benefit from less experienced writers because their area of focus was writing. Kaitlyn made occasional statements about her hesitancy to offer feedback since she was sure that GTAs in English knew much more than she did and that, since she had not taken the same writing-intensive classes, she felt she did not have as much to offer. Even though both Renee and I assured

Kaitlyn that her unbiased outside perspective on our writing as a reader was of great value to us, the same hesitancy remained.

When it was Kaitlyn's turn to present her writing, she primarily shared pieces of creative nonfiction and narratives about mental health that stemmed from her research interests. Kaitlyn's writings focused on a young woman who dealt with a multiple personality disorder and was on the Autism spectrum. Kaitlyn used her background in psychology and personal narratives to inform her writing, and she wanted the themes in the story to transcend beyond a simple work of creative nonfiction into a therapeutic piece to which others sharing similar diagnoses as that of the primary subject could relate. Consequently, her apparent valuing of an academic critique appeared higher than that of Edwin, the student writer in the group. Renee and I would offer both higher-order and lower-order critiques of a more academic nature, while Kaitlyn and Edwin would discuss the creative writing elements, such as dialogue. Kaitlyn accepted feedback with an attitude that displayed genuine appreciation and interest, whether it was from Renee and me, who could almost be considered peers to Kaitlyn (as graduate teaching assistants and adjuncts are only one step away from each other on the academic hierarchy), or it was from Edwin, a first-year writer with similar interests but below Kaitlyn in education and writing experience. Kaitlyn served as a mentor for Edwin, helping him craft a more mature approach to his work by sharing her own ups and downs when she was a new writer. Kaitlyn's faculty experience allowed her the ability and comfort to have difficult conversations with Edwin, the student member, when he would get off track not just in conversation but in writing content. Kaitlyn's writing could be categorized as creative nonfiction since her narratives applied her academic experience in the field of psychology along with her personal experiences with family mental health and her work in the field as a licensed therapist. Because of the need for anonymity while writing about more sensitive mental health issues, Kaitlyn embraced the genre of creative nonfiction for much of her academic writings.

As the writing group meetings continued throughout the semester, Renee and I brought fewer pieces to critique since we were writing on tighter deadlines, and we would often already have a paper written and submitted to our professors and advisors for evaluation before the writing group would meet. Since our work was already being evaluated for a grade, we did not feel the need to receive additional critiques. Edwin also seemed to prefer critiquing other people's writing over having his own writing examined by the group, presumably because of his insecurities about constructive critiques. Thus, Kaitlyn became almost the sole contributor of writings for the group to discuss in the last couple of months the group met. This arrangement, while perhaps not seeming equitable at first glance, worked well for the group members as we settled into a comfortable routine. Renee, Edwin, and I were all happy to give Kaitlyn insight into her work, and Kaitlyn made statements about how she would never run out of things to bring since she had been working on her writings for a long time and enjoyed hearing other perspectives. Kaitlyn did not have a standing office at the university and did not have frequent opportunities to interact with her academic colleagues or to share professional work. The writing group became her outlet for academic collaboration. Given Kaitlyn's apparent view of Renee and me as peers with equal or superior knowledge of academic writing, Kaitlyn's adjunct faculty status did not appear to impede her ability to accept the group's critique or to function on a similar level. Being the teacher of record for freshman comp classes while in grad school appeared to help lessen any perceived gap in ranking between Kaitlyn and me. Even though Kaitlyn chose to often write narrative and creative nonfiction, her academic research within those writings focused on similar themes as Renee's. These shared research interests of social justice within writing centers (Renee) and social justice for mental health diagnoses (Kaitlyn) created cohesion within the writing group even though we had several different faculty disciplines and levels represented.

The writing group continued meeting for about two months following the same established pattern until the onset of two challenges to the group's long-term preservation. Often, when the group had completed an hour's worth of writing-focused dialogue and the meeting had officially concluded, Renee, Kaitlyn, and I would remain for up to thirty minutes longer conversing about personal perspectives and shared experiences, typically academic in nature but sometimes strictly personal. Group comfort increased with continued personal conversations causing the participants' personalities to become more readily apparent. While the group was cordial and collegial with these casual conversations, Kaitlyn would often interject with information or personal anecdotes which did not align or correlate with the given topic, creating difficulties in completing critiques of writing or even politely ending the group meetings so that the members could disperse to their next obligation. As a result, when Renee and I were able to conclude the group meetings after only one hour, we discussed feeling a sense of relief since conversations involving Kaitlyn became more scattered. We believed that Kaitlyn used the writing group as a personal social outlet as well as a place to receive academic writing feedback, while Renee and I only viewed the group as an academic and professional development group. Even though Kaitlyn was a faculty member, it appeared that her tendency to stray off topic was an individual issue and not something that would be characteristic of all faculty members in a multi-level writing group. Another challenge to group persistence came when a full-time faculty member joined the writing group.

Samantha, a non-tenure track lecturer (contingent faculty) in history, joined the group approximately one month before official writing group meetings ceased. Samantha was new to the university and appeared eager to find her niche even within mixed groups with non-faculty. She arrived with knitting needles and yarn, silently listening and entertaining herself with her knitting during her first meeting. After she gained comfort with the group, she also began to offer critiques of the other participants' work, although she declined to present work of her own, relaying that she was working on something and would share it when it was nearer an intermediate draft stage. She seemed hesitant to share her own writing, perhaps because of holding the most senior academic role in the group. Yet, she was comfortable giving feedback, a task she would have utilized heavily as a faculty member. Although Renee and I were initially excited to have attracted another faculty participant to our writing group, we soon realized that Samantha's motivation for participation in the writing group stemmed from the opportunity to discuss academic knowledge and subject matter with an attentive audience. Edwin, being a student in one of Samantha's classes, readily engaged with her in debates over the meaning behind historic events or the value of one type of education over another, while the other group members tried to retain focus on the text being critiqued. After several of these meetings, attendance dissipated as Renee and I struggled to keep the group's focus on the original goal of the group (participants' writings). Samantha's dominant dynamic in the group, not only in personality but also in possessing a higher faculty status, manifested in discernible hesitancy within Renee and me. We grappled with how to maintain a role of authority within the group without appearing in opposition to Samantha's position on campus as a full-time faculty member. The authority of Samantha's position, along with her dominant personality, made it difficult to address her added dynamics within the group given that I felt my lower (GTA) status did not allow me to more directly steer the group. Kaitlyn, Renee, and I had tried on several occasions to bring the group back to a focus on the text and our academic work, but subtlety was lost on Samantha, and we did not wish to cause bad feelings or resentment. I wondered if Samantha's reaction was caused by her assumed authority as a higher-ranking faculty member or if it was simply personality driven, but either way, I was hesitant to potentially damage my relationships within her department by pressing the issue or trying to be an overly dominant group leader. Kaitlyn, who initially engaged in conversation with Samantha and Edwin, privately expressed to Renee and me that she felt Samantha's presence was intrusive and overbearing in that Samantha showed little interest in the original intent of the group and formed a distraction. Each faculty member had a distinctly different approach and formed a different role within the group, even though they served in similar academic roles. Given the repeated challenges of the group and Renee's and my busy schedules—Renee was entering the last phase of her graduate thesis and I had since graduated and was adjuncting in addition to teaching at a local campus— the writing group's attendance waned until we no longer officially met.

Vis's Narrative of the Second Writing Group

The second writing group began as a project assigned to the graduate assistants of Babcock. As graduate student workers within the same college of our university, we shared an office space with other part-time faculty. Graduate assistants, graduate teaching assistants, and adjunct faculty all shared this same space. Due to this proximity, I believe that graduate teaching assistants at our university are more aligned with faculty through their responsibilities as educators of students than research assistants who may not have contact with students. Depending on our supervisors and status in our respective graduate programs, graduate students may strictly conduct research, assist with teaching, or instruct our own class independently. During each of our own appointed graduate assistantships, we assisted with developing lectures for specified courses, grading assignments, and meeting with students to help develop their thoughts and ideas further outside of class discussion, before being assigned as teachers of record while still graduate students. Regardless of title, all occupiers of this office would hold some agency associated with faculty teaching.

One day, Sue expressed that she was responsible for the writing group happening locally on campus. I took interest, since writing groups have always been an interest of mine. I had been unable to participate in a writing group since my own cohort could not meet to establish one due to the distance that comes with online learning. Sue was facing similar issues with attendance, so Emily and I decided to join her group to provide data for the writing group project.

We went into the project fully aware that this group would be studied and gave our consent to being recorded during the meetings. Since the three of us were colleagues of a similar age and academic background, our relationship was casual, and we met as friends. Sue had established a weekly time to meet at the local university coffee shop, and we met there a few times. Unfortunately, due to technical issues and errors, the recordings of these sessions were incomplete. Even more unfortunate was the fact that our university coffee shop kept inconvenient hours. For one of our sessions, we met at a local Starbucks to discuss our writings, joined by an additional participant who is a faculty professional (Taft). Since we felt comfortable with each other, we were fine with abandoning our post at the university and taking our small group off-campus in disregard of Sue's employment requirements. Sue led the group as facilitator and was most concerned about her status as a university employee. She often kept us on a strict schedule because her work was paid by the hour. Although her work supervisor (Babcock) was not a part of the group, her supervisor's presence was felt during each session through Sue's actions, which called attention to the writing group as one of Sue's job responsibilities.

However, Sue's association with the group is two-fold for its faculty presence. Sue, through her writing, established another indirect connection to another faculty's influence, her thesis supervisor. All members of the group have had some experience with Sue's thesis supervisor either through taking the supervisor's courses at the undergraduate and/or graduate levels or by being employed by said faculty member. Due to this shared experience, we all had some knowledge and understanding of the faculty member's expectations and their opinions on writing feedback. Though not explicitly stated within our sessions, the faculty presence was felt in the ways in which we approached Sue's writings. Consequently, faculty presence within this group expanded from Sue's own status as an adjunct faculty member because of the role of her immediate supervisors within the department and graduate program. Her teaching assistantship supervisor contractually obligated her to facilitate and participate in this studied group, *and* her thesis director discouraged this kind of group feedback. Therefore, the thesis director's influence upon this group was felt by all members due to their own experiences with this specific faculty member. The intricacies of faculty presence cannot be reduced to the traditional professor-student authority system, but must be analyzed through marginal and liminal identities, such as graduate teaching assistants, adjunct faculty, and non-tenure track lecturers.

Taft's Narrative of the Second Writing Group

My participation in the second writing group came by way of an accidental meeting at a local coffee shop. I had recently attained a full-time faculty position at a local college and was at a coffee shop grading student work and returning emails when a former classmate, Emily, approached and invited me to join their writing group meeting. Emily had known of my former role as a writing group facilitator and appeared eager to have another person join. The regular group consisted of Emily, a psychology graduate student, Vis, a Spanish graduate student, and Sue, an English graduate student. I had either attended a class with each of the members or had known them as a casual acquaintance at the university.

The focus of the group's critique was a portion of Sue's master's thesis. She appeared discouraged and apathetic about her writing as she gave hard copies to the group. I recall her making several comments pertaining to her thesis supervisor's recent critical feedback over her efforts. Sue expressed her struggle with conceptualizing the vision that her thesis supervisor had for Sue's thesis with her own ideas. Since Emily, Vis, and I had all taken several classes from this same faculty member and felt familiar with her expectations, we tried to offer helpful feedback. As a former classmate who held equal academic ranking with Sue, I did not give a great deal of thought to how my current faculty role might impact the reception of my feedback to Sue. The complex nature of this dynamic would materialize later during the writing group session.

Since Sue could not anticipate my presence at the meeting, she only had two hard copies of her writing, which created a natural split in the group—Vis and Sue, and Emily and me. Seating arrangements and proximity primarily dictated the two sub-groups. Also, my more immediate familiarity with Emily caused me to sit next to her when I initially joined the group, making it natural that we share one copy of the writing and work through it together. I recall asking clarifying questions of Sue, "But that's the example you're using to prove your point? It's Ovid's?" and asking Emily for confirmation, which I received, that I had correctly arrived at a particular misgiving about the meaning and interpretation of a specific passage. Being a newcomer to the group and lacking the immediate camaraderie that I had lost since progressing to a different level of academia than the rest of the group, I sought clarification of Sue's purpose and thoughts before offering suggestions on her writing. I had read some of Sue's writing before as a classmate, which led to a small bias in my expectations of what I would read. This expectation was met when some of Sue's responses appeared to vacillate in uncertainty as her disheartenment with the project became more evident.

As I offered suggestions, I felt some resentment stemming from Sue. She made an emphatic statement in reply to one critique, saying, "I thought that I did!" The resentment did not appear to be directed at anyone physically present, but more towards the thesis chairperson and her compelled participation in the group. However, her reaction caused me to think about the level of critique I was giving and scale back my honest response to some of the writing. I realized that as a faculty member I had been conditioned by grading and giving feedback on student essays, yet I had not considered the different relationship I had with Sue—thus, I had not adjusted the language of my critique to fit the dynamics of the group. Sue's patience with the feedback from everyone in the group was waning at this point in the session. Other assertions from Sue, such as, "I'm to the point where I just want to get this over and done with so I can start writing something else," allude to her eagerness to complete the writing project. Much like the group I co-founded, Sue, a graduate assistant, had been directed by her faculty work supervisor to establish and facilitate the group to contribute to ongoing research.

At this point, I knew that a more in-depth critique of Sue's writings would only further discourage her. Given my status as an invited participant to the meeting and as someone of a higher academic status, I did not feel I was privy to all of the information and critiques the group had previously offered Sue, and I had not been given the non-verbal social permission to share at the same level as the others in the group. Given this, I felt I needed to take a step back so as not to become an unwelcome presence. With that in mind, I tried to soften my feedback to structure, word choice, and grammar or low-order concerns. Since Sue and Vis were working on the other side of the table, I do not have a strong recollection of their focus during the group. In fact, the recording transcript shows that two different conversations were going on at once within the group. We continued with this same pattern of feedback until the prescribed hour for the meeting had elapsed. Sue abruptly announced to the group that we did not have to do any more since she had fulfilled the hour requirement and began to pack up her belongings. At this point, the writing group session ended, and everyone prepared to leave the coffee shop.

DISCUSSION AND CONCLUSION

Two of the faculty members in the first group, Kaitlyn and Samantha, apparently used the group as a social outlet in addition to a writing group. Aitchison and Guerin (2014) noted that, many times, "the companionship of the group imparts a sense of connectedness and belonging to an academic community for those in the process of developing researcher identities" (p. 12). Kaitlyn was an adjunct who desired full-time teaching work, and Samantha was a lecturer (contingent faculty) new to the area. As such, they were seeking belonging in an academic community. Also, they could have been using the writing group for their own personal social needs. Kaitlyn's and Samantha's use of the writing group for social engagement was not initially problematic until it overtook the group's intended purpose as an academic writing and critique group. Renee and Taft were not looking for a group that served as primarily a social outlet, so a mismatch of priorities within the group caused interpersonal tension between the members.

Some of the issues we noticed at hand in the second iteration of the group were a focus on grammar and structure of the paper. Also interesting to note was the fact that the group conversation at one point broke down to two separate conversations. The faculty member, Taft, was able to use her expertise in commenting and correcting papers to help the group member to improve her paper in grammar and punctuation. In the first group, however, Taft felt pushback from the freshman student, Edwin, when commenting on his creative writing, so retreated to offering grammatical and technical feedback rather than substantive critique, as grammatical advice can be seen as less of a face-threatening act than direct critique of the writer's content. Babcock and colleagues (2012), in their review of qualitative studies of writing tutoring, found that in tutoring, "dyads worked on grammar when they could not find a personal connection, or when they felt uncomfortable with each other" and that tutors find working on grammar to be easier and something they turned to if they "lacked confidence in a session" (p. 102). Although not a tutoring session, in the first writing group, Renee and Taft could not establish a personal connection with Edwin, which caused an organic shift in the feedback to grammar, particularly when creative writing was the object of the critique. What is more, the interpretation of creative writing as a more personal and intimate style of writing may influence the writing group's perception of feedback. To fall back upon grammar, feedback protocol may have served as a miscommunication between the disciplines of academic and creative writing.

In the second writing group, the same shift to lower-order concerns like grammar is also notable. Taft perceived an uncomfortable environment, which she concluded resulted from her informal participation and Sue's resistance to critiques being added to her thesis supervisor's feedback. Perhaps Sue, expecting a higher-order discussion with respect to her thesis work, grew more anxious with the feedback focused upon grammar and syntax after stating her concerns in previous meetings in which Taft was absent. Also, in the first writing group as a graduate student and teaching assistant, perhaps Edwin saw Taft as just an English language expert. Perhaps he did not see her as an expert on creative writing. As Aitchison (2014) explained, "One of the strongest reasons for rejecting feedback centered on an author's judgement of the authority and capacity of the feedback giver or reviewer" (p. 57). On the other hand, Edwin was an eager participant when Taft offered him advice on his paper for a course similar to the one she was teaching at the time. Apparently, he recognized her expertise in that area.

In the first group, issues of authority were present when the freshman student and the faculty member in psychology were at first hesitant to offer critique, likely in the face of the expertise of the two English graduate students in the group, one of whom was teaching her own freshman class. On the other hand, when Samantha joined the group, as Edwin's classroom teacher, she tended to dominate the critique. This is in marked contrast to the model that Ings (2014) set up in which the doctoral faculty supervisor purposefully takes a step back in the critique, allowing the collective to step in. Ings writes:

> As the candidate's supervisor I initially adopt the role of
> facilitator, as skills in productive questioning, recording and

> reflection develop, this position is increasingly assumed by members of the collective. The role of the facilitator is to question astutely, not to offer advice. This shifts the dynamic towards collective problem solving and away from a traditional tutorial. (p. 194)

Samantha did not choose to go this route. Given that Samantha had only newly acquired the faculty position and was new to the university, it was apparent that her palpable eagerness for social connection and intellectual affirmation overtook her ability to act as a faculty facilitator and take a less dominant role in feedback. In addition, since Samantha was a history professor, it is possible that she was not as familiar with writing pedagogy as the other group members, several of whom were graduate students in English. One of the editors of this collection noted that it was possible that she did not "know what her role should be, so she defaulted to being the teacher when in a group with students." Perhaps we assumed that people would just know how to conduct a writing group, but perhaps before each group we should/could outline the "rules" of the group for optimal participation.

In the second group, Sue's thesis supervisor was a distinct present absence, as Sue mentioned not knowing what she was supposed to do—"I don't know where it's going"—and being worried about the quality of her product: "I don't want to turn in crap. I don't want to show her, I am too embarrassed." Aitchison (2014) noted, "For writing group members the supervisor was omnipresent" (p. 60). Although in Aitchison's research, "Interviewees reported that it was not uncommon for supervisors to ask about the views of the writing circle when there was a piece of text or an issue in dispute. On occasions supervisors had suggested an author seek the views of the writing circle" (p. 59). In Sue's case, her thesis supervisor was not enthusiastic about her getting feedback from a writing group.

Faculty identity held a great presence within the second writing group based upon the members' attitudes and dialogue about faculty in the recorded sessions. Babcock et al. (2012) found in several studies over tutoring that the instructor was an absent presence in tutoring sessions (pp. 32–34). It stands to reason that in writing groups a similar phenomenon would occur; the faculty member who has assigned the work or who will be judging the outcome of the writing in the form of the master's thesis was felt by all the members. The effects of faculty influence emerged via Sue twofold: her relationship with her thesis supervisor influenced how Sue's writing was approached, and Sue's immediate GA work supervisor, Babcock, who is faculty, affected how members of the group reacted to involvement/expectations of the group. In the group, Taft's faculty identity does not display any asymmetrical status over Sue's writing; however,

Taft's faculty status may influence how she approaches Sue's writings. Finally, pre-existing relationships within the group, e.g., Taft and Emily, Emily and Vis, faculty and student, etc., may or may not influence how the writing group conducted themselves. Each of the members were at one point or another a student of Sue's thesis supervisor; perhaps assumptions about/expectations of the faculty member influenced the sessions indirectly. Aitchison (2014) noted, "intimate knowledge of their peer reviewers facilitates the agency, direction and uptake of feedback by writing group members" (p. 62) and, we might add, knowledge of non-present faculty members does so as well. Sue's thesis supervisor was a clear influence and presence in the group, even though not physically present.

We concluded that identities within writing groups depend upon the multidisciplinary nature of writing and of writer identities. Within the groups studied, each participant held various overlapping identities. Whereas each participant may be perceived superficially to hold a primary identity such as undergraduate/graduate student or faculty, additional identities may hold just as much weight within the writing group. These identities ranged from student to employee to colleague and to friend; whereas faculty presence did hold some authority within certain social contexts, the immediate faculty influence dominated each of the identities therein. Issues such as respect, seniority, and scope of responsibility may have swayed how identities are managed during the writing groups' sessions. Within the second group, we noted that physical faculty presence took on a radically different influence than indirect faculty influence. Faculty influence directed what was focused upon, how long it was focused upon, and in which manner it was appropriate to address various concerns. Within the first group, faculty presence was challenged due to the variable nature of multidisciplinary presence and academic achievement— and perhaps motivation to join the group. Participants may have questioned the effectiveness of the feedback received based upon perceptions of the potential of writing groups. The perceptions of identities of those who gave feedback may have also been questioned due to variable interpretations in levels of expertise and understanding of the writing being analyzed. Further research on multilevel groups including faculty in various academic ranks from graduate teaching assistants to tenured faculty along with students, from freshmen to graduate, will yield interesting and important insights not only on writing but also on authority and group dynamics. Future studies may want to interview group participants to confirm their attitudes and perspectives toward the group.

REFERENCES

Aitchison, C. (2014). Learning from multiple voices: Feedback and authority in doctoral writing groups. In Aitchison, C. & C. Guerin (Eds.), *Writing groups for doctoral education and beyond: Innovations in practice and theory* (pp. 51–64). Routledge. https://doi.org/10.4324/9780203498811.

Aitchison, C. & C. Guerin. (2014). Writing groups, pedagogy, theory, and practice: An introduction. In Aitchison, C. & C. Guerin (Eds.), *Writing groups for doctoral education and beyond: Innovations in practice and theory* (pp. 3–17). Routledge. https://doi.org/10.4324/9780203498811.

Babcock, R. D., Manning, K., Rogers, T., Goff, C. & McCain, A. (2012). *A synthesis of qualitative studies of writing center tutoring, 1983–2006*. Peter Lang.

Bosanquet, A. Cahir, J., Huber, E., Jacenyik-Trawöger, C. & McNeill, M. (2014). An intimate circle: Reflections on writing as women in higher education. In C. Aitchison & C. Guerin (Eds.), *Writing groups for doctoral education and beyond: Innovations in practice and theory* (pp. 204–217). Routledge. https://doi.org/10.4324/9780203498811.

Chai, P. R., Carreiro, S., Carey, J. L., Boyle, K. L., Chapman, B. P. & Boyer, E. W. (2019). Faculty member writing groups support productivity. *The Clinical Teacher 16*(6), 565–569. https://doi.org/10.1111/tct.12923.

Clark-Oates, A. & Cahill, L. (2013). Faculty writing groups: Writing centers and third space collaborations. In A. E. Geller & M. Eodice (Eds.), *Working with faculty writers,* (pp. 111–126). Utah State University Press.

Dwyer, A., Lewis, B., McDonald, F. & Burns, M. (2012). It's always a pleasure: Exploring productivity and pleasure in a writing group for early career academics. *Studies in Continuing Education 34*(2), 129–144. https://doi.org/10.1080/0158037X.2011.58073.

Edwards, J., M. McGuire & Sanchez, R. (2021). *Speaking up, speaking out!* Utah State University Press. https://researchers.westernsydney.edu.au/en/publications/writing-groups-pedagogy-theory-and-practice-an-introduction.

Galligan, L., Cretchley, P., George, L., McDonald, K. M., McDonald, J. & Rankin, J. (2003). Evolution and emerging trends of university writing groups. *Queensland Journal of Educational Research 19*(1), 28–41. http://www.iier.org.au/qjer/qjer19/galligan.html.

Garcia, E. M.A., Eum, S. H., Watt, L. & Boice, R. (2013). Experiencing the benefits of difference within multidisciplinary graduate writing groups. In A. E. Geller & M. Eodice (Eds.), *Working with faculty writers,* (pp. 260–278). Utah State University Press. https://doi.org/10.2307/j.ctt4cgs6g.

Geller, A. E. & Eodice, M. (Eds.). (2013). *Working with faculty writers*. Utah State University Press.

Guerin, C. (2014). The gift of writing groups: Critique, community, and confidence. In C. Aitchison & C. Guerin (Eds.), *Writing groups for doctoral education and beyond: Innovations in practice and theory,* (pp. 128–141). Routledge.

Guerin, C., Xafis, V., Doda, D. V., Gillam, M. H., Larg, A. J., Luckner, H., Jahan, N., Widayati, A. & Xu, C. (2013). Diversity in collaborative research communities: A multicultural, multidisciplinary thesis writing group in public health. *Studies in Continuing Education 35*(1), 65–81. https://doi.org/10.1080/0158037X.2012.684375.

Gumm, L. (2021). Disunity in a writing community: A post-PhD memoir of professional transitions. In J. Edwards, M. McGuire & R. Sanchez. (Eds.), *Speaking up, speaking out!* (pp. 145–157). Utah State University Press.

Haas, S. (2014). Pick-n-mix: A typology of writers' groups in use. In C. Aitchison & C. Guerin (Eds.), *Writing groups for doctoral education and beyond: Innovations in practice and theory* (pp. 30–47). Routledge.

Ings, W. (2014). The studio model: Developing community writing in creative, practice-led PhD design theses. In C. Aitchison & C. Guerin (Eds.), *Writing groups for doctoral education and beyond: Innovations in practice and theory* (pp. 190–203). Routledge.

Joseph, N. & Ashe-McNalley, N. (2021). Collaboration as antidote to NTTF pressures. In J. Edwards, M. McGuire & R. Sanchez (Eds.), *Speaking up, speaking out!* (pp. 193–206). Utah State University Press.

Maher, M. (2014). Transparent transactions: When doctoral students and their supervisors write together. In C. Aitchison & C. Guerin (Eds.), *Writing groups for doctoral education and beyond: Innovations in practice and theory,* (pp. 82–93). Routledge.

Mewburn, I., Osborne, L. & Caldwell, G. (2014). Shut up & Write!: Some surprising uses of cafés and crowds in doctoral writing. In C. Aitchison & C. Guerin (Eds.), *Writing groups for doctoral education and beyond: Innovations in practice and theory* (pp. 218–232). Routledge.

Mulally, D. (2021). Faculty community building: Portfolio-assessment groups as teaching circles. In J. Edwards, M. McGuire & R. Sanchez. (Eds.) *Speaking up, speaking out!* (pp. 221–234). Utah State University Press.

Murray, R. (2014). Doctoral students create new spaces to write. In C. Aitchison & C. Guerin (Eds.), *Writing groups for doctoral education and beyond: Innovations in practice and theory* (pp. 94–109). Routledge.

Penney, S., Young, G., Badenhorst, C., Goodnough, K., Hesson, J., Joy, R., McLeod, H., Pickett, S., Stordy, M. & Vaandering, D. (2015). Faculty writing groups: A support for women balancing family and career on the academic tightrope. *Canadian Journal of Higher Education* 45(4), 457–479. https://doi.org/10.47678/cjhe.v45i4.184534.

Smith, T. G., Molloy, J. C., Kassens-Noor, E., Li, W. & Colunga-Garcia, M. (2013). Developing a heuristic for multidisciplinary faculty writing groups: A case study. In A. E. Geller & M. Eodice (Eds.), *Working with faculty writers* (pp. 175–188). Utah State University Press. https://doi.org/10.2307/j.ctt4cgs6g.

CHAPTER 3.

FACULTY WRITERS AS PROXIMAL WRITERS: WHY FACULTY WRITE NEAR OTHER WRITERS

Jackie Grutsch McKinney
Ball State University

Abstract: *Based on a survey of writers in both formal and informal settings, such as retreats and coffee shops, I examine motivations behind "proximal writing," where writers work near each other. Findings reveal that writing in proximity fosters accountability, enhances focus, and builds community. This chapter identifies the appeal and efficacy of proximal writing among faculty and underscores its role in creating supportive, low-stakes environments conducive to productivity, especially in academic contexts.*

For a few years now, I have been hosting a faculty writing time in the writing center I direct. Every Friday morning before the center opens for feedback sessions, faculty sign in, find a spot and write. As host, I go each week to turn on some background music and write alongside the dozens of other writers. Over the years, I've asked myself many times: What makes these faculty members get to campus so early to write in one another's presence? More broadly, *what makes anyone with a writing task decide to do that task in the presence of others who are writing?* From making writing dates with others online or in person, to joining a writing retreat, to using a hashtag like #amwriting or #nanowrimo, to going to a coffee shop to write knowing other writers will be there, writers often opt to write in the presence of other writers. Why? This curiosity has led to a study on what I call *proximal writing*: writing done purposefully in the presence of others who are writing.

In this chapter, I begin to answer this question as I report on a survey of people who have used proximal writing. Survey participation was not limited to academics/faculty, but a majority of respondents identified as such; those participants will be the primary focus of this chapter. Participants in the study have used formal and informal proximal writing: a writer who pays to attend a planned writing retreat with other writers would be a formal arrangement. Less formal would be finding your way to a space where others are likely writing—perhaps a coffee shop, library, or other public areas. Participants have also engaged in proximal writing with differing degrees of proximity. Some proximal writers work in proximity, sitting at the same physical table with another writer, or, as one person in my study noted, sitting on the couch next to her partner. Other proximal writers might be more distant: in the same room, on the screen via video conferencing (Zoom is popular for long-distance writing dates), or even more loosely proximal when connected by a shared goal document (like a spreadsheet where a writing group tracks their progress) or a hashtag like the aforementioned #amwriting or #nanowrimo. Though many in the study have had both successful and unsuccessful proximal writing experiences, participants note the importance of proximal writing for their productivity, accountability, time on task, and emotional well-being.

As a writing teacher, scholar, director of graduate writing projects, and a writing center director who programs faculty and graduate student writing times, I was curious what writers say they gain from proximal writing, particularly if we consider proximal writing one way that a writer shapes a writing environment. As such, this study aligns with other recent scholarship in writing studies, which focuses on the materiality, spaces, and geographies in the writing process (Craig, 2019; Faris, 2014; Hedge, 2013; McNely et al., 2013; Pigg, 2014a; Pigg, 2014b; Prior & Shipka, 2003; Reynolds, 2007; Rule, 2018; Spinuzzi, 2012). Understanding the motivation to shape one's writing environment to include the presence of other writers could help shape my practices as a teacher, administrator, and writer, and could help the discipline understand more about "world-shaping" habits of proximal writers (Prior & Shipka, 2003). Furthermore, as I got into the data, I found that participants attribute many significant, positive outcomes to proximal writing—outcomes worth understanding better for anyone who works with writers.

REVIEW OF LITERATURE

Proximal writing, as defined for this study, is writing done intentionally in the presence of other writers, a choice a writer makes when shaping their writing environments. I concede that there are proximal writing situations that are less intentional, such as when students are given an in-class writing prompt and expected to write alongside classmates during the class period or when roommates happen to be writing simultaneously. However, participants for this project were asked to opt-in to the survey only if they had intentionally sought out proximal writing situations.

Proximal writing as I've defined it here is *not* synonymous with collaborative writing in which two or more writers work on the same product (Ede & Lunsford, 1990, 2001; Hunter, 2011). It is also *not* about getting feedback from others in writing groups (Gere, 1987, 1994; Maher et al., 2008; Mosset al., 2014; Nelson & Murphy, 1992; Spigelman, 2000) or peer feedback (Connor & Asenavage, 1994; Lockhart & Ng, 1995).[1] However, a writer's prior experiences with any or all of these might affect their experiences with proximal writing and might come before or after a proximal writing experience.

Proximal writing does *not* necessarily constitute a relationship or even what would be considered interaction between writers. Instead, the writers situate themselves among other writers for what that presence or environment provides or provokes. It calls to mind Micciche's (2017) conception of "writing partners," which she says might include "animals, feelings, technologies, matter, time, and materials interacting in both harmonious and antagonistic ways" (p. 44). Micciche emphasizes how environmental and material conditions can greatly influence texts and textual production but do so without attention or recognition; likewise, there has been plenty of attention paid to relational and interactional work between writers, but not as much on how writers use one another's presence to shape their work.

It's useful, also, to consider proximal writing arrangements as what Prior and Shipka (2003) have called ESSPs, environment selecting and structuring processes, which are "the intentional deployment of external aids and actors to shape, stabilize, and direct consciousness in the service of the task at hand" (p. 219). For example, one writer in their study said she purposefully did laundry while she wrote so that the dryer buzzer every 45 minutes or so forced her to get up and walk away from the draft. Prior and Shipka note, "ESSPs involve not only setting up a context, but also the ways the writer inhabits and acts in the space" (p. 222). Of course, with proximal writing, the writer joins a context but cannot necessarily predict or control how the other actors in that space will act. People—other writers in this case—are less predictable than dryer buzzers.

Related is the relatively recent phenomenon of freelance and other mobile workers who opt to work in shared co-working spaces—often for monthly fees (see for example Gandini, 2015; Garrett et al., 2017; Spinuzzi, 2012). Those who work in co-working spaces include writers but aren't limited to writers. Similar, too, is the concept of behavioral synchrony, which is the tendency of animals (including humans) to synchronize their actions with others around them (Tarr et al., 2016). Both of these areas of study overlap with proximal writing but are not entirely similar.

---

1   Some participants in this survey did note asking a question or pausing for feedback during a proximal writing session. I've made distinct writing times vs. feedback times for emphasis, but in practice, many writing partners/groups do both as needs arise.

This study builds on others that have started to cohere under the umbrella "new process studies" or simply a more broadly understood materialism in writing studies—such as Rule (2018), who makes the case for understanding where writing is physically done, and Haas (1996), who showed how tools significantly alter text production. Rule (2018) writes, "Writing is social, expressive, cultural, political, affective, historical, cognitive, *and* it is also fundamentally physical and material, the orchestrated and improvisational activity of bodies and things" (p. 429). Proximal writing is concerned with the "orchestrated and improvisational activity" of bodies among other bodies.

Of the different iterations of proximal writing experiences, only one type has been studied extensively: the participation in writing retreats by faculty and early career academics (Bozalek, 2017; Grant, 2006; Kornhaber et al., 2016; MacLeod et al., 2012; Moore, 2003; Murray & Newton, 2009; Paltridge, 2016; Petrova & Coughlin, 2012; Rud & Trevistan, 2014; Schendel, 2010; Schendel et al., 2013) and in so-called "dissertation bootcamps" (Blake et al., 2015; Lee & Golde, 2013; Powers, 2014; Simpson, 2013). Overall, the research on retreats and bootcamps marks their effectiveness in improving both writers' productivity and sense of well-being. The impetus for this study was to understand proximal writing for faculty inside and also outside of formal arrangements, like writing retreats, as many faculty do not work in institutions where retreats are offered or they cannot attend because of their schedule, care responsibilities, or work preferences. Further, I wanted to understand more deeply what is gained from proximal writing experiences for faculty in general.

SURVEY METHODS AND PARTICIPANTS

Given that I wanted to cast a wide net to see *what makes anyone with a writing task decide to do that task in the presence of others who are writing,* an online survey made the most sense for data collection. I created the survey in Qualtrics with the aim to create a survey that would be relatively short, would address my research question, and would be comprehensible to anyone 18 or older. I drafted the survey and piloted it with a few colleagues; it was too long. So I dropped and combined some questions together in a revised version and ended up with a total of 22 questions. Eight of the questions were multiple choice, 7 were short and open-ended (gender, occupation, etc.), and the remaining 7 were long and open-ended. See Appendix A for the survey instrument.

After obtaining IRB approval, I distributed the survey to those who attended the faculty writing time at my institution, my departmental colleagues, and those in my professional and personal networks via email and social media in the spring of 2019. I encouraged recipients to take the online survey and then to share it within their professional and personal networks—a sort of snowball sampling technique. A total of 361 participants began the survey, but 16 of those did not complete any questions beyond the initial informed consent question; thus, 334 surveys were usable.

Because of the sampling technique, survey participants skew toward those in my networks and the networks of my connections. Participants resemble the population of higher education (and maybe more specifically writing studies) more so than the general population. To this point, about 90% of survey participants are under the age of 50, about 80% identified as female, and about 85% as white. All participants had at least a high school degree, over 60% had a master's degree, and just under half (48%) had doctoral degrees. The vast majority of the participants list occupations that confirm their status in higher education; 80% list at least one of the following: faculty/instructor, graduate assistant/teaching assistant, higher ed administration, academic advisor, and/or writing consultant. As such, the findings here are not necessarily generalizable to or representational of the general population.

Said differently, my invitation to participate in the study reached and compelled participants who mostly work in the same industry and fit the same demographic categories as me, so my findings should not be seen as the "norm." As an academic myself with a Ph.D., who is also a white woman under 50, there's no doubt that my own identity and ways of being in the world limited who participated in the survey, who even saw the survey, and thus the study more broadly. Moreover, as someone who led and even championed proximal writing opportunities as part of my job, I had a stake in what I would find in this survey. That said, the stakes were pretty low. This study had no direct consequences for my work as a writing center director because proximal writing sessions fell outside of my official reported duties, nor on my faculty status as I was fully promoted prior to beginning this project. Though one can never set aside worldviews, identities, or positionality to put on a neutral, objective researcher stance, I was conscientious about leaving as many questions as open-ended as possible to not force participants into a particular set of responses I could imagine, and likewise used emergent analysis in order to not squeeze their open-ended responses into codes or categories I had set before data collection began.

The recruiting texts instructed only those who had experience with proximal writing to take the survey. Participants were asked if they had a "productive or good" proximal writing experience (98% said yes) and if they had ever had an "unproductive/not good" proximal writing experience (60% said yes). When participants were asked to check the types of proximal writing they have experience with, most selected more than one type. At least three-quarters of participants have met other writers in person for writing, have gone to a location to write where there would be others writing and have participated in writing hours/writing retreats. Thus, to generalize about participants in this study: they have had positive experiences with proximal writing and have tried multiple ways of proximal writing.

Participants were generous in their responses; most answered all questions with specificity. For example, for Question 16 (describe a positive proximal writing experience) respondents collectively wrote over 26,000 words. All told, if I printed the responses to the long, open-ended questions in manuscript format, I would probably need more than one ream of paper (over 500 pages). For this chapter, I pulled out the responses from participants who identified as faculty or instructors in higher education (n=138) for the purposes of this collection. These participants largely resembled the larger population of all respondents; however, 87% of these respondents have doctoral degrees and 98% were below the age of 60.

Additionally, I'm focusing my discussion on just four of the long, open-ended questions:

- Q10. Why did you (or do you) write in the proximity of other writers?
- Q11. What would you say are the effects of proximal writing on your writing process, products, and/or progress?
- Q16. Describe a proximal writing experience that you participated in that was productive/good.
- Q18. Describe a proximal writing experience that you participated in that was unproductive/not good.

To analyze the faculty responses to these four questions, I downloaded the responses into a spreadsheet, and I read through all of them. The number of responses varied by question. I then went through and assigned each response one or more codes based on patterns that emerged in my first reading; codes were both emergent and, sometimes, *in vivo*. For example, for Question 10 (why use proximal writing?), some codes that emerged or came from the responses were: motivation, accountability, set time, fun, and not alone/lonely. Doing so allowed me to notice the variety of responses and the frequency of particular codes. Next, I did a second round of coding to group codes into categories. Finally, I looked across questions to notice any themes that emerged when looking at faculty responses to all four questions.

FINDINGS

The faculty participants report using proximal writing for 44% of their writing tasks. They have used proximal writing for work (94% of respondents), for research (90%), for reflection (54%), for fun (41%), for civic duty (17%), and for school (17%). More have participated in physical proximal writing experiences than online experiences, and more have participated in synchronous versus asynchronous experiences, as seen in Table 3.1.

Table 3.1. Types of Proximal Writing Experiences for Faculty Participants (n = 138)

	# of respondents	% of faculty respondents
Met another writer at shared physical specific location and time for a writing "date"	105	76%
Participated in writing hours or writing retreat with other writers at the same physical location	103	75%
Went to a location to write where others would be writing	90	65%
Used email, social media, or other digital means (e.g., a shared google doc) to asynchronously plan writing time/goals with other writers or to record writing	61	44%
Participated in an online writing retreat or challenge with other writers	58	42%
Met another writer online for a synchronous writing "date"	84	61%
Used social media/hashtags to participate in a writing challenge (like NaNoWriMo) or shared writing experience (#amwriting)	29	21%
Other	6	4%

Q10. WHY DID YOU (OR DO YOU) WRITE IN THE PROXIMITY OF OTHER WRITERS? (N = 125)

Faculty are typically required to write for their jobs—research, reports, teaching materials, internal documents, and the like. Therefore, this question did not ask why they write what they have to—but why they decide to write near other writers. Faculty writers gave many reasons for opting for proximal writing experiences. However, a handful of reasons emerged as important to many respondents; faculty respondents to this survey use proximal writing because they want accountability, motivation, support, a set time/focus, and to not be alone or lonely. Many use proximal writing to get more than one of these results, as illustrated in these responses:

Response 1: I think better with others. I'm also motivated both by thinking with others and also by the "energy" I get when I am writing and others are writing, even if we're not writing together. It's like parallel play. I might see them really cranking something out or scribbling or typing and it helps me stay motivated to keep working. It's also sometimes helpful emotional support when the writing I'm working on is stressful or anxiety-provoking.

Response 2: It's motivating, there's accountability, and you just feel the energy and "brain pulse" flowing!

Response 3: Accountability, inspiration, companionship. It is easy to procrastinate so having to be somewhere at a certain time can help with structure. Writing can be isolating, so this makes it seem less lonely. I also like to have someone I can bounce an idea off if I get stuck, and some people to celebrate the small accomplishments with, whether at the end of the day or end of a larger project.

We don't know the degree to which faculty get any of the benefits from proximal writing elsewhere—for example, how else are faculty motivated to write? But the responses here potentially speak to gaps in the way faculty jobs are imagined and structured. For instance, faculty often have responsibilities to teach, but teaching is much more structured and scheduled than writing. Faculty know when and where to be for their classes, and classes have specific start and end dates. Moreover, that teaching schedule is sacrosanct: faculty wouldn't be asked to miss a class for a quick phone call, a meeting, or a university function. But faculty have no guard rails around their writing time: it isn't scheduled by the institution and if scheduled by the individual, it is seen as interruptible. To this point, some respondents noted needing to have a place to write other than their assigned faculty office to hide from others and to focus. Thus, the responses to Q10 suggest that faculty are using proximal writing, in part, to make writing more like their teaching; they say they want a set time, a place, accountability, focus, and other people participating in the same activity.

Q16 AND Q18: POSITIVE AND NEGATIVE EXPERIENCES WITH PROXIMAL WRITING

Question 16 asked writers to describe a proximal writing experience including questions such as: How did you meet writer(s) you write in proximity to? How did your proximal writing begin? What was the proximal writing plan/rules? Did you meet in person and if so where? Why? How long did each session last and how long did the arrangement last? Question 18 asked about negative and unproductive proximinal writing experiences. These questions included: How did you meet writer(s) you write in proximity to? How did your proximal writing begin? What was the proximal writing plan/rules? Did you meet in person and if so where? Why? How long did each session last and how long did the arrangement last?

Q16 and Q18 were written to see what participants would name as positive and negative about their previous proximal writing experiences. Almost all faculty respondents (97%) said they have had a positive experience with proximal writing, and many (55%) say they've had a negative experience. I was curious if positive and negative evaluations would map onto the degree of formality and the closeness of the experience. For instance, would respondents favor structured, in-person meetings with people they knew, versus looser arrangements like just showing up at a coffee shop to write? In some ways their responses did and in some ways they did not map to the degrees of formality and proximity.

The participants classified a wide variety of experiences as productive—planned and not planned, in-person and virtual—though many noted leaving their home or office to write in coffee shops, cafes, libraries, writing retreats/residencies, writing centers, and study rooms, and most participants knew their fellow writers in productive experiences (calling them "friends," their "cohort," "partners," or "colleagues" in responses). For positive experiences, most people described formal arrangements. They often talked about a repeating, scheduled meeting where goals would be shared at the beginning of the session. Some arrangements had built-in rewards (breaks, talking, or food were common). Many respondents wrote about arrangements forged in graduate school/while dissertating/with their graduate school cohort. Many respondents (unless describing a writing retreat) said the proximal writing experience was typically 1–2 hours or 2–3 hours. Here are some examples of the formal proximal writing experiences participants described:

> Response 1: I take part in the Shut-up-and-write sessions at my university. We meet in person or virtually, which works well for me because I'm often off campus. If we meet in person, we meet at a venue on campus. The facilitator brings snacks. We use WhatsApp to meet virtually. We'll get together / get a WhatsApp message 15 minutes before we start just to prepare and get settled. We then write in 25-minute bursts (pomodoro technique). The facilitator and other participants are encouraging and supportive. We usually do 2 to 4 pomodoros (total of 1 to 2 hours) depending on how many writers can stay.

Response 2: My best proximal writing arrangement was with a friend in grad school. She was not in my department, but we met through graduate life activities, including weekly writing sessions organized through the grad life office. We started writing together during those dedicated times organized by the university but later started writing together informally because the rules of our prior group changed but we still wanted to write together under the old rules. We planned weekly times and made appointments on our calendar for "writing dates." We met at coffee shops or sometimes our homes (because having caffeine and sustenance is important for long writing sessions!) and both knew that the other was counting on us to be there. Our sessions started with sharing what we would be working on that session and setting goals to work toward. We checked in periodically and sometimes talked through ideas we were struggling with, but most of our time was spent writing. Then at the end of our time, we reported back what progress we made. We met in person about 95% of the time and were most productive that way (versus checking in at the start and end via text). Typically, we met for about 4–6 hours at a time. We continued this arrangement for about 18 months, until I relocated for my new position after graduation. We have continued to share our experiences and recently started meeting virtually via Skype. I have had several other writing groups that were also structured this way (sometimes with more people), but I believe this relationship was the most productive and positive for me because I was able to depend on this individual to be there and hold me accountable for my writing and also because we were (and still are) able to be vulnerable with one another and share in the fact that it is hard to do this work sometimes! Knowing that someone else was in the same position was good for my mental health.

Unproductive proximal writing experiences also described some similarities with the productive ones. These experiences often included friends or colleagues writing together in coffee shops and libraries at regular meeting times. However, participants note unproductive experiences involve "too much chatting!" a space/group with too many distractions, outside stress, and members who stopped showing up. Many suggest there weren't clear ground rules or shared expectations about the experience and goals. Several also note that distant proximal writing did not sufficiently motivate them. Of all of these, however, the amount of talking or timing of talking was the most prevalent theme followed by a more general "noise" complaint. As illustrated below, many unproductive arrangements suffered several of these pitfalls:

> Response 1: Proximal writing goes rogue when people chat and don't actually come to do work. I've had that happen with friends I've tried to write with, so we don't write together anymore. Trying to write bi-weekly on Saturdays with a group of friends/colleagues at a coffee shop this past academic year was nice, socially, but not particularly productive for me. It was set up by a friend who was hoping to make better progress on her dissertation, but because it has functioned mostly as a drop-in format without clear ground rules about how we would spend the time, what we would work on, or how we would hold ourselves accountable, it hasn't been very effective. Too much of the time is spent catching up on the past two weeks, and it is very easy to avoid writing even while there because we didn't set up processes for mutual accountability and commitment. I think it works for some participants in terms of fighting some feelings of isolation, but I'd like to see it be more.

> Response 2: I thought I might be more productive in a location other than my office (where there's lots of ambient noise and interruptions) or home, so I went to Panera one morning. Three other people were also there working on their laptop computers, and initially I was productive. Unfortunately, about 10 minutes into my writing session one of the other patrons was talking loudly and impossible to ignore. I tried to work for about 45 minutes, hoping she might leave, but when she didn't leave, I did.

As is perhaps to be expected, the data doesn't show just one successful or unsuccessful arrangement for faculty proximal writing experiences. No magic formula bears out because writers have different preferences when shaping their writing sessions. In retrospect, it would have perhaps been interesting to also ask faculty what their optimum proximal writing experience would look like, as many respondents suggested a sort of compromise in working conditions to work in the presence of other writers.

Q11. WHAT WOULD YOU SAY ARE THE EFFECTS OF PROXIMAL WRITING ON YOUR WRITING PROCESS, PRODUCTS, AND/OR PROGRESS?

In asking what effect proximal writing had on their writing, I was trying to gauge benefits and drawbacks faculty noticed on their writing when using proximal writing. Though there was some overlap in what participants named as effects and how they answered Q10 (why use proximal writing?), such as motivation, mostly faculty responded more directly about production. In brief, faculty in the survey report overwhelmingly positive effects of using proximal writing. In fact, out of curiosity, I did a third round of coding for the responses to this question and marked responses as positive, neutral/mixed, or negative effects. Of the 125 responses, 94% were positive; none were negative. Specifically, many report being able to better focus, to write for longer periods of time, to write better, to write more, to form a more consistent writing habit, to be more motivated to write, and to feel better (about writing), as seen in these responses below:

> Response 1: It helps me focus (different location/less distractions), it motivates me (I'm with colleagues doing the same work/going through the same experience), and it helps me feel productive (I set goals and check my progress after each session).
>
> Response 2: I work longer. I stay more encouraged and motivated. I am more likely to bring projects to a close because I have encouragement to finish and SEND rather than keep working toward perfection (that never arrives or exists!).
>
> Response 3: Before joining my writing group, I had never gotten scholarly work done on such a regular basis during the semester (while teaching). I have gotten *much* further with my current book project than I otherwise would have. I rarely get completely blocked, I work on multiple projects at once, and I take reflective notes on my reading.

I was surprised and not surprised by the responses to this question. As someone who has led different proximal writing experiences, I had participants over the years tell me how being involved had helped them complete projects, stay on task, and prioritize writing. I had seen similar effects in my own practice. However, I had suspected that participants overall might be more neutral on the effects—that they would name both benefits and drawbacks. The responses here affirm that faculty respondents work through the challenges of proximal writing because they gain a lot from shaping their writing environment to include others who are writing.

DISCUSSION AND IMPLICATIONS

So, *what makes anyone with a writing task decide to do that task in the presence of others who are writing?* In short, for faculty who participated in this study, they use proximal writing because they believe it greatly benefits their writing and productivity. Most of the respondents who have tried it have had both positive and negative experiences, but they still opt to do it for almost half of their writing tasks. As detailed above, proximal writing experiences can help faculty shape the time, space, focus, structure, and connectedness for writing that they likely have in their teaching and other faculty responsibilities. Previous research on formal proximal writing arrangements (retreats and bootcamps) showed positive outcomes, and this study shows similar positive outcomes for different types of proximal writing arrangements.

Moreover, throughout the data, the idea of writing as an emotion-laden activity emerged. Many named writing time as lonely and isolating, echoing Faris (2014) who says he writes in coffee shops "to make writing less isolating" (p. 23). Respondents felt insecure about their struggles, especially because the struggles of fellow faculty writers were typically invisible to them. Others talked directly about their mental health and how writing alone activated their anxiety. Similarly, Craig (2019) found that affect plays a significant role in the writing processes and writing environment selection of the writers in his case study. Faculty in this study use proximal writing to combat the negative feelings associated with the pressure to write and publish and the isolation of the act of writing.

For those who aim to support faculty writing, this study draws our attention to what faculty want in their writing experiences: space, time, structure, colleagues/peers, and camaraderie (and, yes, food and coffee are appreciated). The survey does not tell us that all faculty would benefit from proximal writing experiences, but it does suggest that some will. It does not tell us who fares better—those who use proximal writing or those who do not. However, faculty in this survey self-report that using proximal writing improves the quality and quantity of their writing. Also important, for many faculty in this study, the use of proximal writing experiences to shape their writing environments began in graduate school; several note an ongoing proximal writing arrangement with graduate student colleagues. Thus, consideration should be given to how supporting faculty begins in graduate school programs.

In closing, one challenge of programming proximal writing experiences for faculty is allowing for different levels of formality and proximity in the programming. Though there was more discussion of formal and close proximal writing arrangements in the responses to "good experiences," there was also reference to distant, asynchronous arrangements as positive. Nonetheless, this study points to the potential for faculty to benefit from proximal writing arrangements generally, so any proximal writing programming offered will likely be utilized.

REFERENCES

Blake, B., Bracewell, J. & Stivers, C. (2015). "Just write?" . . . Not quite: Writing "procedure'" for STEM-focused dissertation boot camps. *The Writing Lab Newsletter, 39*(9–10), 13–17.

Bozalek, V. (2017). Slow scholarship in writing retreats: A diffractive methodology for response-able pedagogies. *South African Journal of Higher Education, 31*(2), 40–57. https://doi.org/10.20853/31-2-1344.

Connor, U. & Asenavage, K. (1994). Peer response groups in ESL writing classes: How much impact on revision? *Journal of second language writing, 3*(3), 257–276. https://tinyurl.com/4fndvsya.

Craig, J. W. (2019). Affective materialities: Places, technologies, and development of writing processes. *Composition Forum*, 41. https://files.eric.ed.gov/fulltext/EJ1213662.pdf.

Ede, L. & Lunsford, A. A. (1990). *Singular texts/plural authors: Perspectives on collaborative writing*. SIU Press.

Ede, L. & Lunsford, A. A. (2001). Collaboration and concepts of authorship. *Publications of the Modern Language Association of America, 116*(2), 354–369. https://doi.org/10.1632/pmla.2001.116.2.354.

Faris, M. J. (2014). Coffee shop writing in a networked age. *College Composition and Communication, 66*(1), 21–24.

Gandini, A. (2015). The rise of coworking spaces: A literature review. *Ephemera, 15*(1), 193–205.

Garrett, L. E., Spreitzer, G. M. & Bacevice, P. A. (2017). Co-constructing a sense of community at work: The emergence of community in coworking spaces. *Organization Studies, 38*(6), 821–842. https://doi.org/10.1177/0170840616685354.

Gere, A. R. (1987). *Writing groups: History, theory, and implications*. SIU Press.

Gere, A. R. (1994). Kitchen tables and rented rooms: The extracurricular of composition. *College Composition and Communication, 45*(1), 75–92.

Grant, B. M. (2006). Writing in the company of other women: Exceeding the boundaries. *Studies in Higher Education, 31*(4), 483–495.

Haas, C. (1996). *Writing technology: Studies on the materiality of literacy*. Routledge. https://doi.org/10.4324/9780203811238.

Hedge, S. L. (2013). *Investigating student identity practices across material spaces and social software: From the classroom to digital environments* [Unpublished doctoral dissertation]. Ball State University.

Hunter, R. (2011). Erasing "property lines": A collaborative notion of authorship and textual ownership on a fan wiki. *Computers and Composition, 28*(1), 40–56.

Kornhaber, R., Cross, M., Betihavas, V. & Bridgman, H. (2016). The benefits and challenges of academic writing retreats: An integrative review. *Higher Education Research & Development, 35*(6), 1210–1227. https://doi.org/10.1080/07294360.2016.1144572.

Lee, S. & Golde, C. (2013). Completing the dissertation and beyond: Writing centers and dissertation boot camps. *Writing Lab Newsletter 37*(7–8), 1–5. https://doi.org/10.1080/03075079.2010.527934.

Lockhart, C. & Ng, P. (1995). Analyzing talk in ESL peer response groups: Stances, functions, and content. *Language learning, 45*(4), 605–651.

MacLeod, I., Steckley, L. & Murray, R. (2012). Time is not enough: Promoting strategic engagement with writing for publication. *Studies in Higher Education, 37*(6), 641–654. https://link.springer.com/chapter/10.1007/978-3-658-27602-7_8.

Maher, D., Seaton, L., McMullen, C., Fitzgerald, T., Otsuji, E. & Lee, A. (2008). "Becoming and being writers": The experiences of doctoral students in writing groups. *Studies in Continuing Education, 30*(3), 263–327.

McNely, B., Gestwicki, P., Gelms, B. & Burke, A. (2013). Spaces and surfaces of invention: A visual ethnography of game development. *Enculturation 15*. https://enculturation.net/visual-ethnography.

Micciche, Laura R. (2017). Acknowledging writing partners. The WAC Clearinghouse; University Press of Colorado. https://doi.org/10.37514/PER-B.2017.0872.

Moore, S. (2003). Writers' retreats for academics: Exploring and increasing the motivation to write. *Journal of Further and Higher Education, 27*(3), 333–342.

Moss, B. J., Highberg, N.P. & Nicolas, M. (Eds.) (2014). *Writing groups inside and outside the classroom.* Routledge.

Murray, R. & Newton, M. (2009). Writing retreat as structured intervention: Margin or mainstream? *Higher Education Research & Development, 28*(5), 541–553 https://doi.org/10.1080/07294360903154126.

Nelson, G. L. & Murphy, J. M. (1992). An L2 writing group: Task and social dimensions. *Journal of Second Language Writing, 1*(3), 171–193.

Paltridge, B. (2016). Writing retreats as writing pedagogy. *Writing & Pedagogy, 8*(1). 199–213. https://doi.org/10.1558/wap.v8i1.27634.

Petrova, P. & Coughlin, A. (2012). Using structured writing retreats to support novice researchers. *International Journal for Researcher Development, 3*(1), 79–88. https://doi.org/10.1108/17597511211278661.

Pigg, S. (2014a). Coordinating constant invention: Social media's role in distributed work. *Technical Communication Quarterly, 23*(2), 69–87.

Pigg, S. (2014b). Emplacing mobile composing habits: A study of academic writing in networked social spaces. *College Composition and Communication, 66*(2), 250–275.

Powers, E. (2014). Dissercamp: Dissertation boot camp "lite." *Writing Lab Newsletter, 38*(5–6), 14–15.

Prior, P. & Shipka, J. (2003). Chronotopic lamination: Tracing the contours of literate activity. In C. Bazerman & D. Russell (Eds.), *Writing selves, writing societies: Research from activity perspectives* (pp. 180–238). The WAC Clearinghouse; Mind, Culture, and Activity. https://doi.org/10.37514/PER-B.2003.2317.2.06.

Reynolds, N. (2007). *Geographies of writing: Inhabiting places and encountering difference.* Southern Illinois University Press.

Rud, L. G. & Trevisan, M. (2014). Jumpstarting junior faculty motivation and performance with focused writing retreats. *The Journal of Faculty Development, 28*(1), 33–40.

Rule, H. J. (2018). Writing's rooms. *College Composition and Communication, 69*(3), 402–432.

Schendel, E. (2010). Retreating into the center: Supporting faculty and staff as writers. *Writing Lab Newsletter 34*(6), 1–6.

Schendel, E., Callaway, S., Dutcher, V. & Griggs, C. (2013). Assessing the effects of faculty and staff retreats: Four institutional perspectives. In A. E. Geller & M. Eodice (Eds.), *Working with faculty writers (*pp. 142–162). Utah State University Press.

Simpson, S. (2013). Building for sustainability: Dissertation boot camp as a nexus of graduate writing support. *Praxis: A Writing Center Journal 10*(2), 1–9.

Spigelman, C. (2000). *Across property lines: Textual ownership in writing groups*. Southern Illinois University Press.

Spinuzzi, C. (2012). Working alone together: Coworking as emergent collaborative activity. *Journal of Business and Technical Communication 26*(4), 399–441.

Tarr, B., Launay, J. & Dunbar, R. I. (2016). Silent disco: dancing in synchrony leads to elevated pain thresholds and social closeness. Evolution and Human, 37(5), 343–349. https://doi.org/10.1016/j.evolhumbehav.2016.02.004.

APPENDIX A: SURVEY INSTRUMENT

1. Are you 18 years or older and consent to participate in this survey?
   - Yes, I agree. [2]
2. Why do you write? (Select all that apply.)
   - for work
   - for school
   - for research
   - for fun/hobby
   - to archive/keep track
   - for reflection/introspection
   - for an organization/club
   - for civic duty
   - other _____
3. What's your age?
   - 18–24
   - 25–29
   - 30–39
   - 40–49
   - 50–59
   - 60–69
   - 70 or older

---

2   The informed consent form was the first page of the survey but is not shown here for brevity.

4. What is your occupation or occupations? (Students can list "student" as occupation.)
5. Gender:
6. Race/Ethnicity:
7. Where do you live? (City, State/Province, Country)
8. Degree(s) completed (select all that apply):
    - High school
    - Associate's degree
    - Bachelor's degree
    - Master's degree
    - Doctoral degree
    - None of these
    - other _____

This is a study about proximal writing: people who opt to write around or at the same time as another person or persons who are writing their own texts. It is NOT a study about collaborative writing (two or more people working on the same writing). Proximal writing, as defined here, includes writing in close proximity (meeting at a physical place to write) and distant proximity (connecting with other writers online through activities like NaNoWriMo and using hashtags like #amwriting).

9. What proximal writing (writing alone together) experiences have you had? (Select all that apply.)
    - Met another writer at shared physical specific location and time for a writing "date"
    - Met another writer online for a synchronous writing "date"
    - Participated in writing hours or writing retreat with other writers at the same physical location
    - Went to a location to write where others would be writing
    - Participated in an online writing retreat or challenge with other writers
    - Used social media/hashtags to participate in a writing challenge (like NaNoWriMo) or shared writing experience (#amwriting)
    - Used email, social media, or other digital means (e.g., a shared google doc) to asynchronously plan writing time/goals with other writers or to record writing progress.
10. Why did you (or do you) write in the proximity of other writers?
11. What would you say are the effects of proximal writing on your writing process, products, and/or progress?
12. What percentage of your writing do you typically produce while proximal writing?
    [slider from 0–100%]

13. What kinds (genres) of writing do you typically do while proximal writing?
14. What kinds (genres) of writing do you typically do when you write alone?
15. Have you ever had a productive/good proximal writing experience?
    - Yes
    - No

If Have you ever had a productive/good proximal writing experience? = yes

16. Describe a proximal writing experience that you participated in that was productive/good. How did you meet writer(s) you write in proximity to? How did your proximal writing begin? What was the proximal writing plan/rules? Did you meet in person and if so where? Why? How long did each session last and how long did the arrangement last?
17. Have you ever had an unproductive/not good proximal writing experience?
    - Yes
    - No

If Have you ever had an unproductive/not good proximal writing experience? = Yes

18. Describe a proximal writing experience that you participated in that was unproductive/not good. How did you meet writer(s) you write in proximity to? How did your proximal writing begin? What was the proximal writing plan/rules? Did you meet in person and if so where? Why? How long did each session last and how long did the arrangement last?
19. Anything else you'd like to say about your experiences with proximal writing?
20. Would you be willing to participate in an interview about your proximal writing habits/experiences?
    - Yes
    - No

If Would you be willing to participate in an interview about your proximal writing habits/experiences?

21. Name:
22. Email address:

CHAPTER 4.

PEOPLE KEEP KNOCKING (OR, I HAVE ANSWERED 50 EMAILS TODAY): BALANCING WORK AND RESEARCH AS A WPA

Lars Söderlund
Baymard Institute

Jaclyn Wells
University of Alabama, Birmingham

Abstract. *We examine the challenges faced by writing program administrators (WPAs) balancing administrative work with research obligations. Based on interviews with rhetoric and composition scholars, this chapter identifies how administrative tasks impede writing and scholarly productivity. We highlight the unexpected extent to which WPA responsibilities disrupt research, arguing for institutional support structures to alleviate this burden. We propose strategies for WPAs to navigate these conflicting demands and emphasize the need for broader recognition of the unique pressures on WPAs in higher education.*

We interviewed 20 published rhetoric and composition scholars for an IRB-approved study about their research and writing processes. We anticipated that we would hear about writer's block, the challenges of dealing with academic publishers, and other barriers to a successful scholarly agenda that are known by many of us but not often discussed. However, we did not anticipate that the interviews would lead to this chapter about WPA responsibilities and their surprising effects on research. In the interviews, we asked each participant 11 questions focused on their writing and publishing experiences, with just one question about how they are affected by teaching, service, and other commitments. (See Appendix A for our full list of interview questions and Appendix B for the pre-interview survey we used to gain contextual info). But as we coded the data, separately and then together, a strong theme appeared: the challenges of writing program administration (WPA), especially the challenge of balancing

WPA work with publishable research.[1] Our participants' comments on WPA work had a frequency and an intensity that stood out from the other data we gathered, even in a dataset that yielded insights into graduate student mentorship and the relationships between academic writers, editors, and reviewers (see our articles in *Pedagogy* [Wells & Söderlund, 2018] and *College Composition and Communication* [Söderlund & Wells, 2019], respectively).

In this chapter, we identify the connections between the WPA case studies in the data and move toward a holistic picture of what makes WPA work especially fatiguing and disruptive to scholarship. Two participants' comments provide great examples. When asked to describe the amount of time she spends on research every week, one WPA participant responded: "There have been times when I was doing administrative work—I remember whole stretches of days going by when I didn't touch anything, like writing or research. I mean that [admin work] takes just a huge dent of time." A different WPA participant responded similarly to the question: "I do not spend time on my research every week at all. I think especially in the last five years that I have had this administrative position, I have really only spent time on research in the weeks if I've had something pressing that I had to do." These comments are representative of many others that explain how administrative roles can lead faculty to set their research aside entirely.

The issue is pressing because many of our research participants noted that rhetoric and composition faculty are often associated with WPA positions, whether writing center directors, WAC/WID coordinators, first-year composition directors, directors of writing majors, or something else. As one participant, a writing center director, put it when describing his own balance between administrative work and research: "being someone in Rhet/Comp, part of what we do is work with other people and administrate things." Given that so many rhetoric and composition faculty take on administrative roles—often in pretenure, non-tenure-earning, or even graduate student positions—recognizing how WPA work challenges research productivity matters greatly for our field, even if we have already recognized that fact many times.

Over the rest of the chapter, we support our argument that producing scholarship is uniquely challenging for WPAs by reporting specific trends from the data.

---

1   Throughout this chapter, the term *WPA* denotes the distinctive work of writing program administration while the more general *administrator* includes WPA work as well as other administrative roles, such as graduate program director or dean. Further, *WPA* is used to include directors of all kinds of writing programs, including first-year composition and professional writing, writing majors, writing centers, WAC/WID programs, etc. When participants spoke about administration, they were generally referring to WPA-type work, but some participants had held other kinds of administrative positions.

We begin by discussing how participants noted that the scholarly restrictions of WPA work intensify one another. The result is a role that is more draining, more time-intensive, and harder to ignore than other administrative positions: WPA interviewees reported that their work can carry a higher level of responsibility than similar administrative academic positions. Toward the end of our results, we also share findings from participants who had held upper administrative positions, like deanships and chairships. Although we argue that WPA work is particularly draining in comparison with administrative work generally, we also learned from our findings that some of these upper administrative positions can create significant barriers to research time, since such admins cannot put aside administrative work when the buck stops with them. We believe this finding is important for writing studies because WPAs may aspire to such positions and because they may be particularly equipped to manage the challenges given their practice balancing their administrative work with other responsibilities.

We conclude the chapter by offering limited suggestions derived from the data for WPAs who want to improve their experience with scholarship, and we call both for others to advocate for the research needs of WPAs and for more research into this area, specifically in documenting the daily time spent by WPA tasks.

POSITIONALITY

Before proceeding, we provide an overview of our positionality in relation to the topic, as our positions inspired our research, shaped our interpretation of the data, and influenced our suggestions for supporting WPAs' experiences with scholarship. Specifically, we are both professors who serve in WPA positions ourselves: Jaci is an associate professor who directs the Writing Center at the University of Alabama-Birmingham, an R1 institution, and Lars is an associate professor who directs the Professional and Technical Writing program at Western Oregon University, a regional comprehensive. We began this study as assistant professors, when neither of us had tenure, and our friendship and writing partnership started even earlier, as graduate students at Purdue University when we discussed the challenging prospect of publishing research. Our interest in research helped spur our IRB-approved interviews, revealing tips and generating articles that helped us achieve tenure. But what we did not expect was that our WPA positions would be so time-consuming as to slow our research progress, in Lars's case even threatening to derail his tenure goals and influencing a move away from the university where he was initially employed.

While our positions are not identical, we have experienced similar timelines in work and in life: Lars completed graduate school just one year after Jaci, we both experienced moving from our first tenure-track positions to new ones after a couple of years, we earned tenure only a few years apart at our second tenure-track jobs, and we even became parents within a few years of each other. Our close friendship and overlapping professional and personal experiences have generated lots of great conversations about how faculty roles and expectations shift over time and about balancing research with other responsibilities. For example, we have learned together that research challenges do not end with achieving tenure, as growing service obligations at the associate level cut deeply into research time. As WPAs, we have even experienced getting tapped for perhaps more service obligations than other associate professors, as our administrative work often makes us visible within the university. In a different example, we have learned how parenting responsibilities factor into the balance of faculty life. This is true for all faculty, of course, but we have shared with each other that the physical presence required by WPA work can be especially tricky to navigate as parents who are also trying to fulfill research, teaching, and service responsibilities.

Further, we see our own checkered experience with the demands of WPA work in light of our colleagues at other institutions who are in far more difficult positions: WPAs on limited-term contracts hoping to generate research for permanent roles, WPAs whose workload is unacceptably high because it is ill-understood by their colleagues, and of course WPAs subject to acute institutional discrimination both inside and outside of the university. We feel lucky to have made tenure, and to have supported each other through the process, but we can easily imagine being in conditions that prevented gaining tenure. That is why we wrote this article.

We proceed now to the direct context for our present study, since some of these issues have received research attention in the past.

BALANCING WPA AND OTHER ADMIN WORK WITH RESEARCH: WHAT WE ALREADY KNOW

Two lines of research are most relevant to a study of WPA administration-research balance: 1) research about faculty writing practices in rhetoric and composition, and 2) research about writing program administration, particularly the expectations put on WPAs' administrative work and publishing record. Also relevant are position statements in the field, including the Council of Writing Program Administrators' (2019) statement "Evaluating the Intellectual Work of Writing Administration" and the Conference on College Composition and Communication (2018) statement "Scholarship in Rhetoric, Writing, and Composition: Guidelines for Faculty, Deans, and Chairs." These statements are generally intended to help writing program administrators advocate for their work by positioning it as scholarly and worthy of counting toward academic rewards like tenure and promotion. The mere need for such statements shows the challenges that WPAs face in balancing administrative work with other expectations, particularly publishing, and in making their case for tenure and promotion.

Rhetoric and composition scholarship in the past 10 years reflects a growing interest in the experiences of faculty writers. This work includes our own articles in *College Composition and Communication* (2019) and *Pedagogy* (2018), Johnson's (2017) and Tarabochia's (2020) articles in *Composition Studies*, Tulley's (2018) *How Writing Faculty Write: Strategies for Process, Product, and Productivity*, and Gallagher and DeVoss's (2019) edited collection *Explanation Points: Publishing in Rhetoric and Composition*. While this list is small, it is significant that the field has seen several articles and books in just the past five years, when previously there were relatively few publications about faculty writing in the field.

Older research about faculty writing and publishing seems mostly concerned with inculcating graduate students into the field's scholarly practices, so it may be more in line with traditional work on helping student writers than more recent work on examining how faculty write. Examples include Roen et al. (1995); Vandenberg (1998); Micciche and Carr (2011); and Olson and Taylor's (1997) edited collection *Publishing in Rhetoric and Composition*. Peer review in the field has also received some attention. This work can be found mostly in two symposia on peer review, one a full special issue of *Rhetoric Review* in 1995 and a shorter, two-article symposium in *CCC* in 2012. The former symposium discussed the changing relationship between authors, editors, and reviewers in the peer review process and how collaborative such relationships should be, while the latter symposium's two articles focus on the peer review process for tenure at most institutions and the effects of writing technologies on publishers' peer review, respectively. This peer review focus differs from the earlier articles' focus on assimilating graduate students into academic writing, but its practice is not on faculty writing practices per se.

Our field's recent interest in faculty writers may have been catalyzed by some universities' increased support for faculty research programs, such as those facilitated by and in writing centers and other programs that rhetoric and composition faculty traditionally administer. Geller and Eodice's (2013) edited collection *Working with Faculty Writers* provides evidence for this assertion. The collection contains 16 chapters that report on faculty writing support programs, many of which are in writing centers, WAC programs, or university-wide initiatives like teaching and learning centers that the chapter author leads. In the introduction, Geller writes, "The emergence of institutionalized writing support (writing centers, writing across the curriculum) for students and faculty shares a history with the emergence of faculty development initiatives and teaching centers" (p. 9).

In other words, support programs for student writers and faculty writers have grown alongside each other. This seems important given that rhetoric and composition faculty often lead such programs, directly in the case of writing centers and WAC programs, and less directly in the case of teaching and learning centers whose faculty writing support they may be asked to consult on.

For the present study, it is interesting but perhaps unsurprising that rhetoric and composition scholars' frequent role of coordinating faculty writing support may have led to an increase in research about faculty writing experiences. After all, most of us want research that will inform the programs we help direct; if those programs help support faculty writers, it makes sense that we would see increased research about how faculty write and what kinds of support they may need. Further, WPAs are commonly advised to keep up a research agenda by publishing about their administrative work, so rhetoric and composition faculty directing programs that support faculty writers may find themselves motivated to research those writers or the resources they have access to. Our own findings reveal that administrator-scholars heed this advice, as many of our participants discussed WPA work as generative for research and publication. Others, however, found it difficult to generate research in their WPA roles due to burnout or other reasons (see findings for more).

WPAs can find many texts that illuminate the challenge of keeping up a research agenda while performing the overwhelming, and often low status, work of administering a writing program, as well as strategies for managing the challenge. Bailiff et al.'s (2008) *Women's Ways of Making It in Rhetoric and Composition* discusses women's struggles and successes in the field, and one issue that appears is the challenge of balancing administration and research. In a chapter dedicated to this challenge, the authors write:

> It is no secret that the time and energy required to administer a writing program is time and energy not spent on researching and publishing—often resulting in negative consequences when an untenured WPA is reviewed for tenure and promotion. (p. 119)

Later in the chapter, the authors offer practical advice for pre-tenure WPAs managing this challenge. This advice includes publishing on administrative work as discussed above, educating tenure committees about WPA work, and balancing administrative loads and publishing expectations relative to one another.

Some publications that address the challenges and strategies for balancing WPA roles with a research agenda include the edited collections *The Promise and Perils of Writing Program Administration* (Enos & Borrowman, 2008) and *Untenured Faculty as Writing Program Administrators* (Dew & Horning, 2007), as well as Charlton et al.'s (2011) *GenAdmin: Theorizing WPA Identities in the Twenty-First Century*. In *GenAdmin*, the authors focus on the generation of WPAs who, like themselves, received specific training in writing program administration. Without denying the challenges WPAs face, the authors consistently consider the opportunities presented by the work, a mindset that may come from how their training positioned writing program administration as scholarly rather than merely managerial. In the book's prelude, Charlton et al. ask, "What are the possibilities afforded to scholar-teacher-activist-administrators in various WPA roles?" (p. xvii). This group may be more likely than others to publish about WPA—indeed, the book *GenAdmin* itself may be evidence of such—since their training pushed them to think of themselves as administrator-scholars even in graduate school, when research goals and interests are forming. Still, the book offers a clear-eyed perspective on the tension we discuss above: the advice given to faculty attempting to balance the demands of administration with publishing, educate others in their institutions about WPA work as scholarly, and avoid burnout may be insufficient or unrealistic for some.

While the publications listed in the previous paragraph are a start, they are dated (particularly important given the more recent challenges brought about by the COVID-19 pandemic) and do not fully address the way faculty WPAs *do* manage their research. In other words, WPAs do publish. We wanted to know how, and the existing scholarship does not drill into the question as clearly as we would like. We were particularly motivated to learn how WPAs research and write because we believe this knowledge could yield better advice for graduate students and pre-tenure WPAs, many of whom may have only been provided general advice to do things like protect their time and mine their administrative work for research questions. Other advice commonly offered to WPAs is to educate others in their institutions about WPA work, particularly tenure committees and department chairs. This advice appears regularly in the publications cited above, and it is also apparent in statements from the Council of Writing Program Administrators (CWPA, 2019) and the Conference on College Composition and Communication (CCCC, 2018) intended to help WPAs educate others in their institutions.[2]

---

2 The MLA also has a report that may help departments improve tenure and promotion processes, "The Report of the MLA Task Force on Evaluating Scholarship for Tenure and Promotion" (2007). This report contains 20 recommendations, but none specifically address handling tenure cases for faculty with administrative roles. In fact, the recommendations do not acknowledge administration as part of faculty work at all, instead standing by the traditional research/teaching/service triad. Recommendations include: "Scholarship, teaching, and service should be the three criteria for tenure. Those responsible for tenure reviews should not include collegiality as an additional criterion for tenure" (MLA, 2007, p. 11). WPAs are left trying to fit their administrative work into one of those three buckets. While most of them will view the

The CWPA statement (2019) clearly positions writing program administration as scholarly, a positioning that many WPAs must explicitly make to their colleagues who see their work as mere management or service. The statement begins:

> It is clear within departments of English that research and teaching are generally regarded as intellectual, professional activities worthy of tenure and promotion. But administration . . . has for the most part been treated as a management activity that does not produce new knowledge and that neither requires nor demonstrates scholarly expertise and disciplinary knowledge.

In this statement, the CWPA acknowledges another difference between teaching and administrative work: the former is comfortably recognized as intellectual, where the latter may be viewed as non-disciplinary pencil pushing or service. The statement continues: "… by refiguring writing administration as scholarly and intellectual work, we argue that it is worthy of tenure and promotion when it advances and enacts disciplinary knowledge within the field of Rhetoric and Composition." The writers establish that WPA work is intellectual when it "advance[s] knowledge—its production, clarification, connection, reinterpretation, or application . . . [and] results in products or activities that can be evaluated by others" (CWPA, 2019). The writers also list and describe five categories of WPA work that fit both criteria: 1. Program Creation, 2. Curricular Design, 3. Faculty Development, 4. Program Assessment and Evaluation, and 5. Program-Related Textual Production.

The statement overall and these categories are relevant to the present study for two reasons. First, the mere existence of the document speaks to the challenges WPA-scholars often face in seeking tenure and promotion, a process that privileges traditional scholarly publishing. Second, the categories make room for different types of writing than traditional scholarly publications. The last category, program-related textual production, suggests that the documents WPAs write frequently should be viewed as scholarly. The CCCC statement "Scholarship in Rhetoric, Writing, and Composition: Guidelines for Faculty, Deans, and Chairs" (2018) also advocates for WPA work as scholarly. The original version of this statement, published in 1987, came before the CWPA statement (first published in 1998) and was initially subtitled "A Description for Department Chairs and Deans."

The addition of "Faculty" to the guidelines' subtitle may imply greater expectations of, or opportunities for, self-advocacy in the tenure and promotion

---

work as scholarship, they may face tenure committees and departments that view it as service, and this MLA report offers no advice for addressing that dilemma.

process. Most relevant to the present study is the CCCC Statement's section "How Writing Program Administration and Scholarship in Rhetoric, Writing, and Composition Are Linked." This section of the statement begins:

> The boundaries between scholarship, teaching, and service are quite porous for faculty members working in rhetoric, writing, and composition. This is because much of what we study is about pedagogy and practice: how writing is taught and learned in courses, programs, and extracurricular sites. This is also because many rhetoric, writing, and composition scholars administer (and study) writing programs of various kinds. ...

This section of the CCCC Statement also notes the availability of courses in writing program administration and "increasing attention paid to the ways that programmatic work can be considered scholarship." The existence of the CWPA statement and the section of the CCCC statement discussed here remind us that faculty in WPA positions do face unique challenges. This may be especially true for pre-tenure faculty trying to publish enough to clear the tenure bar. Our study sought firsthand perspectives from faculty writers about their writing and publishing experiences. While we did not explicitly seek perspectives about how WPA work influenced these experiences—though we did ask general questions about the balance between research and other demands—we learned a lot about how our participants thought about administration and research.

METHODS

Our IRB-approved study used interviews to learn about the writing habits and experiences of 20 published scholars in rhetoric and composition. To identify participants, we went to 10 major journals in the field.[3] From each journal, we selected authors who had published an article between 2008 and 2013. We contacted potential participants until we had two authors from each of the 10 journals. While we attempted to create a diverse group, particularly in terms of position and institution, the group skewed toward tenure-track faculty and institutions with higher research activity. Our participant group is a limitation of our study. Future research should investigate scholars who are not on the tenure track and/or who are working in institutions with lower research activity. Future research should also include a participant group that is more racially diverse to investigate experiences of scholars of color.

---

3 *College Composition and Communication, Composition Studies, WPA: Writing Program Administration, Writing Center Journal, Enculturation, Present Tense, Computers and Composition (online and print), Kairos, Rhetoric Society Quarterly,* and *Rhetoric Review*

We used surveys to collect demographic and basic work information, such as the participant's job title and publishing histories, which included how many journal articles they had published. See Appendix B for survey questions. Interviews lasted one hour and included questions about the participants' writing habits and schedules, their balance of research with other commitments, their resources used, and their experiences with reviewers and co-authors. See Appendix A for interview questions. All interviews were recorded and transcribed.

We used a grounded theory approach to analyze the data. First, we each looked through the interview transcripts separately to identify possible themes. Then we consulted the data together in a videoconference, discussing what we saw and determining preliminarily how we would code the data. Then we returned to the data individually to organize our findings by the themes we decided on, and took multiple passes to calculate the frequency and content of references to each theme. These initial findings that emerged are discussed in our *Pedagogy* article, which focused on preparing graduate students for academic publishing. We identified a theme of WPA work and its effects on research, but that was not a focus of our article. We coded again for our *CCC* article, finding new themes and incidents of helpful comments, especially on the topic of editing and peer review. Finally, for this chapter on WPA work, we reconsidered our previous coding and identified themes together, and we again consulted the data and coded it separately according to what it had to say about writing program administration and research, ultimately sharing our findings with each other and merging them.

In the next section, we discuss the study's findings about the experiences of administrator-scholars in rhetoric and composition.

FINDINGS

Because of our limited sample size and the nature of our interviews (20 interviews of around an hour in length), our findings do not represent a definitive picture of how WPAs' research is affected by their administrative duties, but they identify issues of WPA administration-research balance so powerful that they manifested even in a dataset not initially focused on that issue. Thus, we present our findings as a set of case studies whose overlapping narratives create an outline of how WPA work affects WPAs' research.

You Can't Just Shut the Door (Because People Will Knock)

As discussed in the introduction, nearly all participants talked about administration taking time away from research. These comments were based on either the participants' past or current experiences as administrators or, for a couple of participants, their sense that they had been productive researchers partly because they had been protected from administrative work. The quotations we share in the introduction are representative of many comments that speak to the time administration demands, as is the following quotation from a participant: "Since that kind of work just takes up as much time as you give to it, it can be a huge distraction to doing research, and it was." This participant had directed a PhD program in rhetoric and writing, but we heard similar comments from many kinds of administrators, including directors of writing centers and first-year composition programs, department chairs, former deans, and more.

Our participants' experiences illustrate potential problems with common productivity advice. Such advice, found in books like Silvia's (2007) *How to Write a Lot* or writing "bootcamps" hosted by university faculty development programs, can sometimes boil down to "just protect your research time." The specific strategies offered may include putting writing time on the calendar, refusing meetings during that time, and/or shutting your office door while writing. One of our first participants, a composition director, showed within the first five minutes of our interview the limitations of the last strategy: she had shut her office door to do the interview, someone knocked, and then the person knocked again until she went to the door to ask them to come back later.

Could the participant have worked from home that day if she had needed to focus on research? Perhaps. However, she described for us a weekly schedule chock-full of meetings that required her presence on campus, so staying home for a day or even just an afternoon simply may not be reasonable for a WPA like her.[4] When we asked how her research time was affected by other responsibilities, the participant responded:

> Well, I could send you my schedule for this week and you can see how it's affected by it because I really don't have any time blocks this week to sit down and write. As you saw at the beginning of this interview, I had people coming in the door, I had to talk to them, I had to shut the door, and it still didn't work. I have a lot of people who come in and want to see me about all kinds of stuff.

---

4 Our interviews were conducted before the COVID-19 pandemic. During the pandemic, faculty members like this participant would of course be more likely to work remotely than at the time of the interviews, and working remotely may be more common for WPAs even post-pandemic. We wonder how this change may help administrators like our participant, as working from home may provide more flexibility and privacy (we hope no one would show up at this participant's home to interrupt an in-progress interview). Of course, working remotely presents its own challenges, so we do not want to make any claims about how it may protect research time for WPAs. We do think this area would be fascinating for future study.

As this participant suggests, a busy administrator's schedule may be filled not just with official meetings but also with less formal conversations that, even if quick, still add up to frequent interruptions that can get in the way of dedicated writing time. This may be particularly true for someone like this participant, who directs a large first-year composition program with dozens of graduate teaching assistants who are brand new to teaching and thousands of first-year students who are brand new to college.

THE "HEADSPACE" OF ADMINISTRATION

Several participants discussed how administrative work not only takes up a lot of time but also requires a different kind of thinking than research. When asked how research time was affected by other job responsibilities like teaching, service, and administration, one participant remarked:

> Administration made it just virtually impossible even if I had wanted to be writing in the weeks [during the semester]. It's not just the time, it's what it does to your brain, that it is a completely different mindset and skill set. You're not even in an intellectual space for the majority of your waking life. You're in this strange bureaucratic weird space and it's just hard, at least it was hard for me to even get my head where it would be to even read. I couldn't even really read anything intellectual, it's terrible.

Interestingly, the original question was only about *time*, but the participant pushed on the question to note that administrators face challenges beyond the well-documented time limitations. As this participant suggests, they may also struggle to concentrate on research, since administrative work may demand a kind of thinking that differs from, or is even incompatible with, scholarly work. One participant acknowledged common advice to keep up a research agenda by publishing on WPA work and commented that he would like to write about his administrative work, particularly in curriculum development. He also explained that he has not done so because of burnout: "To do so much of that [admin] work all the time, I don't want to then turn around and write a 9,000- or 10,000- word article about it. I'm like, 'I'm done.'"

For these participants, teaching did not seem to distract from research in the way administrative work does. This is partly practical, as participants described teaching subjects that were related to their research, which allowed them to connect research with course prep. When asked about his balance between research and other parts of his job, one participant commented: "[Research time] is mostly affected by administrative work. The teaching not so much, because often I'm teaching topics or subjects that are related to things that I'm writing. Part of my preparation for instruction in the class entails writing sections of pieces that I intend to publish on my own." Other participants simply noted that teaching did not drain their intellectual and emotional energy in the same way administrative work does. One participant even seemed resentful of how administrative work and service could take away time for research but explicitly said she did not feel the same about teaching, which she views as a central part of her job: "Teaching I don't really count as an intrusion of my writing time because that's my job and really, if I'm going to be a professor, my job is to teach students." While this participant is talking about time and not necessarily "headspace," her perspective of administration as a drain and teaching as a central part of the job seems significant in how she viewed and approached the work in relation to her research.

Importantly, not all participants viewed administrative work as a drain on their intellectual energy, even if they did agree that the work took up a lot of time. Several participants spoke of WPA work as generative for their research in the kind of ways the participant quoted above sees her teaching. One participant talked about how both teaching and administration work into her research:

> I tend to try and teach things that will feed into my research, so I see teaching as really productive and generative in that way. Most things that I have written have come out of teaching, actually pretty directly . . . It is the same thing with administration. Actually, [an article about WPA work] has come from my own experience as an administrator. I see all these things as very much in relationship and feeding one another. No doubt giving the time is a challenge, but I'm a note taker so if I'm having a problem in administration, I'm usually writing notes about it to myself to say, this is my thinking and this is what is going on so I can come back to it later.

This participant went on to describe a detailed process of how she uses One-Note's feature to keep detailed notes on her administrative work and on every course she teaches. She described using the notes to keep a log of her thinking and generate ideas for conference papers, which she then could turn into journal articles. The participant described her work process: "I try to work really methodically in stages like that and not feel like I have to produce something from scratch all at once but try to build up to it." Keeping consistent notes on her WPA work was a major part of this. While this participant described the most detailed, methodical process of reflecting regularly on her administrative work, several other participants also spoke generally about gaining research ideas from their roles as WPAs.

Of course, we do not want to create a binary between seeing administrative work as an intellectual drain *or* as generative for writing scholarship. Wells, a writing center director of 10 years, feels that it can be both. Wells has published articles and a co-authored book that were certainly prompted and helped along by her experiences in the writing center and her access to writing center data and potential research participants and collaborators. At the same time, Wells has experienced weeks when the writing center demanded such draining bureaucratic work, like budgeting, that intellectual energy for research was nil.

Emails, Proposals, and Some More Emails: What "Counts" as Writing?

If comments about the headspace of administration raised questions about what counts as intellectual activity, other comments raised questions about what counts as writing. In addition to discussing more traditional forms of scholarly writing like books and journal articles, many participants discussed the writing they do as administrators. These findings provide a perfect example of how a research methods foible can have a silver lining. One of our interview questions was, "Please describe the kinds of writing you do most regularly." We had in our minds *scholarly* writing, since that was the focus of the study, but with the general way we worded the question, many participants understandably answered with a broader notion of writing. Our ambiguously phrased interview question garnered great findings about all the kinds of writing participants do in their work, as well as some comments about how this writing compares to more traditional scholarly writing.

The writing of administration, like administrative work in general, simply takes up a lot of time. One participant, a new writing center director, commented: "I'm just surprised how much time email takes up now. . . . It's funny how something as simple as that is just a time suck." Many participants made similar comments, but the best example came from one of our first participants, a tenured associate professor and first-year composition director at a major research university. When asked about the kinds of writing she does most regularly, this participant responded immediately and emphatically: "Email." Looking back at the transcript, we cringe at our clumsy attempt to redirect and specify that we had in mind more traditional forms of scholarship, like journal articles and grant proposals. Our participant was polite but firm in explaining that she knew exactly what we meant by the question but wanted us to understand how much time she spent on email alone as an in-demand WPA:

> I just wanted to tell you that I sent about 30 emails today. So that you understand what it means to be an administrator and

when you talk about what other things do you write mostly, I'm pointing out to you that I still have six more [emails] to do, which means I probably write about 50 emails a day. In terms of WPA scholarship, I think that's significant.

The participant's last comment is particularly interesting to us, as she suggests that for WPAs, email forms an important part of scholarship. She went on to describe the other types of writing she does, including IRB proposals, journal articles, conference presentations, and grant proposals. She mused that it would be interesting to research the writing life of a WPA. In particular, it would be fascinating to study how WPAs toggle constantly between day-to-day writing like email and research writing like journal articles and conference presentations. We briefly discuss this idea in our conclusion.

Several other participants spoke to the pressure they faced in responding quickly when the emails were about immediate concerns. This is particularly true for administrators who get email not only from their own students but from others' students as well. One participant, a first-year composition director, commented about her research, "It gets pushed aside. It's hard when I have my own teaching responsibilities, and then I'm getting emails daily from instructors, who are having their own issues with their students. I'm getting emails and requests from other people's students." She went on to speak to the immediacy of those emails and the need to respond quickly: "[When] there's email from a student who needs to meet with me like tomorrow, there's an immediacy for those concerns that can't really be brushed aside."

We say more in the next section about the life of upper admins, but being unable to ignore email may be especially the case for administrators who are in charge of whole units or programs. One participant, a department head, spoke of having two instructors come to her the week of her interview with students who had written explicitly of self-harm and suicide. She commented that she simply could not set such issues aside in the name of protecting her research time, as the issues were life-or-death. While the participant noted the same may not be true for "junior administrators" (her words—she seemed to mean anyone in charge of a unit smaller than a department), we could easily see a first-year composition director or writing center director facing similar challenges, albeit perhaps not as regularly due to the smaller size of the programs. Wells, for example, has received emails from student tutors who were experiencing health or other problems that she simply could not set aside in favor of research. Of course, email is only one kind of writing that administrators do regularly. When asked what she writes the most, one writing center administrator responded, "Memos, paperwork, forms and bureaucratic things that universities require for one purpose or another . . . there's always a form for something." The same participant also talked about social media posts. Even though she had mostly handed off responsibility for the writing center's social media to tutors, she is still responsible for handling any problematic or poorly received posts. A different participant wrote that when she directed her department's graduate program, "I used to spend a lot of time just writing emails and one-page proposals and that kind of stuff to advance the program." Like these two participants, several others talked about proposals, bureaucratic writing like forms, and memos and other kinds of communication they wrote for tutors, instructors, and colleagues.

Comments about these types of administrative writing were less emphatic than comments about email, but we were still struck by how many participants discussed programmatic documents like proposals. In retrospect, we wish we had asked more follow-up questions about the participants' experiences with these forms of writing. As a follow-up, we did ask the writing center director from the previous paragraph if her writing process differed when writing the administrative documents she discussed versus more traditional forms of scholarship, like conference proposals and presentations, which she also talked about. She responded that she mostly followed the same process but was able to dive into administrative documents a little more easily, since she had more experience with writing them.

WHEN EVERY PROBLEM IS YOUR PROBLEM: THE LIFE OF SENIOR FACULTY ADMINS

While most of our participants were either early- or mid-career faculty, we did interview four full professors, all of whom had held a variety of administrative roles throughout their careers. At the time of interviews, two were chairs (one an English department chair, one chair of a large rhetoric and composition program within an English department), and one had been an interim department chair, an associate dean, and the chair of a large rhetoric and composition program. The fourth had developed and then directed a professional writing program. Two participants—the current English department chair and the former interim chair and associate dean—spoke most directly to how senior administrative work could challenge research. We end our findings with these comments because they remind us that the challenges do not end when one achieves tenure and not even when one becomes a full professor.

In fact, the current English department chair we spoke with pointed out that research can become more of a struggle for senior administrators. Junior administrators, she claimed, could generally prioritize their research time, but more senior admins like department chairs cannot because the buck stops with them.⁵ She explained that administrative work simply must take priority in many situations:

> Admin must take preference sometimes. You are in charge, so when a foreign dignitary wants to speak to you or a VP needs you to counsel their child on being an English major, that's what you have to do. Junior faculty can shrug it off because the buck rarely stops there. They are protected.

The participant who had been an interim department chair, associate dean, and chair of a rhetoric and composition program offered similar comments and specified that being a department chair could most challenge research time:

> You've got to just be so draconian in your schedule to do it [research] when you're an administrator. The hardest job in the university is to be a department chair or head depending upon whatever they call it in the university. The former president of [participant's university] who was a person I knew and respected said it was harder than his job because you are the point person for the students, the faculty, other administration. It all triangulates on you. You can't do a half-assed job. You have to do it because every problem is your problem.

This participant went on to talk forcefully about how he always discouraged assistant and even tenured associate professors from being department chairs, as he felt strongly that such a move could hinder their research enough to keep them from becoming full professors.

While these comments offer important cautionary tales about taking on senior administrative work, we are also reminded that rhetoric and composition faculty can serve as important allies when they are in these roles. In talking about his work as associate dean, the participant quoted above described explaining constantly to other administrators how time-consuming writing instruction can be:

> This is the point I keep getting across to administrators. When you are, for example, reading student papers, it is an enormous time commitment and it's exhausting at the end of it. Then after . . . we do a full set of papers, we're expected to

---

5   As we commented previously, "junior administrator" is this participant's term. She seemed to mean those who were directing any program that was smaller than a department. The participant who had been an interim department chair and associate dean also used the term junior administrator and seemed to share this participant's general definition.

do our best research between 10:00 at night and 1:00 in the morning, when we're exhausted, right?

This participant also described writing tenure and promotion documents during his time as an associate dean. We imagine writing faculty would benefit if more of us were positioned to talk to senior administrators about writing instruction and to advocate for working conditions and tenure and promotion guidelines that serve us best. For that reason, we do not believe the answer to protecting one's research time from administration should come down to, "Don't be an administrator." As mentioned before, that is unrealistic for rhetoric and composition faculty and, as we see from this participant's comments, rhetoric and composition faculty can serve as important advocates as administrators. Instead, we believe what's needed are research productivity strategies that account for administrative responsibilities, as well as strategies for positioning one's admin work as scholarly. In the chapter's conclusion, we turn to these ideas.

WHERE WE GO FROM HERE

At this point in the chapter, a reader may reasonably expect us to offer strategies that faculty can use to balance a scholarly agenda with administrative demands. Unfortunately, we cannot offer such strategies. To be more precise, we *could* offer some strategies, but they would likely be suggestions our readers have already heard. During interviews, many participants recounted the very faculty productivity advice we might summarize here, as well as some of the most common advice given to current and future administrators. In our study, we found that common productivity advice, like shutting one's office door, can be impractical for WPAs, and common career advice, like not taking on administrative roles pre-tenure, can be unrealistic for rhetoric and composition faculty who may have trained to direct writing programs.

Still, we do not wish to dismiss common productivity advice or advice about administrative work commonly given to current and future rhetoric and composition faculty. Surely many faculty members benefit from productivity advice in books like Silvia's (2007) *How to Write a Lot* or Boice's (1990) *Professors as Writers*, as well as strategies offered in faculty success programs held by university centers and national organizations.[6] In fact, we have ourselves implemented and benefited from common strategies like writing in small chunks, putting research time on the schedule, and keeping accountable by checking in with a writing partner or group. Additionally, many rhetoric and composition faculty

---

6   As an example, visit the website for the National Center for Faculty Development and Diversity at https://www.facultydiversity.org/fsp-bootcamp.

have surely benefited from advice to be cautious about taking on administrative work pre-tenure. Even when faculty, like Wells, choose to take pre-tenure WPA positions, they may benefit from suggestions to proceed cautiously and consider how they may need to adjust their work habits to find balance and meet their tenure requirements.

Without dismissing current advice outright, we do wish to discuss how common faculty productivity advice may be limited for administrators, as well as how common advice for current or future admins may be unrealistic for rhetoric and composition faculty. While we cannot offer new advice, we can offer ideas for additional research and points readers may want to bring up with their departments and within our field. All of the sections below are both areas for future research and points for discussion.

THE WRITING LIFE OF AN ADMINISTRATOR

One of the most interesting ideas for future research came directly from one of our participants, who discussed her own all-day balance between different types of writing and suggested that someone should research this experience. We agree. Research could investigate the types of writing administrators do most commonly that are not viewed as scholarly in the traditional sense of journal articles and books. We are thinking here about email, social media and web content, program proposals and reports, and forms and other kinds of bureaucratic documents required by the university. Research could also study the process of administrative writing, like what it is like to shift regularly between this kind of writing and more scholarly forms; investigate how the writing of administration differs from more traditional forms of scholarly writing in terms of process and strategies; and question how common types of administrative writing reflect disciplinary knowledge and experience.

Profiles of administrators' writing lives alone would be interesting in and of themselves, of course, but we also imagine the research would prove directly useful for individuals and for the field. First, this research could help faculty administrators find new opportunities in their everyday writing, including opportunities for teaching and collaborating with students. In one example, it strikes us now that the social media writing one participant discussed doing with her writing center tutors and students could offer a faculty-student collaboration that diverges from the co-authored articles we normally think of. In a different example, many participants discussed writing proposals, reports, and other kinds of program documents that could provide valuable examples for professional and technical writing courses or even projects for student interns.

Care Responsibilities, Research, and Admin Work

We did not explicitly ask participants about parenting or other care responsibilities. Still, several participants, particularly those with children, talked about these demands. Interestingly, many of these participants talked about such demands during the same conversations about administrative roles, possibly because both topics were prompted by our question about balancing research time with other demands.

Some noted the overall positive effect of care responsibilities on their work habits and work-life balance. For example, one participant described how having children motivated her to stay focused during the day so she would not have to work after they came home from school:

> When you have kids, trying to work from 4:00–8:00 [PM] is like a nightmare. You don't want to have to do it, so you force yourself to be more productive [during the day]. It's like having a deadline. Four o'clock is your deadline, and when you have a deadline, it imposes a certain sense of urgency that makes working more productively during the daytime easier.

However, other participants made different comments. During one particularly interesting interview, a participant laughed at the way a well-known faculty productivity program marketed itself by claiming faculty could learn strategies to avoid working after hours or on weekends: "[They claim] you can do it so you're not working on weekends [because] you're doing the work during the week, yadda, yadda, yadda. I don't think these people have children, but that's another story." As this participant suggests, common research productivity advice may be limited for faculty who are balancing work with care obligations. We imagine that the pandemic has only exacerbated this problem.

Of course, lots of faculty, not just administrators, are caring for others, including children, aging parents, or both. However, what we heard in several interviews is that care demands, like administrative demands, can challenge common strategies for maintaining a research agenda. When a faculty member is both an administrator and a caretaker, the challenges may double. The participant we quote second in the previous paragraph discussed the challenges of being a nursing mother:

> I will tell you when I was pregnant and nursing . . . that was really difficult. I remember having two hours and I have to get all this stuff done because I have to go back and nurse. . . . I would go to Starbucks or someplace like that and I would just write like the wind for two hours so I could get back and feed

my baby. I remember that was kind of difficult, but it was also good because I got it done, but it was a challenge.

This participant describes enacting common writing productivity advice: carve out time for research, go somewhere they will not be distracted (or shut the office door), and use that time to focus completely on writing. From the participant's description, one can imagine how difficult this would be for a nursing mother who has a deadline to return to her hungry baby. For an administrator who must balance all of this with meetings, many of which may be on campus, the balance becomes even more difficult. At a different point in the interview, this participant commented about the balance of research with other demands: "I think that you have to kind of figure out what are the constraints that shape when and how you can write. I definitely think that administration and family life affect that."

Her comments remind us that scholar-admin-parents need support and advice that recognizes all the roles they play. Just as future studies may investigate the challenges faced by faculty administrators, studies that investigate the challenges faced by faculty parents may help us develop support programs and advice that better reflect their realities. In particular, we imagine the field may benefit from interview studies that, like our own, attempt to uncover "real" faculty writing experiences, including what strategies they use to cope, but are focused on faculty parents.

ADVICE AND ADVOCACY FOR WRITING PROGRAM ADMINISTRATORS

Participant comments suggest that common advice about protecting research time may be difficult for in-demand WPAs. For example, productivity books and blogs often suggest faculty create a writing schedule and protect it fiercely by, for example, ignoring email and shutting the office door for two hours every day (or an hour a day or two afternoons a week or whatever). We do not question the usefulness of this advice, but participants' comments suggest admins may have trouble setting and sticking to a writing schedule when emails with immediate needs come in so regularly. As one participant comments, some emails simply cannot be set aside, and administrator-scholars need productivity advice that is more attuned to this reality.

Additionally, common advice to simply avoid administrative work pre-tenure may be unrealistic for rhetoric and composition faculty, given that our disciplinary training makes us prime candidates for directing writing centers, first-year composition programs, and other writing initiatives. Instead of being advised to simply avoid administrative work, current and future rhetoric and composition faculty need research productivity strategies that are more attuned to the realities of WPAs. Such faculty may also need strategies for advocating for their administrative work as scholarly, given how colleagues, non-WPA university administrators, and tenure committees seem to remain ignorant of the subject.

REFERENCES

Ballif, M., Davis, D. D. & Mountford, R. (2008). *Women's ways of making it in rhetoric and composition*. Routledge. https://doi.org/10.4324/9780203929841.

Boice, R. (1990). *Professors as writers: A self-help guide to productive writing*. New Forums Press.

Charlton, C., Charlton, J., Graban, T. S., Ryan, K. J. & Stolley, A. F. (2011). *GenAdmin: Theorizing WPA identities in the twenty-first century*. Parlor Press.

Conference on College Composition and Communication (CCC). (2018, April 4). *Scholarship in rhetoric, writing, and composition: Guidelines for faculty, deans, and chairs* [CCCC Position Statement]. http://cccc.ncte.org/cccc/resources/positions/scholarshipincomp.

Council of Writing Program Administrators (CWPA). (2019, July 17). *Evaluating the intellectual work of writing administration* (WPA Position Statement). http://wpacouncil.org/aws/CWPA/pt/sd/news_article/242849/_PARENT/layout_details/false.

Dew, D. F. & Horning, A. (Eds.). (2007). *Untenured faculty as writing program administrators: Institutional practices and politics*. Parlor Press.

Enos, T. & Borrowman, S. (Eds.). (2008). *The promise and perils of writing program administration*. Parlor Press.

Gallagher, J. R. & DeVoss, D. N. (Eds.). (2019). *Explanation points: Publishing in rhetoric and composition*. Utah State University Press. https://doi.org/10.7330/9781607328834.

Geller, A. E. & Eodice, M. (Eds.). (2013). *Working with faculty writers*. Utah State University Press.

Johnson, K. (2017). Writing by the book, writing beyond the book. *Composition Studies, 45*(2), 55–72.

Micciche, L. R. & Carr, A. D. (2011). Toward graduate-level writing instruction. *College Composition and Communication, 62*(3), 477–501.

Modern Language Association Task Force on Evaluating Scholarship for Tenure and Promotion (MLA). (2007). *Report on evaluating scholarship for tenure and promotion*. Modern Language Association. https://www.mla.org/Resources/Research/Surveys-Reports-and-Other-Documents/Publishing-and-Scholarship/Report-on-Evaluating-Scholarship-for-Tenure-and-Promotion.

Olson, G. A. & Taylor, T. W. (Eds.). (1997). *Publishing in rhetoric and composition*. State University of New York Press.

Roen, Duane H., Villanueva, V., Brown, S., Kirsch, G., Adams, J., Wyche-Smith, S. & Helsley, S. (1995). Revising for publication: Advice to graduate students and other junior scholars. *Rhetoric Society Quarterly, 25*, 237–246.

Silvia, P. (2007). *How to write a lot: A practical guide to productive academic writing*. APA Life Tools.

Söderlund, L. & Wells, J. (2019). A study of the practices and responsibilities of scholarly peer review in rhetoric and composition. *College Composition and Communication, 71*(1), 117–144.

Tarabochia, S. L. (2020). Self-authorship and faculty writers' trajectories of becoming. *Composition Studies, 48*(1), 16–33.

Tulley, C. E. (2018). *How writing faculty write: Strategies for process, product, and productivity*. Utah State University Press.

Vandenberg, P. (1998). Composing composition studies: Scholarly publication and the practice of discipline. In C. Farris & C. M. Anson (Eds.), *Under construction: Working at the intersections of composition theory, research, and practice* (pp. 19–29). Utah State University Press.

Wells, J. & Söderlund, L. (2018). Preparing graduate students for academic publishing: Results from a study of published rhetoric and composition scholars. *Pedagogy: Critical Approaches to Teaching Literature, Language, Composition, and Culture, 18*(1), 131–156. https://doi.org/10.1215/15314200-4216994.

APPENDIX A. INTERVIEW QUESTIONS

1. What do you see as your primary areas of research within rhetoric and composition?
2. How did you learn to write for/publish in our field?
3. On average, how much time do you spend on your research every week and how does that time break down?
4. What resources do you use regularly to complete your research?
5. What types of collaborative writing and research do you do? How does collaborating affect your process?
6. If you're faculty: Describe the tenure requirements in your institution. If you're a graduate student: Describe the amount of published research you anticipate doing at the job you hope to get.
7. How is your writing time affected by teaching, administration, service, other responsibilities?
8. What types of writing do you do most often (ex: grant proposals, conference presentations, articles, etc.)?
9. How do you know you're ready to submit a document?
10. What have been your greatest writing/research successes? What have been your biggest obstacles?
11. Talk about the kinds of feedback you've received from reviewers. What's been most helpful? Most discouraging?

APPENDIX B. SURVEY

1. Where did you attend/are you attending graduate school?
2. What year did you graduate, if you have matriculated?
3. What is the name of your current academic institution and what is your position? (Place and title and/or administrative role, e.g., Wright State University, Assistant Professor, Director of Professional and Technical Writing)
4. How many peer-reviewed book reviews have you published?
   a. none
   b. 1–2
   c. 3–4
   d. other____
5. How many peer-reviewed articles have you published?
   a. 1–2
   b. 3–4
   c. other____
6. How many peer-reviewed books have you published?
   a. none
   b. 1
   c. 2
   d. other____
7. Are you at a tenure-granting institution? If so, are you tenured or untenured? How long since has it been you were awarded your last rank, and how long before you anticipate receiving your next rank (if applicable)?

CHAPTER 5.

COMPLICATING TECHNO-AFTERGLOW: PURSUING COMPOSITIONAL EQUITY AND MAKING LABOR VISIBLE IN DIGITAL SCHOLARLY PRODUCTION

Paul Muhlhauser
McDaniel College

Jenna Sheffield
Salem College

Abstract: *We explore digital scholarship in composition studies, specifically focusing on labor visibility and compositional equity. We critique the traditional preference for print scholarship over digital forms and argue for acknowledgment of the labor-intensive process of digital publication. By examining born-digital publications, we advocate for equity in assessing digital scholarship and encourage a shift in evaluative criteria to appreciate diverse modes of academic production. This work pushes for a more inclusive understanding of what constitutes scholarly labor, especially in digital contexts.*

It has been nearly 30 years since *Kairos: A Journal for Teachers of Writing in Webbed Environments* (now *Kairos: A Journal of Rhetoric, Technology, and Pedagogy*) first published, and *Computers and Composition Online*'s digital scholarship archives go back as far as 2000. In other words, it has been quite a while since the excitement of born-digital scholarship flooded into the rhetoric and composition field, establishing itself as a vital and vibrant form of scholarship conveyed through digital texts/web texts, wikis, and multimodal works. The credibility and excitement, however, of digital texts more or less trickled through English departments. Scholars producing digital work found themselves needing to argue for the merits of digital scholarship, justifying its value and equality with traditional scholarship (Ball, 2004; Purdy & Walker, 2010).

Now, at least in rhetoric and composition circles, digital scholarship seems to be getting closer and closer to being considered "real" scholarship. There are more established spaces for publishing in the field (e.g., *JOMR* and *Computers and Composition Digital Press*). Teaching "digital literacy" has become a somewhat cliché and redundant phrase. It is just what happens in the rhetoric and composition classroom. Though substantial progress has been made in the field, it's still a little early for digital scholars to bask in techno-afterglow—to "rest on their laurels" and cease pursuing compositional equity. Digital scholarship remains stigmatized in the larger worlds of English and communication, as well as across our institutions—tenure committees and/or administrators often don't "get it."

Fundamental to supporting this stigma are the important differences in composing processes between digital scholarship and traditional scholarship that are glossed over—differences that would help challenge the stigma and add prestige to digital scholarship. These unseen differences are the invisible labors inherent in digital scholarship composing processes, labors not always part of traditional scholarly processes. Understanding these differences makes clear the compositional inequities inherent in how digital scholarship and traditional scholarship are defined, how they function, how they are created, and what they do.

Compositional equity is our term for acknowledging these differences and for inciting a change in perspectives between what digital scholars and traditional scholars do. We suggest compositional equity is a helpful framework for valuing the invisible labors of scholarship, in particular the product and processes of digital scholarship. We complicate the idea that digital scholarship has "made it," that there is some kind of techno-afterglow to indulge. Digital scholarship remains stigmatized as "easy" (i.e., easy to create), less rigorously peer reviewed, and, well, fun, at least when compared to traditional scholarship. The stigma is not something easy to quantify or qualify beyond a feeling, beyond microaggressions we have experienced about our work. However, the CCCC's statement on digital scholarship helping scholars express its value, as well as book chapters like "Making Digital Scholarship Count" (Kelly, 2013) and articles like "Valuing Digital Scholarship: Exploring the Changing Realities of Intellectual Work" (Purdy & Walker, 2010) and "Engaging Digital Scholarship: Thoughts on Evaluating Multimedia Scholarship" (Anderson & McPherson, 2011) point to an "othering," a less-than position for digital scholarship when compared to traditional scholarship. Digital scholarship, in other words, is regularly framed as having to continually "prove" itself.

Besides highlighting that almost Sisyphean task, another purpose of our survey was to, in a sense, "prove" the stigma's existence beyond framings and our own feelings. By doing so, we hope to make clear the labors of process and the process of labor in born-digital productions. In our study, we investigate digital scholars' composing processes, the technologies they know or have had to learn to be successful, their motivations for publishing digital scholarship, and the invisible labors (including emotional) that may be inherent in their work. Our study, we hope, will assist digital scholars in making visible the work inherent in their compositional processes *and* products. We hope the trends we identify in this study can be used to develop stronger faculty writing support programs, elucidate helpful publishing practices in the field, and make clear the compositional inequity between digital and traditional scholarship, in an effort to move toward equity.

COMPLICATING CORE CONCEPTS: INVISIBLE LABOR, EMOTIONAL LABOR, AND COMPOSITIONAL EQUITY

Invisible labor is an important concept currently pervading rhetoric and composition studies research. The gist of the concept is to make visible and explicit the diverse and overlooked kinds of labor rhetoric and composition scholars perform. Teaching to a class for fifty minutes, grading/evaluating papers, and meeting with students are the obvious, stereotypical, visible aspects of rhetoric and composition labor. Prepping for classes, creating assignments to assess, the recovery from exhausting individual conferences with students, and conducting research and writing about it, on the other hand, are invisible labors—work of rhetoric and composition teaching and scholarship that often goes unnoticed and unappreciated by larger non-rhetoric and composition publics.

Rhetoric and composition scholars have applied the invisible labor "lens" in a variety of ways. In relation to Writing Program Administration (WPA) work, scholars argue that substantial aspects of the WPA's job are invisible, undervalued, and often go completely unnoticed (Day et al. 2013; McIntyre, 2019; Micciche, 2002). Much of the work of WPAs has been treated as work that does not produce new knowledge or require scholarly expertise (Council of Writing Program Administrators, 2019). In particular, the invisibility of emotional labor (resolving conflicts, gaining trust, mentoring, advising) of WPAs goes unnoticed (Jackson et al., 2016), and the work products (e.g., policies or curriculum development) of WPAs are often not valued by tenure and promotion committees or the discipline at large (McIntyre, 2019).

The lenses of invisible labor and emotional labor are being applied to more aspects of rhetoric and composition experiences and work. Sano-Franchini (2016) examined emotional labor in the culture of the rhetoric and composition job market. Last year, *The Journal of Multimodal Rhetorics* (2021) devoted two special issues (4.2 and 5.1) to invisible labor, exploring a range of invisible labors in academics (e.g., invisible labors experienced by people of color, differential invisible labor of single mothers, and how digital literacy can be considered a free form of labor students possess/don't possess in classrooms).

The consequences of invisible and emotional labor are significant and perceptible, often leading to exhaustion, burnout, job dissatisfaction, and "emotional angst" (Micciche, 2002). We argue that many of these problems hold true for another unique subset of rhetoric and composition scholars: scholars who produce digital scholarship.

While there are studies examining the work of the digital rhetoric and composition scholar, the research is focused more on defining digital scholarship (Ball, 2004), theorizing ways to legitimize digital scholarship, studying how users experience digital scholarship (Tham & Grace, 2020), or theorizing about the challenges and opportunities of publishing in new media environments (Journet, Ball & Trauman, 2012; Sheffield, 2015). Few studies focus on the actual composing processes of digital scholars or the factors that influence or inhibit scholarly productivity for these scholars, who consider themselves "technorhetoricians" (Maid, 2000) or computers and writing researchers. Though it does mention many of the issues associated with digital scholarship (e.g., collaborative nature and time), even the helpful advice in the Conference on College Composition and Communication's (2015) "Promotion and Tenure Guidelines for Work with Technology" position statement lacks references supporting assumptions about digital scholarship. To that end, the extant research or scholarly statements are mostly anecdotal or driven by case studies, which are valuable but may not offer the scope necessary to incite change or convince non-digital scholars of its legitimacy.

Our study takes up this challenge, as we employ quantitative research methods to more fully grasp the extent of digital scholars' composing processes and the labor of their work. Therefore, much of our study extends into a concern about equity, a concern which has been on the minds of digitally focused rhetoric and composition scholars for a long time, especially with regards to access, student techno-literacies, and interface bias (e.g., Selber, 2004; Selfe, 1999; Selfe & Selfe, 1994). And Chamberlain, Haver, and Hartline (2015–2016), more recently, dispute the Do-It-Yourself ethic, noting it is not an equitable position and plays into white techno-patriarchal assumptions as well—do it alone, without help or consultation. Almjeld and England (2015–2016) show the value in creating equitable spaces for girls to learn digital technologies in their webtext, guiding scholars on how to work with the larger community and facilitate larger scholastic and community buy-in.

Muhlhauser and Self (2019) make equity explicit, describing the ways Tinder and Bumble perform "technological equity" and "technological equality" via gender performance, critiquing how the apps treat power differentials in dating cultures between men and women. Muhlhauser and Salvati (2021) define "rhetorical equity," arguing for texts to practice transtextuality and accommodate a variety of audiences through multiple textual versions. *Compositional equity* is an effort to make explicit the ways texts are not the same, either in outcome or in their processes. In other words, there is a difference between compositional equity and *compositional equality*—the notion that composing processes are identical or egalitarian performances. With compositional equality, there's a presumption about process and product—that author processes are, though they may be different, regarded equally, even when the products, too, may be vastly different. Compositional equality's ethic rests on a value system that ignores differential composing processes and types of texts scholars produce.

Compositional equity, on the other hand, is *more* inclusive and empathetic to author processes and products, presuming processes and types of products are differentiated, requiring different expertise, invisible and emotional labors, time constraints, and difficulties. Compositional equity recognizes that processes and products are rarely equal. Compositional equity comes from an "all texts are created *equitable*" instead of an "all texts are created *equal*" position, acknowledging a diverse range of scholar creation processes and products.

METHODS

To understand compositional equity and the emotional labors inherent in digital scholarship, we sent a questionnaire to digital scholars in rhetoric and composition or closely related fields, asking them about their composing processes. Our pool of respondents came from the most recent research published over a five-year span in *Kairos, Computers and Composition Online, The Journal of Multimodal Rhetorics, Harlot of the Arts*,[1] and *Computers and Composition Digital Press*.

We selected the works that met our definition of digital scholarship and emailed the authors, asking them to participate in our survey. Though there is overlap between what we call traditional scholarship and digital scholarship, we provided the definitions of the concepts for our respondents for two reasons: (1) to provide conceptual foundations for our respondents, and (2) to help respondents understand why they were selected and how their works are examples of digital scholarship:

- *Traditional (Print) Scholarship:* Scholarship that primarily uses the written channel of communication (i.e., uses alphabetic text either

---

1 Though no longer publishing new work, *Harlot* was an important outlet for webtexts in rhetoric and composition. We looked at their last five years of publication.

in physical print or as a digital artifact). Presentation of product (research/article) is prescriptively formatted by the publisher's "house" rules. Though such scholarship may include non-linguistic aspects (tables, diagrams, bold-faced headings, and images), the creation of new imagery and formatting is limited. The arguments being made in traditional texts are generally meant to be experienced linearly.

- *Digital Scholarship*: Digital scholarship may take two forms:
  - Linguistic-centric scholarship, which uses a variety of communication channels beyond just alphabetic text to present arguments. Authors have agency in design and are involved in creation of new, not exclusively written, content.
  - Non-linguistic-centric scholarship (such as an argument made using images), in which other modes of communication take precedence over the written (if included at all). Authors have agency in design and are involved in creation of new, not exclusively written content.

Both forms of digital scholarship tend to "break away from linear modes of print traditions" (Ball, 2004, p. 403). Digital scholarship can be linear; however, regardless of linearity, the presentation of scholarship is generally not prescriptive. An important aspect of digital scholarship is how authors are highly involved in presentation, setting the scene for how their scholarship is displayed and experienced by audiences.

We used "linguistic-centric" and "non-linguistic-centric" to distinguish types of digital scholarship, as "linguistic" is the common parlance for describing multimodal and multimedia work using primarily *words* to communicate. Examples of additional modes include visual, aural, spatial, and gestural. Additionally, "linear" is also common parlance in digital scholarship referring to the "direction" a text can be read: beginning to end where a reader is "supposed" to experience a text in a linear order or a text with multiple entry points where linearity is not assumed necessary for readers to understand or engage with the text.

After creating a list of all authors who had published digital scholarship in the above-listed outlets, we then individually emailed each author who composed digital scholarship, asking them to respond to our questionnaire. Our list resulted in 188 possible respondents, and we received 58 total responses, for a 31% response rate.[2] The survey was open from June 29, 2021 through July 14, 2021.

The questionnaire was designed to address a few key areas:

- *Respondent demographics:* The demographic information we collected included (1) the race/ethnicity with which respondents identified,

---

2   We removed individuals from the pool if we could not find their current email address.

(2) gender, (3) type of school at which the respondent works (liberal arts college, community college, etc.), (4) respondents' faculty status (tenured, tenure-track, etc.), (5) their department, (6) the amount of digital scholarship they had published, and (7) their familiarity with a variety of technologies and technological principles.

- *Perceptions of digital scholarship:* We asked respondents closed- and open-ended questions regarding how they felt others perceive digital scholarship work. These questions were meant to help us understand the possible emotional labor of digital scholarship work and how scholars feel it is or is not valued amongst colleagues and others. (See Appendix A for all survey questions.)
- *Composing processes:* We asked a variety of questions about how respondents compose—what approaches are most successful for them.
- *Scholarly labor and affective dimensions of composing digital scholarship:* We also asked questions aimed at understanding scholars' feelings about composing digital scholarship that would help us understand the invisible labors involved in producing digital scholarship as compared to traditional scholarship.

In addition to analyzing responses to all closed-ended questions, we coded open-ended responses for common themes where applicable. In many cases, there were not enough responses for us to identify trends; however, we use the quotations in the results section to further illustrate responses from the open-ended questions.

POSITIONALITY

It is important for us to acknowledge our positionalities in relation to our study's population, the topic we selected to research, and our research process. In doing so, we are acknowledging known biases and assisting readers in assessing how our identities have shaped our research. When we began this study, we were both operating from a privileged position, in the sense that we both had already successfully achieved tenure and promotion to associate professor, and we had achieved this success publishing some digital scholarship. We came into this project aware that our respondents might not have earned tenure or might not be in tenure-track positions. We also realized that even though our respondents had published digital scholarship, they might not solely publish digital scholarship and might not consider themselves digital scholars. We generally considered ourselves "insiders," part of the community within which we were conducting our research (Huberman & Miles, 2002). We had both been active in the computers and writing community for years, had published in some of the journals from which we selected respondents, and identified as digital scholars. In the end, we had a mix of respondents who identified as digital scholars and who did not; most had published some digital scholarship but had not done so exclusively. As such, we had a range of respondent types in terms of their level of comfort, familiarity, and identification with digital scholarship. Additionally, we're both white and have worked primarily in private institutions. In terms of demographics for our respondents, they were mostly white and worked at public universities or colleges. Though we tried to mitigate our own bias as much as possible in leaving space for respondents to provide their own identities and recontextualize questions, we understand that our positions in scholarship have certainly shaped our research process and product.

For example, our questions were certainly framed not just by the research in the field of computers and composition but by our own experiences. When we brainstormed the kinds of strategies respondents might have used to successfully defend their digital work, we used strategies we had successfully implemented in our own reviews as multiple-choice options. Our questions were also led by our own curiosities. In particular, we wanted to know whether others resorted to print projects after struggling to complete a digital scholarship project and, if so, why they had done so.

SURVEY RESULTS

Our results are divided into three major sections followed by our conclusion:

- *Respondent Demographics* provides context for our findings, reflecting the various positionalities of our respondents.
- *Making Visible the Pressures of "Resort to Print"* examines respondents' answers to questions involving the differences and similarities of traditional and digital scholarly composing processes.
- *Making Labors Visible: Emotion and Effort* describes respondents' answers to questions about their and others' perceptions of digital scholarship's value and respondents' experiences with and feelings about being digital scholars.

Both *Making Visible the Pressures of "Resort to Print"* and *Making Labors Visible: Emotion and Effort* are subdivided. Each subdivision provides "Results" sections, where we report our findings, and "Interpretations" sections, where we interpret our findings, describing their significance as well as larger compositional implications.

Respondent Demographics

A vast majority (77.78%) of the respondents work at public universities and colleges. At the time of taking the survey, 19 respondents were tenured, 14 were tenure-track, 4 were non-tenure-track (e.g., lecturers), 3 were no longer faculty members, none were adjuncts, and 5 selected "other" when asked their faculty status. Most of these faculty work in English departments, while some work in interdisciplinary departments or rhetoric & writing departments. The respondents' reported genders were as follows:

- Man: 37.78%
- Woman: 44.44%
- Non-binary/third gender: 6.67%
- Prefer not to say: 6.67%
- Prefer to self-describe: 4.44% (1 - gender fluid, 1 - cis male)

In terms of reported race/ethnicity, of the 46 respondents who answered this questions they selected as follows:

- White: 39
- Asian or Asian American: 3
- Prefer not to say: 2
- Hispanic or Latino: 1
- One respondent self-identified as Eelam Tamil
- No respondents identified as Pacific Islander, African American or Black, American Indian or Alaska Native, Middle Eastern, or Multiracial.

To gain a sense of how much work the respondents had done in the realm of digital scholarship, we asked them to estimate how much of their published, peer-reviewed research would be considered digital scholarship, rather than traditional scholarship. Nearly 50% of the respondents selected 0–25%, meaning that less than 25% of their overall body of published scholarship would be considered digital scholarship. 31 percent of respondents selected 26–50%; 11 percent of respondents selected 51–75%, and 8 percent of respondents indicated that 76–100% of their scholarship is digital.

Making Visible the Pressures of "Resort to Print"

To better understand the cultural and structural pressures undergirding resort-to-print dispositions, we "complicated" or examined three aspects of respondents' answers: perceptions of digital scholarship, digital composing processes and differences from traditional scholarship, and emotional labor and the extra efforts put forth in composing digital scholarship.

Results: Complicating Perceptions of Scholarship: Digital and Traditional

To determine how respondents perceived others' view of digital scholarship, we asked respondents (Question 1) to rate their level of agreement with the following:

1. Digital scholarship is as highly valued as traditional scholarship at my university/college.
2. Digital scholarship is as highly valued as traditional scholarship in the field of rhetoric and composition (or related fields).
3. Learning new technologies is a practice that is valued by my university/college in faculty evaluation processes such as annual reviews or tenure and promotion.

As Figure 5.1 shows, most respondents "somewhat agreed" that digital scholarship is as highly valued as traditional scholarship at both their institutions (21) and in the field of rhetoric and composition (22), indicating some level of uncertainty and inequality in the ways the two are valued. We found that 39% of respondents somewhat or strongly disagreed that learning new technologies is valued by their university or college in faculty review processes, and 20% were neutral.

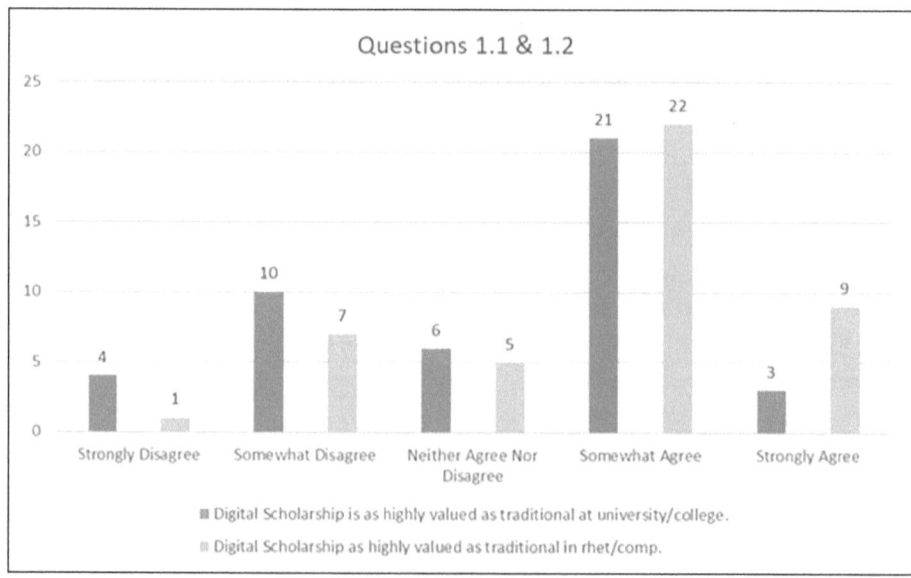

Figure 5.1. Value of digital scholarship in faculty review process

When we further sorted this data by respondents' self-identification as either digital scholars, traditional scholars, both, or neither, it was clear that those respondents who considered themselves digital scholars or "both" digital and traditional scholars felt more strongly that learning new technologies is not valued by their institutions.

Similarly, in Question 10, we asked respondents, "To the best of your knowledge, how has your digital scholarship been treated, valued, or understood by others during faculty review processes, such as annual reviews or tenure and promotion cases?" 15 respondents said the two types of scholarship were treated the same; 11 said digital scholarship was treated as inferior to traditional; 17 marked unsure; and 2 noted that their digital scholarship was treated as superior to traditional.

Interpretations: Complicating Perceptions of Digital Scholarship: Digital and Traditional

> Every time I complete a digital project, I swear I'm never going to do one again :).
>
> – Survey Respondent

Though the above respondent's oath is a humorous take on the time and effort involved in digital projects, there is an important kernel of truth in the respondent's declaration, what we refer to as "a resort-to-print mentality"—a publishing disposition in which outside forces drive authors towards more traditional forms of scholarship. We are fearful the resort-to-print disposition is or may become a tendency in rhetoric and composition, creating a kind of digital scholarly wasteland where "pushing the envelope," so to speak, is hegemonically discouraged. Resort to print or the choice to pursue traditional scholarship has, in other words, become a disposition we hope our current study makes visible.

The driving force behind our resort-to-print disposition is connected to the stigma surrounding digital scholarship; the effort and time it takes to compose digital scholarship (i.e., the learning curves for creating custom digital scholarship like Muhlhauser and Self's "Swipe Right on Find/Replace" and Sheffield's "Thinking Beyond Tools" are monumental in comparison to traditional scholarship); and a sense that there is an underappreciation of the knowledge, experience with programs, and non-alphabetic literacies digital scholars possess.

Overall, the results are encouraging. It's heartening to see digital scholarship being "somewhat" as highly valued as traditional scholarship in both the rhetoric and composition field and with the wider faculty. Yet, why only "somewhat"? Or why are there only two examples of digital scholarship being treated as superior to traditional, when it's clear that many of our respondents find digital scholarship to take more time and skills to produce? In other words, there is nothing "somewhat" in digital scholarship's value: it remains stigmatized as inferior to traditional scholarship even though digital scholars acknowledge the ways digital scholarship should be as highly valued or even superior. Lastly, and somewhat ironically, it is noteworthy that learning new technologies is only moderately valued in review processes, since it is that learning that makes digital scholarship possible. It isn't that we expect the final product to be considered better because it took more time. Currently, and in a general sense, audience culture doesn't value time as part of the quality of a product, though certainly the time something takes to read is being featured more prominently in linguistic-mode-oriented texts (i.e., articles with read time included). Instead, the quality of the product—audience members' experiences with it—is valued: that is, it's "good" or "bad" or "alright."

However, with regard to the more specific audiences, specifically those evaluating faculty research (e.g., stakeholders like provosts, chairs, and other tenure-track evaluators), we do feel that it is appropriate and fair that time be an important consideration, one that acknowledges engagement and output. The time it takes authors to create digital text means there likely will be fewer publications per year. While our focus is on the competencies and skills digital scholars acquire and use to produce digital scholarship, we acknowledge that other activities take time—such as learning a new research methodology, doing archival research, etc. This, too, should be acknowledged in the context of evaluations of faculty productivity—it is just not the focus of our current study.

Results: Complicating Composing Processes: Digital Scholarship and Differences from Traditional Scholarship

We asked a range of questions about respondents' composing processes so that we could glean what works, and what doesn't, for writers of digital scholarship. Respondents were asked to rate their level of agreement for the following statements on a scale from strongly agree to strongly disagree

1. Collaboration is vital to composing quality digital scholarship.
2. When composing digital scholarship, I typically write out my research as a traditional manuscript and then convert that research into a digital format.
3. When composing digital scholarship, I usually have an idea of the digital format I want to present my research in from the very beginning of my project.

4. When composing digital scholarship, I compose directly in the technology (such as in the HTML code or Content Management System).
5. Generally, composing digital scholarship takes me more time than traditional scholarship.
6. I often have to learn new technologies before I compose digital scholarship.

In Figure 5.2, we share the responses to each of the above items. The time commitment inherent in digital scholarship work was apparent. A majority of respondents agreed (32 strongly agreed and 7 somewhat agreed, or 70% of all respondents) that composing digital scholarship takes them more time than traditional scholarship (and none strongly disagreed). Nearly all respondents (42) also noted that they often have to learn new technologies before they begin composing digital scholarship. In fact, one respondent made a connection between time commitment, literacies, audience, and stigma: "Scholarship that requires more literacies and more time and that reflects the types of texts people now encounter is often perceived as inferior to traditional print scholarship."

Respondents were mixed in terms of what processes work best for them. For example, 19 respondents somewhat or strongly disagreed that their process begins with writing a print-based manuscript and then converting it into a digital format, whereas approximately 16 indicated that this mirrors their process. What was most common (41 respondents strongly or somewhat agreed) in the question about composing processes was that scholars already had an idea in their minds of the digital format they wanted to use to present their research from the very beginning of the project; the technology choice was not an afterthought.

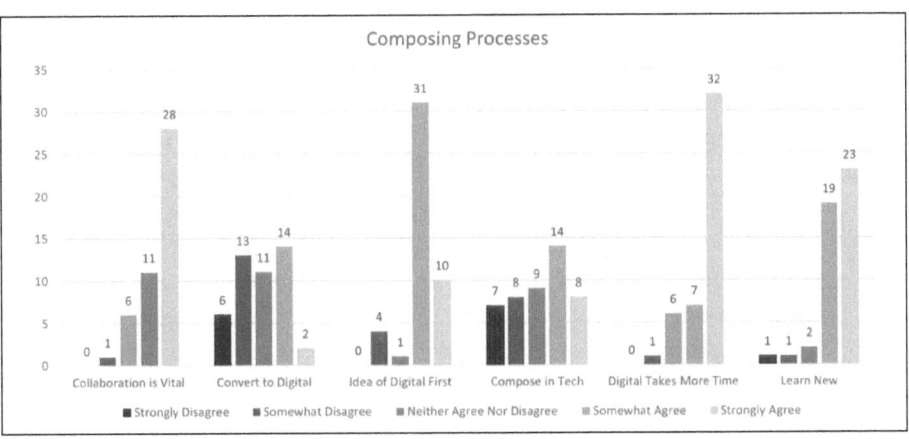

Figure 5.2. Beliefs about digital composing (n=46)

The respondents were mixed when asked if they tend to compose directly within the technology (such as a content management system) as they are writing. Fifteen percent strongly or somewhat disagreed, 22 percent somewhat or strongly agreed, and 9 percent selected neither agree nor disagree. In addition to the closed-ended question regarding composing processes, we asked our respondents to think about one of their most successful digital projects and "Describe your process for composing that work and why you think the process was successful." Responses were understandably varied. After all, composing digital rhetoric comes in all sorts of forms (e.g., podcasts, websites, videos, and/or mixes of forms). However, there were two common touchpoints in composing processes: sketching and iteration. Though sketching may have been keyed into our respondents, since it was an example we provided in the survey question to help our respondents understand what we meant by process, sketching/outlining/mockups (mentioned by 7/14 respondents for this question) was an important aspect of planning projects. The iterative and/or reciprocal aspects of the process (i.e., getting feedback from collaborators, editors, peers, then adjusting the project and getting more feedback) was also important (mentioned by 7/14 in response to this question).

To better understand respondents' technical capabilities and design knowledge, we asked respondents to rate their level of competence related to items such as web design languages, video-editing tools, app creation, accessibility, and usability. Our goal with this question was to demonstrate the many varied composing skills and abilities digital scholars have and/or need, which is ultimately connected to the labor inherent in this work and reveals some of the technical processes involved in digital scholarship. Most respondents indicated at least an average level of competence in WYSIWYG web building tools, content management systems, visual design, and user experience principles. Some of the areas in which respondents indicated the least technical competence included programming languages, video game-editing tools, app creation, data visualization, and image-editing tools.

In another question, we asked respondents if they had begun composing digital scholarship and later changed their mind, converting it into traditional scholarship, or vice versa. Fourteen respondents had indicated starting to compose digital scholarship and then resorting to traditional scholarship, and 13 respondents indicated they had started with traditional scholarship and later turned it into digital scholarship. Five respondents indicated they had done both transformations. In a follow-up question, we asked respondents to explain their decision-making processes when making such moves. When writing these questions, we were aiming to get at whether or not scholars had experienced the resort-to-print mentality, but the responses also revealed information about respondents' composing processes. Respondents turning from digital to traditional scholarship repeatedly mentioned time limits or lack of time to learn technology (6 of 14). One respondent who turned from traditional to digital scholarship even mentioned having time to learn technology, which helped facilitate the change. Respondents transforming from digital scholarship to traditional scholarship also mentioned explicitly not having publication outlets (4 of 14). Respondents making the move from traditional to digital scholarship mentioned how digital scholarship seemed to fit the project better in one way or another (6 of 13)—e.g., "[Showing] possibilities with evidence" and "the message is probably best communicated in a visual (or audiovisual), non-alphanumeric format." One respondent deftly summarizes the difficulty and the complicated decision-making process in deciding between mediums:

> A project's move to traditional or digital has happened when the scope/focus of the project shifted and either a traditional or a digital approach no longer seemed like the right fit. Time is also a major factor, governing how much energy one can put into a particular project at any given moment.

Interpretations: Complicating Composing Processes—Digital Scholarship and Differences from Traditional Scholarship

> With a traditional composing process, I can basically get the draft done on my own or with my co-researchers. With a digital composing process, I needed to learn new technologies and invite additional collaborators to help me create the vision I had in my mind.
>
> – Survey Respondent

In short, we find that digital scholars consider the "right" fit in how projects develop and where their project may go; however, time *and* technical knowledge *and* energy are important factors guiding what a project becomes: traditional or digital. Relatedly, we found that 41 respondents had similar processes, in which they decided on the digital format of their scholarship early in their research processes. When this response is read in conjunction with other questions, it seems that our respondents have thought critically about the technology they want to use early in the process—that it is vital to their scholarship, to their arguments and research. We wish we could have dug deeper, because we now wonder why it was so vital for respondents to present their scholarship non-traditionally with more modal decisions (i.e., decisions beyond the content features of the linguistic mode). Additionally, we are interested in learning more about how respondents negotiated technological dead ends where something didn't work. Given the large number of respondents who agreed with this question, we think this points to opportunities for future research and exploration about these decisions.

The strong agreement on this particular point also led us to thinking about practical and more systemic advice. Practically, scholars creating webtexts should be flexible with technology: if one doesn't work, for instance, it does not necessarily mean switch to print. Instead, be ready to pivot with technologies as projects develops; there is more than one way to "CSSkin a caHTML." More systemically, we recommend that scholars and/or faculty teaching in rhetoric and composition graduate programs develop a (pardon the portmanteau) *technodology*—a technology methodology (maybe a "techno-methodology") for making design decisions for digitally born scholarship. A technodology for learning and considering how technologies can be used to create such scholarship. Developing technodology would assist scholars in making the "right" choice, in being able to pivot, and help a new generation of scholars appreciate the digitally born scholarship.

Furthermore, our study results showed that although composing processes are varied, much like they are for traditional scholarship, digital scholars have more options to consider along with more processes to perform. It makes sense that sketching, iteration, learning new technology, and collaborating with others who may be more *tech-savvy* are important aspects of composing digital scholarship. The process of building webtexts is multidimensional and relies on multiple literacies: planning the interface (sketching), creating the multimodal content (getting feedback on the elements, testing usability, accessibility, and readability), and figuring out how to make the interface function. Resort-to-print dispositions, in other words, may not exist when projects begin and/or as they start to take shape, but such dispositions seem to appear when larger structural and cultural elements become part of the composing process, a process that is *not* compositionally equitable.

Such dispositions have a history and can even be connected to those promoting digital scholarship. Concerns about some digital scholars' lack of technical ability, for example, was a flashpoint at Computers and Writing 2012, where a round table of enthusiastic digital scholars repeated a *learn-to-code* mantra. While encouraging scholars to take chances and be fearless in learning to program, there was simultaneously a shaming and stigmatizing effect on digital scholars whose processes were shaped by WYSIWYG technologies.

Though well-meaning, the mantra forgets digital scholarly processes and time in relation to technology's dynamic nature (i.e., the ways technologies change and how there is more than the most recent scholarship to keep up with, like with traditional linear scholarship). The mantra also forgets time and the positionality of digital scholars (i.e., in terms of work-life balance, institutional labor, and desire to learn such things). In other words, *learn to code* does not need to be the privileged way to compose digital scholarship. Such privilege plays into the resort-to-print disposition, limiting who can do digital scholarship.

At the same time, it is impressive that, as our results show, scholars have solid competence in a range of technology and visual design principles that may not have been a part of their disciplinary training. This illustrates some of the knowledge and labor involved in digital composing, labor which is not always recognized by those who view the end product, an equitable understanding of process differences.

Making Labors Visible: Emotions and Effort

To better understand the differential emotional labors and efforts between digital and traditional composing processes, we complicated how respondents felt about their workload, how they felt about their digital and traditional scholarships—if there were differences, and to describe how they distribute their workloads for digital and traditional scholarship. We also wanted to know if there were differential experiences in labor between both gender and race.

Results: Complicating Emotional Labor

In the survey, we asked a variety of questions to gain a better understanding of the emotional labor that may, or may not, be inherent in composing digital scholarship. We began by asking questions about respondents' feelings about their employment—feelings of stress, burnout, hope, etc.—in general. In a later question, we asked if any of these feelings were connected to their digital scholarship work. We felt that by separating the two questions, we could get a more accurate and less biased depiction of how digital scholarship may or may not affect their emotions about their work.

In Question 13, respondents were presented with the statements below and asked to select how accurately the statements reflected their feelings on a 5-point Likert scale:

- I feel that I have control over my workload.
- I feel that I have sufficient time to learn.
- I am satisfied with my job.
- I feel stressed.
- I feel burned out.
- I feel supported by my colleagues.
- I feel supported by my college/university.[3]

---

3   Some of the categories we measured, such as stress, control over workload, and job satisfaction, were inspired by a study on burnout in academic health centers (Locke et al., 2020).

A majority of the respondents selected that "I feel stressed" (38 out of 44) and "I feel burned out" (31 out of 44) moderately, mostly, or clearly describes their feelings. They also felt they had little control over their workload (29 out of 44). At the same time, they also indicated feeling very proud of their work; in fact, 41 out of the 44 respondents to this question said that the statement "I feel proud of my work" moderately (4), mostly (20), or clearly (17) describes their feelings. Respondents reported feeling moderately or mostly supported by their universities and colleagues (30 out of 44), and most (36) reponded that the statement "I feel that others value my work" mostly or clearly describes their feelings. Very few respondents felt cynical about their work, with only 20 indicating that this statement moderately to clearly describes their feelings.

Of course, the respondents' feelings about their work (Question 13) did not necessarily have a direct correlation with their digital scholarship. As such, for Question 14, we asked the respondents to indicate if any of their choices from Question 13 were related to their work in digital scholarship. The most commonly selected statements were the following:

- I feel proud of my work. (23)
- I feel that others value my work. (17)
- I feel hopeful about my work. (17)
- I feel like I work too much. (13)
- I feel that I have sufficient time to learn. (11)
- I feel stressed. (9)
- I feel burned out. (8)

To determine if these connections were positive or negative, we turned to the open-ended question, in which we asked respondents to explain their responses by describing how their work in digital scholarship had impacted their feelings in any of these areas. We also compared their responses in Question 13 and Question 14 to see the correlations between responses. Over half of the respondents who "clearly" or "mostly" felt proud of their work indicated that this was directly related to their work in digital scholarship. At the same time, those who felt that they work too much connected that statement to their work in digital scholarship. And while 11 indicated that the statement "I feel that I have sufficient time to learn" was connected to their digital composing, those responses were generally not positive; in other words, those respondents said that "I feel that I have sufficient time to learn" either "slightly" or "does not describe" their feelings. The respondents who felt stressed or burned out frequently noted that those feelings were connected to their work in digital scholarship. As one stated, "I . . . believe that the time-cost of creating these projects contributes to stress."

On an overall positive note, most respondents felt their digital scholarship work was supported by colleagues.

Most respondents did not indicate that the statement "I feel like I have control over my workload" was related to their digital composing. Only 2 of 29 felt digital composing played a factor in their feelings about their workload.

To better understand the connections between certain emotions and digital scholarship, we asked to what degree respondents' feelings corresponded with the following statements:

- I enjoy composing digital scholarship.
- I enjoy composing traditional scholarship.
- I prefer composing digital scholarship over traditional.
- I feel proud when I have successfully published digital scholarship.
- I feel proud when I have successfully published traditional scholarship.
- I feel pressure to help others in my department with technology issues because I am known as a digital scholar.
- When composing digital scholarship, I worry that my time and effort will be wasted if the publication does not get accepted.
- When composing traditional scholarship, I worry that my time and effort will be wasted if the publication does not get accepted.

Most respondents indicated they feel enjoyment composing digital scholarship (37 of 42 selected "moderate," "mostly," or "clearly describes my feelings") as well as when composing traditional scholarship (39 of 42). Ratings were similar in terms of respondents noting that they feel proud when they have successfully published digital scholarship (36) and traditional linear scholarship (36). In terms of the approach by which they prefer to compose (digital or traditional), responses were mixed, with about half of the respondents preferring digital and half preferring traditional.

As seen in Figure 5.3, when considering the statement, "When composing *digital* scholarship, I worry that my time and effort will be wasted if the publication does not get accepted," 34 out of 44 respondents said the statement moderately describes their feelings (9), mostly describes their feelings (10), or clearly describes their feelings (15). When the same question was asked about *traditional* scholarship, fewer respondents (28 out of 43) said they felt this worry. Additionally, when asked about how they felt about their work, scholars who identified themselves as traditional scholars felt the statement, "I feel hopeful about my work," described their feelings more so than those who considered themselves "both" (i.e., digital and traditional scholars) or primarily digital scholars.

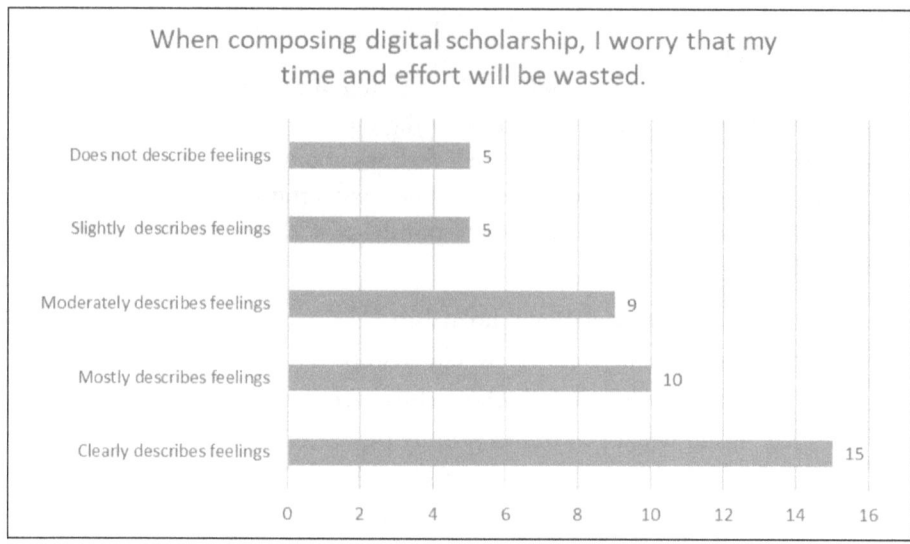

Figure 5.3. Perceptions of "Wasted Time" When Composing Digital Scholarship

Interpretations: Complicating Emotional Labor

> When I compose digitally, I'm reminded of just how much time it takes to learn new tools, and often that will ultimately lead me to create less ambitious projects just because this is kind of an optional or voluntary thing that I'm doing. I don't think my department or university penalizes me for this work, but they also don't reward it. So I have to have internal motivation (belief that it's the best way to pose the argument or make the argument accessible to audiences I care about) in order to do it.
>
> – Survey Respondent

The above respondent's comments summarize the themes we saw throughout the study. And read in conjunction with other responses, it was clear to us that the emotional investment, time investment, and limited outlets for digital publishing factored into the differences in worries and, thus, compositional inequuity between digital and traditional scholarship. There is a nod to the resort-to-print mentality here as well, as the respondent comments on creating less ambitious projects because of the extra work. The respondent also notes that the extra work, while not disregarded, is not rewarded. Still, the respondent reflects the overall importance or value of digital scholarship—that sometimes it is the best way to make the argument one wants to make or that it is the best way to make the argument accessible to the audience one cares about. This *internal* motivation seems to be a driving force for many of our respondents that likely leads to some of the feelings of pride and accomplishment surrounding the final product.

The time and effort of producing digital scholarship was clearly a limiting factor for our respondents reflecting compositional inequity, but despite that fact, it was exciting to see that while most consider themselves both digital and traditional scholars, most were proudest or felt the best about the digital scholarship they composed. Composing digital scholarship, at least for our respondents, was an ambivalent process, simultaneously leaving them feeling stressed and burned out during the process but proud of the product.

Of course, many factors can feed into how one feels about their work and, given that the survey was distributed during the COVID-19 pandemic, we imagine that factors like shifts to remote instruction, illness, deaths in the family, and many other personal concerns influenced respondents' choices.

While we are unsure why respondents did not often connect the feeling of having control over one's workload to their work in digital composing, it is possible, given responses to other questions, that they deem practices such as learning new technologies to be outside of their expected workload.

Results: Complicating Effort

In breaking down the time commitments by task, we asked respondents to characterize the level of time and effort they tend to spend on the following tasks for both digital scholarship and traditional scholarship: (1) conducting research, (2) writing alphabetic text, (3) formatting to submission guidelines set by the publisher, (4) using technology to create and/or edit multimedia elements, (5) designing/organizing the aesthetics of the work, (6) proofreading alphabetic text, (7) editing for accessibility, (8) learning new methodologies, and (9) learning new technologies. To compare time and effort between digital and traditional, respondents were given the option to select "none," "little," "somewhat," "much," "traditional," and a "great deal."

We used the "a great deal" scale response as our way to compare digital and traditional scholarship. Across a range of questions, respondents generally indicated that digital scholarship requires more labor than traditional. For example, for traditional scholarship, only the categories of "conducting research" and "writing alphabetic text" received a higher number of responses to the "a great deal" metric. In all other categories, digital scholarship took more time and effort. The most striking differences were in relationship to accessibility and design. Thirty-six respondents (or 81%) indicated that designing and organizing the aesthetics of digital scholarship takes a great deal of time and effort, whereas only 6 respondents (or 14%) selected "a great deal" for traditional scholarship.

Similarly, using technology to create or edit multimedia elements and editing for accessibility took a great deal of time and effort for 34 and 26 respondents, respectively, when composing digital scholarship. On the other hand, only 3 respondents selected "a great deal" for multimedia and only four selected "a great deal" for accessibility considerations with regard to traditional scholarship.

In addition to the time and effort involved in composing digital scholarship, there may be other factors that influence scholars' abilities to produce digital scholarship. For our study, the most prevalent limiting factors were, in order:

- lack of time (40),
- constraints in their own technological capabilities (21),
- a lack of funds to purchase assets (13),
- perceptions at their institutions that digital scholarship is not as important as traditional (13),
- lack of mentorship from someone who has published digital scholarship (12), and
- a need for funds to learn (12).

On the other hand, respondents generally did not indicate a lack of personal interest in composing digital scholarship, nor had many encountered bad experiences submitting to digital journals in the past. Only 5 respondents noted lack of support from their departments as a limiting factor.

Respondents were also invited to select any resources or opportunities they had used in order to successfully compose digital scholarship. Most commonly selected were free online tutorials (37), collaboration with a colleague and/or co-author on design (31), collaboration with a colleague and/or co-author on content or research (31), mentorship from colleagues who could help with technology or design skills (31), mentorship from colleagues who were willing to offer feedback on drafts/works in progress (29), feedback from a journal's or publisher's reviewers (26), and assistance received from an academic journal's staff (19). It was interesting to note that on-campus faculty development workshops were not selected often (7), nor were graduate school courses (17). This may point to areas for future institution-level improvement. In addition to asking respondents about resources and collaborations, we also asked respondents, "What successful strategies and/or resources have you used to help explain/support the importance of your digital scholarship to others during faculty review processes?" While our initial goal in asking this question was to offer faculty writers specific strategies for ensuring their work is valued, the results also showed us this work complicates the meaning of effort and labor in relationship to digital composing. The most common response, mentioned by 27 respondents, was that respondents used strategies to explain how digital scholarship allows audiences to engage with their research in multiple ways. Twenty-six respondents noted the importance of explaining how digital scholarship is more accessible to broader audiences than traditional scholarship. Another important strategy was taking the time to explain the time and effort that went into the composing process. Sixteen respondents also indicated using position statements from national organizations in the rhetoric and composition field and 16 noted that they found ways to demonstrate the similarity of their digital scholarship to traditional scholarship. Only 7 had used screenshots to illustrate their composing processes.

Interpretations: Complicating Effort

While most of the strategies seemed to prove valuable for the respondents and therefore may serve as helpful to faculty writers in this area, the responses also reveal that there is additional labor in making one's digital scholarship be considered "up to par" with traditional scholarship. Though one respondent noted the opposite—"I haven't had to justify my use of digital scholarship. I have just included the scholarship with my other publications"—most others felt the need to spend time justifying why they were publishing in that format and explaining the work that went into the composing process. Considering how students and faculty negotiate a saturated multimodal media environment in their daily lives, it's important to note the irony in the perceived stigma of digital scholarship. Digital scholars' extra justification points to an academic value system of what English and/or rhetoric and composition is and does: composes scholarship in a very narrow, print-biased way. There remains a lack of equity in the labor of justifying composing traditional and digital scholarship, again, with digital scholarship shouldering a larger burden.

Granted, some of this information may seem obvious at first glance. It's less likely that scholars will spend time on multimedia elements for a print journal even as print is no longer the dominant way journals publish work. However, taken as a whole, the data demonstrates the drastic amount of work scholars put into aspects of their digital composing that may largely go unnoticed, unacknowledged, or unappreciated, such as learning new technologies (which, for example, took a great deal of time for only 4 respondents composing traditional scholarship but which took a great deal of time for 24 respondents when composing digitally).

Results: Complicating Effort—Gender and Race

More men reported that they feel they have the time to learn at their institutions (Question 13). Specifically, 10 out of 17 men indicated that the statement "I feel that I have sufficient time to learn" moderately, mostly, or clearly describes their feelings. Responding to the same statement, women, on the other hand, reported feeling the statement "does not at all" or "only slightly" describes their feelings (13 of 20). In addition, more women (20, or all the women in our study) reported that lack of time has limited their production of digital scholarship as compared to 4 men out of 17.

As indicated in our "Respondent Demographics" section, there were too few (5) People of Color (POC), to draw any conclusions. We speculate on why this is the case below.

Interpretations: Complicating Effort—Gender and Race

In terms of equity related to factors such as gender and race, our study is hopeful in showing how women are composing digital scholarship in numbers similar to men (at least with regards to respondents in our study). And if we superficially evaluated names of the 191 possible participants (which itself is problematic) we contacted, this bears out, too. In fact, this suggests more women are participating in digital projects than men in the rhetoric and composition field. We wish we had more information, however, about the ratio of men and women in the rhetoric and composition field. Adding such context would help us better understand on a more general level the gender equity in composing digital scholarship: for instance, there might be a higher percentage of men in the field participating in digital scholarship than women.

Time, however, pointed towards some unsurprising aspects of gender inequity with regards to digital scholarship and resort to print dispositions. It is difficult to speculate on reasons why this is occurring since we did not specifically lead respondents in this direction with follow-up questions. Still, it is not a reach to apply hegemonic masculinity as an answer to why this is occurring—more specifically, the structures and cultures differentiating how men and women work. It is somewhat banal to bring up such inequity as it is a common practice. Mason, Wolfinger, and Goulden's (2013) comprehensive *Do Babies Matter: Gender and Family in the Ivory Tower* shows clearly how the structures of heterosexual family and invisible labors therein disadvantage women in their academic careers.

Guarino and Borden (2017) show how there is a differential between men and women in higher education, with women performing more service than men. El-Alayli, Hansen-Brown & Ceynar (2018) observed how women are "Dancing Backward in High Heels: Female Professors Experience More Work Demands and Special Favor Requests, Particularly from Academically Entitled Students."

Time is a valuable resource that, for women, is often scarce for research. COVID-19 did not helping this situation. Holding classes online did not mean there was necessarily more time for research, especially for women in academics. For instance, in their survey on how time is affected differently by women and men academics, Deryugina, Shurchkov, and Stearns (2021) found that there was a "disproportionate decline in research time among female academics relative to research time among male academics" (p. 166), yet other activities like teaching and research were not affected. Furthermore, "female academics with children—especially those with young children—were disadvantaged to a significantly greater extent" (Deryuginaet al., 2021, p. 164). Viglione's (2020) *Nature* article summarizes the most recent studies on the effect of COVID-19 on academic production: "across disciplines, women's publishing rate has fallen relative to men's amid the pandemic." This can be explained by invisible labors like childcare, caring for relatives, converting classes to online (with women faculty more often having greater teaching responsibilities). Furthermore, "because many institutions are shut owing to the pandemic, non-research university commitments—such as participation in hiring and curriculum committees—are probably taking up less time. These are often dominated by senior faculty members—more of whom are men. As a result, men could find themselves with more time to write papers while women experience the opposite." (pp. 367–368) It seems that the cards are stacked against women producing digital scholarship. We wonder how much more could have been generated. How many projects were scuttled?

With regards to POC responding to our survey, there were not enough non-white participants for us to draw conclusions about their experiences, but we hope future studies are able to better address why POC are not a larger part of digital scholarship.

Of course the easy answer as to why we had so few POC participate in our survey is to blame the pipeline (i.e., there just aren't enough rhetoric and composition faculty of color to find for our survey). Consider the 2018 National Center for Education Statistics observation about faculty of color (which includes adjuncts and interim professors) in "degree-granting postsecondary institutions" that only 25 percent were faculty of color (this number includes faculty who identify as two or more races). The less easy and more equitable answer has to do with the structures and cultures inhibiting people of color from staying in academics and being successful in technology and in the academy and from even wanting to participate in digital scholarship and/or academics.

Matthew (2016), in her work exploring the academic experiences of tenure-track faculty of color, summarizes the structural-cultural issues people of color in academics negotiate this way:

> Faculty of color always have to do at least two things at the
> same time as they go about their work: figure out how to cope

> with (confront, deflect, or absorb) the daily microaggressions of the academy while trying to navigate structural obstacles that everyone faces in environments that are either maddeningly indifferent or hostile." (pp. xv-xvi)

Faculty of color often face a more difficult tenure path, with more emotional labor, compared to white faculty. White-Lewis's (2020) study on faculty hiring practices shows another dimension of difficulty for POC to negotiate: a candidate's *fit*. In theory, a candidate's *fit* is supposed to be somewhat objective. Yet White-Lewis describes problems with the concept:

> (1) Its application to understanding and justifying hiring decisions is severely overstated, and (2) it obscures the abundance of idiosyncratic preferences throughout the entire hiring process, which perpetuate racial aversion, neutrality, and convenience. (p. 850)

Our results—though we do not have data on the racial breakdown of rhetoric and composition scholars with academic appointments—can be read as a call to action to discover why digital scholars of color are so low in number and then facilitate more ways to be inclusive. Is there a structural and/or cultural paradigm of *fit* in digital scholarship limiting who practices digital scholarship?

TECHNO-AFTERGLOW IS COMPLICATED

While we aren't ready to say the sun is setting on initial enthusiasm for digital scholarship, we do know that the afterglow for composing such scholarship is somewhat fleeting, especially in the current academic environment. The structures and cultures surrounding academia are *still* designed for traditional linear scholarship—for scholarship that doesn't have all the "extras." A resort-to-print mentality may not be occurring explicitly on an individual level where scholars are purposefully avoiding digital scholarship; however, there is a *printism* or *traditionalism*—a bias implicitly limiting digital composing processes and, thus, making it more difficult to make digital scholarship.

As we and our respondents have noted, there is much invisible labor that goes into composing born-digital scholarship, and being the *digital* scholar in an English, writing, or rhetoric and composition department also comes with its own pressures and labors. Digital scholars' research often takes much more time to complete than the average print text because these researchers are not only conducting research and writing the results but then coding websites or designing innovative, interactive ways for audiences to engage with the text.

They take on the extra burden of arguing for the scholarly value of their work. They often spend additional money and time learning new technologies or coding languages, and of course, there is an emotional labor component that many digital scholars take on, mentoring other digital scholars to help them navigate the complexities of creating, defending, and legitimizing one's work. Digital scholars even have to worry more about finding places to publish. At the heart of it, the costs of such invisible labor are about equity/inequity in composition processes and products between digital and traditional scholarship.

The logic behind the superiority of traditional scholarship is somewhat vexing. Though we understand this would not exactly be equitable, we wonder why digital scholarship is not more highly valued than traditional scholarship. With all the *extras* of time, techno-literacies, techno-training, and accessibility knowledge in composing digital scholarship, why aren't they compared differently? Why isn't the default different so that one has to argue for making traditional scholarship instead of the other way around? Digital scholarship, in other words, can easily be viewed as superior to traditional scholarship but isn't treated as such.

It's difficult to imagine how to shift the connotations and stigma still surrounding digital scholarship. Perhaps, time will tell as the perception seems to be heading in a more equitable direction. There are, for example, institutional experiences that are hopeful, as one respondent describes:

> Professional development opportunities in digital literacy and new tools support all of the feelings I've identifies [sic]. My institution also promotes collaboration and many colleagues are excellent collaborators. Digital scholarship is sufficiently complex to benefit from collaboration—which is to say that working in digital scholarship is hard, though not impossible, to do alone, so the need for many kinds of expertise lends authenticity and value to the collaborative process.

Still, the time when we will no longer view traditional linear scholarship as the default is probably a long way off. However, as this respondent and others observed, there are some avenues for improving digital scholarly production and making sure one has the tools to succeed as a digital scholar.

STRUCTURAL IMPROVEMENTS

- *Course releases.* Higher education institutions should provide course releases specifically for learning new technologies, programming languages, and/or design principles to enable scholars to produce well-rounded, accessible digital scholarship.

- *Defining scholarship.* Departments and committees should work on creating definitions of scholarship that are both inclusive and acknowledge the workload, time, and inequity in digital scholarly production processes.
- *Digital opportunities.* More outlets for digital scholarship should emerge, thus reducing some of the challenges related to visibility and credibility.
- *Graduate education.* Graduate programs in rhetoric and composition focusing on digital technology should make sure to embed learning technologies in courses and assist digital scholars in understanding both the time and effort that makes up digital scholarship and the stigma associated with it.
- *Journal assistance.* Born-digital journals should or should continue to offer assistance in digital scholarly design in the editing process. In fact, it might be helpful to have digital mavens or digital editors that are consultants for helping to answer technical questions and learn how to imagine and design webtexts.
- *Collaboration database.* Our leading professional organizations should develop a collaboration database for rhetoric and composition. This would be a useful tool for matching technical skills and research interests. It would serve as a kind of academic matchmaker for rhetoric and composition scholars where they create academic profiles showcasing skills, expertise, and projects they are thinking about and/or working on that could use some digital collaboration.
- *Acknowledgment of gender differentiation.* Departments and committees should work to refine research guidelines and expectations in ways that acknowledge the differences in workload, time, and effort among faculty and how these differences are stratified by gender.

It's unlikely that some of our ideas here will come to fruition in the near future, and these ideas rely upon institutional change in academia, which is overwhelmingly slow. So, in the meantime, we settle by offering practical strategies for digital scholars to help defend their work, recognizing that we may be contributing to inequities by leaning into suggestions that digital scholars must do more to defend their work. Yet we hope these strategies, many used by our respondents, will prove helpful and perhaps encourage some faculty writers to not give in to the resort-to-print temptations.

- *Using disciplinary position statements.* The CCCC position statement on technology, for example, articulates many of the inequities inherent in digital scholarly production, which we have explored, and provides guidelines/advice for how digital scholarship should be understood and valued. The statement also provides helpful case studies examining how different stakeholders view digital scholarship. Granted, the case studies were created in 2001 and appear to have not been updated, so they may only serve as a very general guide for how faculty writers might explain and defend their work. But they provide models on which arguments can be based.

- *Documenting process.* Digital scholars may find it beneficial to fully explain their composing processes, document the hours they spend learning technologies, take screenshots of webtexts in progress, etc. In other words, scholars need to make the labor visible for those who cannot currently see it.
- *Documenting interactions.* In addition to the impacts of citation, the metrics of which can be difficult to locate with webtexts, digital scholars may find it beneficial to track the impact of their work in the form of digital metrics related to their webtext (e.g., visits, time spent on a particular text, links to the webtext). Additionally, scholars may find using social media metrics helpful in arguing about impact and accessibility to larger publics (e.g., "likes" and "shares"). And in addition to numbers, scholars could contextualize who is sharing, providing explanations for how shares by those considered leaders in the field have more weight than other shares.
- *Making rhetorical choices.* The driving force behind many of our respondents' decisions to compose digital scholarship was their conclusion that it best fit the arguments they wanted to make. We suggest considering questions of audience, access, and context early in the composing process and letting those decisions drive whether or not you as a writer choose to compose digitally. Don't shy away from the digital because it isn't valued. Equally important, don't flock toward it just because it's shiny.
- *Embrace what you know, feel you can know, and collaborate.* We support the "readymade rhetoric" approach Muhlhauser and Kachur (2014) take in their webtext, and see their "Love the One You're with Pedagogy" as an inclusive and equitable practice, acknowledging the time and difficulty that goes into creating digital scholarship and the positionality of digital authors. Digital scholars, in other words, should remember to "love" or use the technology they know or feel they can know based on their current positionalities. Learning to code isn't the *only* or *ideal* way to design insightful and cutting edge works or think critically about technology. There is no shame in not knowing

coding or programming. And scholars should continue to be open to collaboration opportunities with scholars whose "readymade" knowledge is different/complementary to their own when imagining digital scholarship.

Composing digital scholarship is valuable and worthwhile. It is work that has made a difference and is often widely cited. However, we do want to be clear to scholars that digital scholarly composing processes are difficult, often take more time than traditional composing processes, and may not be viewed as highly as traditional scholarship. We hope that some of the data and the suggestions we have provided here can serve faculty writers in selecting what they write, how they write, and how they defend those choices.

REFERENCES

Almjeld, J. & England, J. (2015–2016). Training technofeminists: A field guide to the art of girls' tech camps. *Computers and Composition Online*. Professional Development, Fall 2015–2016. http://cconlinejournal.org/fall15/almjeld_england.

Anderson, S. & McPherson, T. (2011). Engaging digital scholarship: Thoughts on evaluating multimedia scholarship. *Profession*, 136–151. https://doi.org/10.1632/prof.2011.2011.1.136.

Ball, C. E. (2004). Show, not tell: The value of new media scholarship. *Computers and Composition, 21*(4), 403–425. https://doi.org/10.1016/s8755-4615(04)00038-600038-6).

Chamberlain, E., Gramer, R. & Hartline, M.F. (2015–2016). Mess not mastery: Encouraging digital dispositions in girls. *Computers and Composition Online*. Theory into Practice, 2015–2016. http://cconlinejournal.org/fall15/dma.

Conference on College Composition and Communication. (2015). *Promotion and tenure guidelines for work with technology*. https://cccc.ncte.org/cccc/resources/positions/promotionandtenure.

Council of Writing Program Administrators. (2019). *Evaluating the intellectual work of writing administration*. https://wpacouncil.org/aws/CWPA/pt/sd/news_article/242849/_PARENT/layout_details/false.

Day, M., Delagrange, S. H., Palmquist, M., Pemberton, M. A. & Walker, J. R. (2013). What we really value: Redefining scholarly engagement in tenure and promotion protocols. *College Composition and Communication, 65*(1), 185–208. https://www.jstor.org/stable/43490813.

Deryugina, T., Shurchkov, O. & Stearns, J. (2021). COVID-19 disruptions disproportionately affect female academics. *AEA Papers & Proceedings, 111*, 164–168. https://doi.org/10.1257/pandp.20211017.

El-Alayli, A., Hansen-Brown, A. A. & Ceynar, M. (2018). Dancing backwards in high heels: Female professors experience more work demands and special favor requests, particularly from academically entitled students. *Sex Roles: A Journal of Research, 79*(3–4), 136–150. https://doi.org/10.1007/s11199-017-0872-6.

Guarino, C. M. & Borden, V. M. H. (2017). Faculty service loads and gender: Are women taking care of the academic family? *Research in Higher Education, 58*(6), 672–694. https://doi.org/10.1007/s11162-017-9454-2.

Huberman, A. M. & Miles, M. B. (2002). *The qualitative researcher's companion*. Sage.

Jackson, R., McKinney, J. & Caswell, N. (2016). Writing center administration and/as emotional labor, *Composition Forum, 34*. https://compositionforum.com/issue/34/writing-center.php.

Journet, D., Ball, C. & Trauman, R. (Eds.). (2012). *The new work of composing*. Computers and Composition Digital Press. http://ccdigitalpress.org/nwc.

Kelly, M. (2013). Making Digital Scholarship Count. In D. J. Cohen & T. Scheinfeldt (Eds.), *Hacking the academy: New approaches to scholarship and teaching from digital humanities,* (pp. 50–54). University of Michigan Press. https://doi.org/10.2307/j.ctv65swj3.14.

Locke, A. B., Fortenberry, K. T. & Van Hala, S.. (2020). Use of a feedback survey as a part of a wellness champions program to improve academic faculty satisfaction and burnout: Implications for burnout in academic health centers. *Global advances in health and medicine, 9*, 2164956120973635. https://doi.org/10.1177/2164956120973635.

Maid, B. (2000). Yes, a technorhetorician can get tenure. *Computers and Composition, 17*(1), 9–18. https://www.sciencedirect.com/science/article/pii/S8755461599000262?via%3Dihub.

Mason, M. A., Wolfinger, N. H. & Goulden, M. (2013). *Do babies matter?: Gender and family in the ivory tower*. Rutgers University Press.

Matthew, P. A. (2016). *Written/unwritten: Diversity and the hidden truths of tenure*. University of North Carolina Press.

McIntyre, M. (2019). Snapshots of #WPALife: Invisible labor and writing program administration. *Academic Labor: Research and Artistry, 3*(8), 64–86. https://wac.colostate.edu/docs/alra/v3/mcintyre.pdf.

Micciche, L. R. (2002). More than a feeling: Disappointment and WPA work. *College English, 64*(4), 432–458. https://doi.org/10.2307/3250746.

Muhlhauser, P. & Kachur, R. (2014). Readymade rhetoric: Love the one you're with. *Computers and Composition Online*. Theory into Practice, Fall 2014. http://cconlinejournal.org/fall14/readymade.

Muhlhauser, P. & Salvati, T. (2021). Unrapunzeling communication: Rhetorical equity in rhet/comp journal practices. *Journal of Multimodal Rhetorics, 5*(1). http://journalofmultimodalrhetorics.com/5-1-issue-muhlhauser-and-salvati.

Muhlhauser, P. & Self, M. (2019). Swipe right on find/replace: Invention, equity, and technofeminist potentials of find/replace technologies. *Computers and Composition Online*. D. N. DeVoss, A. Haas & J. Rhodes (Eds.), March 2019, Special Issue: TechnoFeminism (Re)Generations and intersectional futures. http://cconlinejournal.org/techfem_si/06_Muhlhauser_Self.

National Center for Education Statistics. (2020). *Fast facts: Race/Ethnicity of college faculty*. Institute of Education Sciences. https://nces.ed.gov/fastfacts/display.asp?id=61.

Purdy, J. P. & Walker, J. R. (2010). Valuing digital scholarship: Exploring the changing realities of intellectual work. *Profession*, 177–195. https://colab.ws/articles/10.1632%2Fprof.2010.2010.1.177.

Sano-Franchini, J. (2016). It's like writing yourself into a codependent relationship with someone who doesn't even want you! Emotional labor, intimacy, and the academic job market in rhetoric and composition. *College Composition and Communication*, 68(1), 98–124.

Selber, S. A. (2004). *Multiliteracies for a digital age*. Southern Illinois University Press.

Selfe, C. L. (1999). *Technology and literacy in the twenty-first century: The importance of paying attention*. Southern Illinois University Press.

Selfe, C. L. & R. J. Selfe, J. (1994). The politics of the interface: Power and its exercise in electronic contact zones. *College Composition and Communication, 45*(4), 480–504. https://doi.org/10.2307/358761.

Sheffield, J. P. (2015). Digital scholarship and interactivity: A study of commenting features in networked books. *Computers and Composition, 37*, 166–181.

Sheffield, J. P. (2015–2016). Thinking beyond tools: Writing program administration and digital literacies. *Computers and Composition Online*, Theory into Practice, 2015–2016. http://cconlinejournal.org/sheffield.

Tham, J. C. K. & Grace, R. (2020). Reading born-digital scholarship: A study of webtext user experience. *Computers and Composition, 58.*,1–19. https://doi.org/10.1016/j.compcom.2020.102601.

Viglione, G. (2020). Are women publishing less during the pandemic? Here's what the data say. *Nature, 581*(7809), 365+. https://link.gale.com/apps/doc/A624990968/AONE?u=anon~4a281c10&sid=googleScholar&xid=d0b718bf.

White-Lewis, D. K. (2020). The Facade of fit in faculty search processes. *Journal of Higher Education, 91*(6), 833–857. https://doi.org/10.1080/00221546.2020.1775058.

PART 2. HOW TO SUPPORT FACULTY WRITERS

As a counterpart to *Part I's* focus on how faculty writers are currently writing, *Part II: How to Support Faculty Writers* examines rhetoric and composition-based support strategies from inside and outside the university that seek to support faculty in these areas. Chapter 6, "Writing Support for Faculty of Color," by Laura R. Micciche and Batsheva Guy calls for the need for differential forms of support for faculty who occupy nondominant subject positions using research from surveys and interviews of participants from interdisciplinary writing workshops (face-to-face and, during COVID-19, online) to assess writing and publishing goals and needs. Findings from this study at a four-year Research I predominantly white institution offer applicability to similar institutions where published research is a requirement for promotion and tenure. Extending this look at supporting faculty who often aren't served by traditional university support, Chapter 7: "What Professional Academic Writers Want from Writing Studies Coaching," by Beth Hewett looks at reasons why faculty writers seek external writing support after traditional supports fail. Hewett argues that academic writing coaching companies such as Defend & Publish, which is outside the university structure but founded and staffed by rhetoric and composition faculty, can fill the gaps in faculty writing support. Hewett uses data from Defend & Publish clients and coaches to determine what specific kinds of assistance writers request from coaching and what coaches provide writers in response. These findings offer insight into not only where doctoral students and current faculty might be supported beyond the academy but also how coaches interpret faculty writing needs when navigating client-versus-university interests and in recognition of the best ways to help faculty writers while working within limitations, such as a client's lack of budget to afford extensive coaching or knowledge about scholarly writing practice.

Research within writing studies shows that graduate students often lack both tactical and emotional writing support (Micciche & Carr, 2011) even as writing will become the currency they need to apply for academic jobs, publish, and write grants successfully. In Chapter 8, "Intentional Institutional Support for Future Faculty: A Focus on Grant and Professional Materials," Charmian Lam uses grounded theory and semi-structured interviews of doctoral students, doctoral candidates, and employed graduates to recognize that a sense of belonging and academic success are associated with cultural capital which students seek through departmental and, more often, external training in faculty skills and genre conventions in professional writing. Building on the idea of supporting graduate students as they develop professional identities as writers as well as Wells and Söderlund's focus on the professional development of the facilitator, Chapter 9, "Developing One's Writerly Identity: The Impact of Leading a Faculty Writing Group," by Kristin Messuri and Elizabeth Sharp similarly studies issues of belonging among female faculty members. Because faculty outside of rhetoric and composition rarely identify as writers first, Messuri and Sharp, using grounded theory and the constant comparative method, analyze research from focus groups of faculty who have served as writing group facilitators in a large multidisciplinary women's faculty writing program. Like Messuri and Sharp's chapter, Chapter 10, "Leading Faculty Writing Academies: A Case Study of Three Faculty and Writerly Dispositions," by J. Michael Rifenburg and Rebecca Johnston also focuses on the faculty facilitators of a faculty support program, this time through the lens of a large multi-campus institution. Facilitators discuss how their leadership shapes their writerly identities and how these experiences carry forward into the facilitators' own scholarship. Through semi-structured interviews, faculty facilitators revealed how their experiences resist marketization, competitiveness, and standardization in higher education. Closing Part II, and the collection as a whole, Chapter 11: "Faculty Writers as Collaborators: Writing in Relationships," by Kristina Quynn and Carol Wilusz, bridges faculty writing practice with writing support by drawing on case study data of faculty mentors and graduate student mentees at Colorado State University. Quynn and Wilusz illuminate where writing support programs might develop additional much-needed resources for faculty, directing attention to relational writing processes rather than the more common pedagogical approach.

REFERENCES

Micciche, L. R. & Carr, A. D. (2011). Toward graduate-level writing instruction. *College Composition & Communication, 62*(3), 477–501. https://doi.org/10.58680/ccc201113457.

Wells, J. M. & Söderlund, L. (2018). Preparing graduate students for academic publishing: Results from a study of published rhetoric and composition scholars. *Pedagogy, 18*(1), 131–156. https://doi.org/10.1215/15314200-4216994.

CHAPTER 6.
WRITING SUPPORT FOR FACULTY OF COLOR

Laura R. Micciche and Batsheva Guy
University of Cincinnati

Abstract: *This chapter addresses the unique writing support needs of faculty of color at historically white institutions. Based on our experience facilitating writing groups, we identify the critical need for affinity-based communities, mentorship, and structured writing goals tailored for faculty of color. The chapter highlights institutional barriers and the impact of typically white attitudes and behavioral norms on faculty well-being and retention. It calls for tailored writing support programs that reflect the experiences of faculty of color, advocating for systemic changes in academic culture to foster equity and inclusion.*

As facilitators of faculty writing groups at a historically white institution (HWI) in the Midwest, we have had the opportunity to work with faculty members across rank, college, and discipline in face-to-face and online contexts. During these sessions, we noticed that faculty of color expressed a need for affinity group community, peer mentors, work/life balance, and structured writing goals with more specificity and regularity than did white faculty members. What we were hearing anecdotally motivated the research detailed in this chapter. We set out to learn how faculty of color at our four-year Research I institution describe the conditions under which they write, so that we might develop writing and publishing support tailored to their needs. We anticipate that our findings will have applicability to other institutions where attracting, supporting, and retaining faculty of color, particularly at HWIs, require data-based evidence as well as creative thinking. In this chapter, we use HWI (Historically White Institution) instead of PWI (Predominantly White Institution) to acknowledge the institution's origins and legacy of systemic exclusion rather than its current demographics.

We come to this research with an awareness that unchecked whiteness, or whiteness as a presumed norm that structures entry and advancement in academic institutions, is baked into higher education labor practices. How else to explain the deplorable demographics across U.S. higher education? In 2017, for example, the National Center for Education Statistics found that faculty in post-secondary institutions remain 76 percent white, while student demographics are changing at a much faster rate (Davis & Fry, 2019). This disparity has several negative effects on faculty success. For instance, Brandolyn Jones et al. (2015) argue that women and faculty of color tend to take on more student advising than their white male colleagues, in part because students "gravitate toward faculty members who look like them or [are] of the same race or ethnicity in search of empathy for common cultural experiences and mentoring" (p. 143). In addition, faculty of color face what Sherri L. Wallace et al. (2012) call "roadblocks to productivity and career advancement" (p. 424). Such roadblocks include "getting oriented to the institution and its culture; getting access to informal networks and information, monetary resources, and collegial feedback in research and teaching endeavors; managing expectations for performance, particularly the tenure process; finding collegiality; and creating a balance between professional roles and family life" (Wallace et al., 2012, p. 424).

We have more than a pipeline problem, in other words; we have a culture problem. Previous studies of faculty of color retention rates have shown that, rather than background experiences, "quality of experiences once the individual arrives at an institution have the greatest impact on retention" (Jayakumar et al., 2009, p. 550). If this holds, then impactful faculty support programs can be powerful tools in institutional culture change. Rashida Harrison (2016) describes the dialogic potential of strategic support programs, noting that "excellent support" leads to expanded numbers of diverse faculty, which leads to "inclusive learning environments and more diversified kinds of scholarly inquiries" (pp. 56–57).

To build a case for creating "excellent" writing support, we combine insights from interdisciplinary research on faculty development—most often framed by feminist and critical race theory, educational and labor studies, and the scholarship of teaching and learning—with research in rhetoric and composition. The former rarely addresses writing theory and practice; the latter largely backgrounds cultural and social differences in discussions of writing support (Ballif et al., 2008; Olson & Taylor, 1997; Tulley, 2018). Ensuring that all faculty members are prepared to succeed in research-intensive environments is going to require culture change. While writing support is only one small part of such change, alongside teaching and service support, both of which are better documented in existing research (e.g., Belcher, 2019; Boice, 1990; Boyce & Aguilera, 2021; Pyke, 2011; Rankin, 2001), we believe culturally enhanced writing support can potentially have a big impact on faculty well-being and productivity by nurturing community-building, faculty coalitions around shared interests, access to resources, and cross-disciplinary collegiality.

In this chapter, we report on an institutional survey and group-level assessment (GLA) designed to gather faculty members' experiences with, preparation for, and feelings about writing for reappointment and promotion. Our discussion and analysis below are based on responses from 50 survey respondents and six participants in the GLA, a participatory group method that moves toward an action plan. We focus on the open response portions of our survey in which participants commented on writing needs, and on the results of our GLA discussion, including the action plan developed by participants. These segments of our study highlight three key themes related to writing support: financial and collegial resources, isolation and competition, and time and space issues. Drawing on these themes, we share GLA members' action plan initiatives aimed at writing productivity for faculty of color. We hope our findings offer strategies for thoughtful writing support while also informing efforts to recruit and retain faculty of color in the first place.

POSITIONALITY AND METHODS

The IRB-exempt study we designed grew out of our work with faculty on writing initiatives. We sought a better understanding of writing conditions for faculty of color at our institution and felt a mixed-methods approach would illuminate both faculty demographics and qualitative experiences with writing. However, we also recognized the limitations of our shared positionality from which to conduct this study. As two white women, one tenured in English and one serving as Program Director of Inclusive Excellence in the College of Engineering and Applied Science, we recognize the privilege of our institutional and cultural positions. We believe white people must put in the work to understand how institutions marginalize and undervalue faculty of color so that we can contribute to positive change. Too, we recognize, following standpoint theory, that "groups who share common placement in hierarchical power relations also share common experiences in such power relations" (Collins, 1997, p. 377). As researchers writing about and for those with whom we do not share common placement or access to power, we knew we needed to check our whiteness. The work and knowledge of faculty members who occupy nondominant subject positions are too often devalued and/or misunderstood in HWIs, where whiteness is very often the unacknowledged criteria for good or acceptable work.

To decenter our institutional and racialized perspectives, we developed a two-phase study that prioritized participant-driven data analysis in the second phase. The first phase of our study was a 37-question survey administered online through Qualtrics (see Appendix B for recruitment email and survey questions). The survey was open to faculty of color, nontenure or tenure track, who are required to publish research or creative activity for reappointment, promotion, or tenure. We distributed our recruitment email by tapping campus leaders—deans, associate deans, heads of special centers—sending to transdisciplinary listservs, and reaching out to affinity groups on campus: Black Faculty Association, Latinx Faculty Association, and the Women's, Gender, and Sexuality Studies department. In each case, we depended on recipients' willingness to forward our call to their contacts, creating a snowball effect that we believe worked effectively.

In our recruitment email, we invited colleagues who self-identify as faculty of color to complete the survey. We sought to avoid constructing categories of identity that don't match individual experiences as well as to extend agency for self-definition to our participants. Rather than create a comparative study with whites as the norm against which others are measured, we wanted to focus on the distinct experiences of faculty of color. This approach, in combination with our recruitment email, had its own problems, as we later realized. Fourteen of our 50 respondents identified as white, which we believe resulted from our wording in the first paragraph of our email ("research study of writing support for faculty of color") leading faculty members to think that we were asking how they support faculty of color. In addition, we failed to incorporate skip logic in the identification portion of the survey that would have prevented those who identified as white from completing the survey. As a result, we manually excluded white faculty members' responses in our discussion below.

In the end, the 34 respondents came from 17 disciplines and 11 colleges, two of which are branch campuses of the main campus where we work. Fourteen respondents were born outside the U.S., and 10 identified as administrators. Twenty-two survey respondents identified as women, 10 as men, one as genderqueer, and one preferred not to disclose gender. In terms of respondents' racial and ethnic identification, 16 identified as Asian/Asian American, ten as Black/African American, three as Multiracial, two as Hispanic/Latinx, two as Native American/Alaskan, and one as "other," with a write-in option indicating Hellenic Jew.

At the university, there are 841 faculty of color and 3,091 white faculty. Out of those, there are 506 faculty of color in STEM fields, 1,576 white faculty in STEM fields, 325 non-STEM faculty of color, and 1,487 non-STEM white faculty. The limited diversity of our survey participants, particularly the small number of Latinx and Native American/Alaskan respondents, is reflective of the diversity of the university faculty as a whole (80% white, 11.4% Black, 7.3% Asian) ("University," n.d.). Additionally, more faculty in non-STEM fields (59.5%) filled out the survey than did those in STEM fields (40.4%). As such, our findings in this chapter are preliminary and represent the initial phase of our research.

The content of the survey focused on participants' familial and education background; writing requirements for promotion, tenure, and reappointment;

feelings about writing; and ideal forms of writing support. Two optional open responses at the end invited respondents to add feedback about writing needs and advice for new faculty of color at the institution. In addition, respondents could add an email address if they were interested in being part of a follow-up small group discussion. Twelve people added their email addresses, and seven participated in the GLA: two men and five women. Both men who participated identified as Black, and out of the five women who participated, two identified as Black and three as Asian. Collectively, they represented diverse locations within the university: Asian studies, art history, business, psychology, medicine, health information, nursing, and rehabilitation and nutrition sciences.

To account for the richness and epistemic salience of participant experiences represented in the data, we used a GLA format when meeting with participants remotely. This method allows researchers to foreground participant-generated themes that they see in the data and to outline a collaboratively developed action plan. A GLA is like a focus group in that both include demographically similar people who represent a subset of a larger population. While focus groups typically function through a controlled interview process with predetermined questions, a GLA is a "qualitative and participatory large group method in which timely and valid data are collaboratively generated and interactively evaluated with relevant stakeholders leading to the development of participant-driven data and relevant action plans" (Vaughn & Lohmueller, 2014, p. 336).

We adapted the typical large group format for our smaller number of GLA participants. On the one hand, the smaller group limits the representational validity of our results; on the other, group members were able to have a nuanced, deep conversation that might have been impossible with more participants. In short, we believe that the size of the group and the GLA process itself, which incorporates participants' response, reflection, discussion, and action planning, ended up being an advantage for our first attempt at studying writers who identify as faculty of color. While GLAs are typically hosted in-person, we modified the process to a remote format, detailed stepwise as follows:

1. *Responding to prompts (asynchronous):* Participants were asked to respond to 15 open-ended prompts that we crafted based on hot spots in the survey data (e.g., support, feelings about writing and writing needs). Participants were asked to respond with their first thoughts, using words and short phrases seen only by us.

2. *Reflecting upon answers (asynchronous):* Anonymized responses to prompts were combined into a shared document that all participants had access to via a Google document. Participants reflected upon others' answers and used asterisks (*) to indicate which responses resonated with them.

3. *Introductions & icebreakers (synchronous):* Following the prompt responses and reflection, we met with participants over Zoom, beginning with introductions and an explanation of the GLA process.
4. *Small group discussion (synchronous):* While on Zoom, participants were divided into small groups and assigned a set of prompts and prompt responses. They were instructed to identify 3–5 themes across the prompt responses.
5. *Large group discussion (synchronous):* Small groups shared their themes with the larger group, and as a large group, participants consolidated the themes and developed overarching themes.
6. *Action planning (synchronous):* Based on the key themes, the group as a whole developed action steps to address the issues that surfaced during the large group discussion.

Participants were given two weeks to complete the asynchronous portion of the GLA process. The synchronous portions were completed in a single 90-minute Zoom session, facilitated by the authors. While the GLA was in session, we took notes that were visible to the participants on screen. Near the end of the session, we asked everyone to review the notes and to suggest additions and corrections and/or to ask questions about the written representation of our conversation. The resulting participant-identified themes and action planning, along with the open survey responses, provide a framework for understanding what supports and thwarts writing productivity for faculty of color at our institution.

DATA ANALYSIS

We implemented an iterative data analysis process to integrate the open-ended survey findings with the GLA findings. Responses to the quantitative survey questions were analyzed, and this data was used to create targeted prompts for the GLA. Following the GLA, which included a large group thematic analysis, we coded the open survey responses and, in turn, linked them to the GLA themes. The coded survey responses were largely subcategories of the themes determined by GLA participants.

THEMES & ACTION PLAN

Financial and collegial support, isolation and competition, and time and space issues—these themes might at first appear to be universal concerns among faculty. We found, however, that threaded throughout discussion of these themes was talk about cultural and racial inequity. Behind the themes were concerns that faculty work was not recognized or materially valued, that colleagues were reluctant to invite them to collaborate, that a competitive environment left them feeling isolated from colleagues, and that racial and ethnic bias played a part in all of the above. In what follows, we discuss the themes identified by participants while drawing on examples from the survey and GLA discussion. We then present the action plan developed by GLA members, which includes practical and aspirational changes that would make our university, and likely other HWIs, a healthier and more habitable place for faculty of color.

THEME 1: FINANCIAL AND COLLEGIAL SUPPORT

Support comes in many forms. Perhaps the most obvious is equitable compensation, which emerged as a major concern for survey respondents and GLA participants. When survey respondents were invited to add "any comments related to your writing needs that will help us understand what you see as factors supporting or inhibiting your productivity," they responded by articulating compensation issues that disadvantage faculty of color. One respondent noted, for instance, that our university "rhetorically articulates" support but does not back it up with compensation. As a result, faculty of color spend precious time and energy applying for "each and every funding opportunity," an exhausting process that cuts into research time. When asked what advice they would give to new faculty of color about how to achieve their writing goals, one respondent contended that they wouldn't encourage potential faculty members to accept a position at our university, explaining that "[s]alaries are grossly lower than other schools."

Inadequate compensation also came up in the GLA discussion, as participants described the inflexible spending rules on available funding and problems with allocation. Others articulated the need for on-campus editorial assistance for writing projects, and mentorship for new faculty in order to create a pipeline for success. One participant described an aspirational model for success: teams of senior faculty mentors and new faculty collaborating on a publication to establish momentum and create a network of connected faculty. This idea was offered after the group spoke about the need for collaboration to spark writing and career success. Writing preparation and support came up in other ways, too; for example, participants in one GLA floated the idea of a writing center dedicated to faculty writing needs. And there was wide support for well-timed teaching releases that would allow for the kind of intensive research and publication expected at a Research I. Survey participants, too, commented on this issue in their open responses. One noted that our university "does not offer reduced teaching loads and other forms of institutional support" needed for research (although this varies by department). In the same vein, another warned, "Do not expect to be rewarded or promoted for your accomplishments and understand that others who have produced less scholarship will be promoted through the ranks." One participant commented even more pointedly, "White faculty get more research support and their research is valued more."

Theme 2: Isolation and Competition

In an open survey response, one person explained that people of color are seldom the first asked to collaborate: "We are always the last one to be invited to the party." Instead of a collaborative ethic, GLA participants described a "cloak and dagger" approach to research characterized by secretiveness and evasiveness. As a result, faculty of color say their approach is to "find your pack," "find your tribe," and "figure it out on your own." Their comments reinforce findings by education scholars Gloria D. Thomas and Carol Hollenshead (2001) who developed a qualitative study to learn how women faculty of color cope, resist, and succeed at a research university. Their participants described feeling invisible, colleagues' dismissal of their research, and a lack of support for their intellectual work (2001, pp. 166–167). Unsurprisingly, this isolating experience has a negative effect on research and publication, because faculty need intellectual community and reciprocity to be motivated and productive.

Our participants noted that, as a matter of survival, they try to model behaviors of inclusivity, or model the change they want to see and lead from there—a perspective that indicates the responsibility faculty feel toward the academic communities they are joining, or attempting to join. To be the change they want to see suggests that faculty of color feel that they must produce intellectual and emotional labor to survive in an unwelcoming or downright threatening environment. To that point, a Native American faculty member wrote in a survey response that they were told by former department heads that "Indians are drunks and thieves" and "You have gone off the reservation." In addition, colleagues referred to this faculty member as "Chief."

To counter the isolation and degradation they experience, faculty of color are often left to "figure it out on [their] own," which involves the production of invisible labor, nothing new to under-represented people in most any line of work. Institutional apathy, explicit forms of white privilege, overt racism—all are familiar themes in research about the experiences of faculty of color. Too, choosing between tokenization or being left out, as Anwer (2020) writes, has long been part of the narrative. But these themes and hard choices don't define everyone's experience or mindset when it comes to writing support. We noticed, for example, that our survey respondents offered counter-narratives when asked about giving advice to new faculty of color. Participants described the following deliberate actions to make their research lives more productive:

> Connect with other faculty of color to create a network of support. Do not be afraid to continue your research, even if you are discouraged from it: find grants and outside support to continue your work.
>
> Find colleagues with whom you are comfortable sharing your writing.
>
> The same advice I give everyone: treat writing as a part of your job. Just like you show up to teach at a certain time every day whether or not you feel like it, you show up to write at a certain time whether or not you feel like it, and the work will get done.
>
> Don't limit yourself to co-authors in your department, college or even at UC. Use contacts you make at conferences and via professional email listservs to find writing opportunities and co-authors. These opportunities can be found across the nation and across the globe.

These responses make clear that waiting for the institution to do the right thing is not a viable option for faculty of color. They take matters into their own hands by constructing best practices when institutional collaboration, mentorship, and compensation fall short. GLA participants, too, encouraged faculty of color to find support beyond the institution—for example, through the National Center for Faculty Development and Diversity (particularly their writing bootcamps and faculty success program) and the Biostatistics, Epidemiology, and Research Design program. We acknowledge that this kind of support is not accessible to all, particularly if institutions do not have a membership that enables faculty and graduate students to take advantage of the available resources. Without a membership to NCFDD, for example, the cost burden of $500 per year may be out of reach for many faculty members.

As faculty members shared resources and made plans to connect with one another beyond our group meeting, we could see the importance of "collectivist, peer" mentoring, which Thomas and Hollenshead (2001) found to be critical for the success of women faculty of color. We see potential in applying this model of mentoring to the specific instance of writing support. While all faculty members, to some extent, must proactively support their own writing goals, doing so is made immeasurably more challenging in an environment where faculty experiences are "simultaneously invisible (e.g., accomplishments

Theme 3: Time and Space Issues

During the GLA discussion, faculty members expressed a need for spaces on campus where they can work and get support. Our conversation took place during the COVID-19 pandemic, when most faculty were working from home, so distractions and space limitations on research were on everyone's minds. One participant noted that, before the pandemic, she regularly reserved a library carrel for writing and research, away from the distractions of both home and campus office. She could no longer do that with the library closed, nor could she visit the newly established Faculty Enrichment Center (FEC), also located in the main library on campus. The FEC is a space where faculty can work in open areas, meet in small groups in conference rooms equipped with large screens and white boards, and attend professional development sessions on the institutional review board process, mid-career faculty support, and mindful movement, among other regularly offered sessions.

Even prior to the pandemic, though, several faculty members reported being unaware of the FEC, and others found it inaccessible given their office locations on campus. Despite its rich resources and ample workspace, the FEC seemed inaccessible to some for reasons beyond the center's control: the location in the middle of campus and the lack of close parking. As an urban university, space is a perpetual challenge, as is access to buildings from bus stops and parking lots. One must traverse concrete paths and hills to move from building to building (and then walk some more to get to a car or bus stop). As a result, the physical space of campus ends up reinforcing the intellectual and emotional isolation that faculty of color experience. The geography of the campus and the lack of creative ways to mitigate its effects, in other words, contribute to faculty feeling unsupported and isolated. We contend that the effects of such physical barriers are more costly to faculty of color than to white faculty. Because faculty of color constitute just 18% of overall faculty ("University," n.d.), they are in need of community and sociality, made possible by accommodating spaces and access to them.

In addition to writing and research difficulties presented by spatial limitations, both survey and GLA participants commented on the need for time to write. As noted earlier, faculty of color expressed frustrations with spending precious time on grant applications for research support. A seasoned administrator who completed our survey wrote that faculty of color need something other than sabbaticals to catch up on their research agendas, especially when those agendas are sidelined by heavy service loads. Suggestions included the need for pre-tenure course releases that would better position them to meet the publication requirements of a research university. Faculty described research writing for publication as a "marathon, not a sprint." Just as a marathon involves support and care during each leg of the 26.2 mile course, so should universities offer practical, material, and intellectual support for writers on the road toward tenure or reappointment. GLA members suggested that mentors should share with faculty the realities of time to publication to unmask the timeline of academic publication that might seem hidden from view. Most prominently, participants spoke about the need for protected time, a need that is amplified when understood through the context of unsupportive colleagues, competition and isolation, and a culture of racism or malignant neglect. This point was underscored by a GLA participant who described the experience of being the only person of color in committee meetings—a role that involves a considerable time commitment—as discouraging and as leading to disengagement because faculty of color find themselves "fighting against the tide here."

By weaving space and time issues into our discussion of writing support, faculty of color indicated that larger systemic issues—buildings, parking, workspaces, course releases, research time to compensate for service responsibilities—take on specific importance when viewed alongside the other themes we've discussed. That is, because racism and white privilege structure institutional life in ways that are both invisible and absorbed into the culture of a place, time and space issues should be understood as racially inflected rather than universal issues that affect everyone in the same way.

Action Plan

Following the theme discussion portion of the GLA, participants engaged in action planning to address the aforementioned themes. Specific actions addressed were resources, mentorship, and time and space issues.

Action 1: Resources

GLA participants felt that on-boarding new faculty members could be more useful if meaningful information about resources was disseminated, and opportunities for collaboration were presented upon hire. The "roadblocks to productivity and career advancement" identified by Wallace et al. (2012) and mentioned at the beginning of this chapter align with what we heard from faculty, who indicated that having a more comprehensive handle on funding and research resources available to them would help immensely in the success of their writing and scholarship. Communicating this information early (during the hire and orientation process) and often is critical. Day-to-day tasks sometimes obscure important communications that live on difficult-to-find-or-navigate websites. To that end, participants agreed that having a one-stop shop for resources in an online format would allow for awareness and dissemination of resources to be more effective and efficient for all faculty members. This could manifest as a page on the internal-facing website or a newsletter to the faculty email list. While this sounds obvious and simple enough, we're continually astonished by the number of resources available on campus that are new to us as faculty-staff leaders; we can only imagine how faculty "out of the loop" must feel. Additional sought-after resources include more hands-on writing support, such as professional editing services onsite. We know from our work with faculty writers that quite a few hire writing and editing coaches, form writing groups, and attend university-affiliated writing workshops like ours, as well as ones offered by national organizations. Attending to the needs that drive faculty members to these resources in the first place would amount to a practical intervention with significant consequences for writing productivity, community-building, and perhaps retention. Hosting writing and editing services on campus would benefit all faculty members but would especially serve faculty of color, often lacking institutional and collegial support for their research programs.

Action 2: Mentorship

Faculty participants also determined that a mentorship program or network specifically related to writing and publishing would be ideal. Mentoring as a venue to create community once faculty are here can help improve the retention rates of faculty, and faculty of color, specifically (Jayakumar et al., 2009). For African American faculty, both the need for good mentors and writing with a team lead to increased quality and quantity of writing (Allen et al., 2018). For GLA participants, formalized mentoring that leads to collaborative publication is highly valued. Too, remembering Thomas's qualitative study indicating the positive impact of "collectivist, peer" mentoring (2001, p. 174), we were struck by how GLA participants enacted, but did not explicitly discuss this model. During the discussion, participants entered resources in the chat, for instance, and made informal plans to connect with one another after the session. What was happening dovetails with findings Alexander and Shaver (2020) detailed in "Disrupting the Numbers: The Impact of a Women's Faculty Writing Program on Associate Professors." In their study, Alexander and Shaver found that when women of the same rank spent time together in a common space, they prioritized publication and promotional goals. In their review of national faculty writing programs, they noted that programs provided "emotional support, even facilitating academic alliances and friendships where individuals learn about institutional structures or campus politics" (p. 62). Though our participants were neither all women nor all associate professors, GLA members enjoyed connecting in a common space and spontaneously shared experiences, advice, and resources.

Creating more opportunities for collectivist peer mentoring among faculty of color would likely have similar results as those uncovered by Alexander and Shaver.

Action 3: Time & Space

According to GLA participants, providing faculty members with course release or sabbaticals that specifically focus on writing would require prioritizing writing within colleges and disciplines. Prioritizing faculty writing could involve implementing dedicated weekly blocked time for writing, creating interdisciplinary writing accountability groups, and providing workshops on the topics of writing and publishing. These sorts of formalized initiatives might function as institutionally sanctioned reprieves from the service burden placed on faculty of color, which makes dedicated writing time challenging. As Jones et al. (2015) indicate in their study of African American women faculty, "All the participants in this study shared how burdened they felt in trying to balance scholarship, student advising, service, and teaching" (p. 143). Black faculty members are frequently faced with taking on invisible labor, as our participants attested, including creating networks of support, finding resources outside the university, and dealing with exclusionary and/or racist behavior from colleagues. Space also came up as a point for action planning—the need for more space and free parking so that faculty can easily access designated spaces, as well as reservable spaces in university buildings and practical furniture. While an overarching goal is culture change within academia, incremental steps such as offering course releases, monetary incentives, and physical space for faculty of color to focus on writing can begin to chip away at unconscious bias.

IMPLICATIONS AND CONCLUSIONS

The themes as a whole—the importance of compensation, the negative effects of competition and isolation, and the need for time and space—are likely universal amongst tenure-track faculty attempting to develop their research agendas. We contend that they have particularity when applied to faculty of color. For example, the GLA discussion surrounding inequity, which addressed the lack of recognition or value attached to the work of faculty of color and a need for collaboration and mentorship, was couched in the context of racial bias, microaggressions, and blatant discrimination. These conditions wear on people and exact a real toll. In their Foreword to *Presumed Incompetent*, Bettina Aptheker (2012) comments on the human cost of inequity: "We are in the university. We are in the labs. We are in the law schools and courtrooms, medical schools and operating theaters.

We prevail, but sometimes it is at enormous costs to ourselves, to our sense of well-being, balance, and confidence" (p. xi). The emotional and psychic costs, which are sometimes difficult to quantify, underscore why writing support should not be approached as a universal that applies the same to all. As Sara Ahmed (2012) reminds us in *On Being Included: Racism and Diversity in Institutional Life*, "To recognize diversity requires that time, energy, and labor be given to diversity. Recognition is thus material as well as symbolic: how time, energy, and labor are directed within institutions affects how they surface" (p. 29).

Studies of writing and publishing by writing scholars have considerable room to grow in this context. For example, in *How Writing Faculty Write: Strategies for Process, Product, and Productivity* (Tulley, 2018), *Women's Ways of Making It in Rhetoric and Composition* (Ballif, Davis & Mountford, 2008), and *Publishing in Rhetoric and Composition* (Olson & Taylor, 1997), we learn how successful writers have sustained their commitment to writing throughout their careers while balancing their roles as teachers, administrators, and mentors. We learn about publication venues and processes. Overall, though, these books do not address differential forms of support inflected by culture and identity, about surviving as an outsider in an insider's game.

A study by Sandra L. Tarabochia (2020) demonstrates what such research might look like. She contends that writing studies scholars who work with faculty writers "must honor and promote trajectories of becoming tied to actual bodies, histories, emotional landscapes, emerging identities and lived realities" (p. 19). Tarabochia's qualitative study of faculty writers feature three pre-tenure women working at a "very high research" institution. One participant in her study, Sadie, an education faculty member who identifies as a Black woman, describes how schooling created for her a struggle to trust her voice and experience. By the time she enters higher education as a tenure-track professor, the voice inside her head tells her that "the institution just wants to kill you" (p. 21). Commenting on Sadie's story, Tarabochia addresses the institutional landscape that faculty of color and those from marginalized populations find themselves in:

> [They] face disproportionate challenges as writers and humans fighting to survive systems that not only fail to recognize and support their unique trajectories of becoming, trajectories built around epistemologies of lived experience, but inflict harm on those who contort their trajectories (and epistemologies) to fit traditional 'tales of learning' and pathways to success. (p. 23)

Tarabochia's study illustrates the complexity of faculty writing support for faculty trying to navigate these systems.

In a study of work-life balance, Anwer (2020) describes invisible labor specific to faculty of color pre- and post-COVID-19: We can be sure that Black faculty, and faculty of color more generally, will face (and are already facing) an intensification of the demands on their time, their intellectual-emotional resources. They will find themselves in a bind—to add to their already mammoth workloads or forgo serving on committees, letting them be steered by predominantly white faculty and administrators, as they try to "fix" the problem of racist campuses. Thus, "this quandary—to participate in the toxicity of being tokenized or risk being out altogether—predates COVID-19, of course" (Anwer, 2020, p.6).

GLA participants indicated that their identities and lived experiences were largely overlooked when it came to support for writing success, as many participants reported that the university at large is not supportive of faculty of color (although pockets of support do exist), yet it expects high service commitments, overburdening these faculty and negatively impacting their writing productivity.

Looking forward, we believe our research could have more impact if it were expanded to include the experiences of faculty of color at comparable institutions and a mix of institution types and sizes. We also suggest follow-up research regarding support for women faculty of color, specifically, given their disproportionate mentorship and service loads which could impede writing and publishing. The support needs of other populations are also worthy of study, including faculty members with disabilities and those who identify as LGBTQ+. A comparative study exploring the differences between majority faculty and faculty of color in terms of writing support could shed light onto specific interventions that would benefit faculty of color, specifically, as well as those that would benefit all faculty. Examining the interconnections between faculty support for writing and publishing and teaching and service, as well, would provide a more holistic view of faculty needs. Furthermore, if our suggested action items are implemented at our university, follow-up studies must include the assessment and evaluation of these programs to measure impact and whether such interventions were perceived as valuable by faculty of color. In addition, one-on-one open-ended interviews would yield valuable insights that could shed more light on the way race, ethnicity, and language difference inflect faculty experiences in higher education. In a 2016 interview with Cheryl A. Wall, who has worked on establishing a Black women's literary canon, Rashida L. Harrison (2016) asks Wall about the importance of increasing diversity to fulfill a university's academic mission and commitment to social justice. "If the university is going to continue to produce new knowledge," answers Wall, "it needs to diversify the people who are seeking new knowledge; that includes scholars of color" (p. 55). Supporting the needs of these scholars—writing needs, in our case—is essential to the success of diversity and inclusion initiatives. That is, recruiting faculty of color won't lead to substantive change if they end up leaving because of a culture that neglects their expertise, voices, lived experiences, and needs.

REFERENCES

Ahmed, S. (2012). *On being included: Racism and diversity in institutional life.* Duke University Press. https://doi.org/10.1215/9780822395324.

Alexander, K. P. & Shaver, L. (2020). Disrupting the numbers: The impact of a women's faculty writing program on associate professors. *College English, 72*(1), 58–86. https://www.jstor.org/stable/27114481.

Allen, J. L., Huggins-Hoyt, K. Y., Holosko, M. J. & Briggs, H. E. (2018). African American social work faculty: Overcoming existing barriers and achieving research productivity. *Research on Social Work Practice, 28*(3), 309–319. https://doi.org/10.1177/1049731517701578.

Anwer, M. (2020). Academic labor and the global pandemic: revisiting life-work balance under COVID-19. *Susan Bulkeley Butler Center for Leadership Excellence and ADVANCE Working Paper Series, 3*(2), 5–13. https://www.purdue.edu/butler/documents/5-wps-2020-special.

Aptheker, B. (2012). Foreword. In G. Gutiérrez y Muhs, Y. F. Niemann, C. G. González & A. P. Harris (Eds.), *Presumed incompetent: The intersections of race and class for women in academia* (pp. xi–xiv). Utah State University Press.

Belcher, W. L. (2019). *Writing your journal article in twelve weeks: A guide to academic publishing success* (2nd ed.). University of Chicago Press. https://wendybelcher.com/writing-advice/writing-your-journal-article-in-twelve/.

Boice, R. (1990). *Professors as writers: A self-help guide to productive writing.* New Forums Press. https://archive.org/details/professorsaswrit0000boic.

Boyce, M. & Aguilera, R. J. (2021). Preparing for tenure at a research-intensive university. *BMC Proceedings, 15*(Suppl 2), 14. https://doi.org/10.1186/s12919-021-00221-8.

Collins, P. H. (1997). Comment on Hekman's "Truth and method: Feminist standpoint theory revisited": Where's the power? *Signs, 22*(2), 375–381. https://www.jstor.org/stable/3175278.

Davis, L. & Fry, R. (2019). College faculty have become more racially and ethnically diverse, but remain far less so than students. *Pew Research Center, 31.* https://www.pewresearch.org/short-reads/2019/07/31/us-college-faculty-student-diversity/.

Harrison, R. L. (2016). Building a canon, creating dialogue: An interview with Cheryl A. Wall. In P. A. Matthew (Ed.), *Written/Unwritten: Diversity and the hidden truths of tenure* (pp. 46–63). University of North Carolina Press. https://www.jstor.org/stable/10.5149/9781469627724_matthew.

Jayakumar, U. M., Howard, T. C., Allen, W. R. & Han, J. C. (2009). Racial privilege in the professoriate: An exploration of campus climate, retention, and satisfaction. *The Journal of Higher Education, 80*(5), 538–563. https://choices.gseis.ucla.edu/pdfs/RacialPrivilege.pdf.

Jones, B., Hwang, E. & Bustamante, R. M. (2015). African American female professors' strategies for successful attainment of tenure and promotion at predominantly white institutions: It can happen. *Education, Citizenship and Social Justice, 10*(2), 133–151. https://eric.ed.gov/?id=EJ1064713.
Olson, G. A. & Taylor, T.W. (1997). *Publishing in rhetoric and composition*. State University of New York.
Pyke, K. (2011). Service and gender inequity among faculty. *PS: Political Science and Politics, 44*(1), 85–87. https://www.jstor.org/stable/40984489.
Rankin, E. (2001). *The work of writing: Insights and strategies for academics and professionals*. Jossey-Bass.
Settles, I. H., Buchanan, N. T. & Dotson K. (2019). Scrutinized but not recognized: (In) visibility and hypervisibility experiences of faculty of color. *Journal of Vocational Behavior, 113*, 62–74. https://doi.org/10.1016/j.jvb.2018.06.003.
Tarabochia, S. L. (2020). Self-Authorship and faculty writers' trajectories of becoming. *Composition Studies, 48*(1), 16–33.
Thomas, G. D. & Hollenshead, C. (2001). Resisting from the margins: The coping strategies of black women and other women of color faculty members at a research university. *Journal of Negro Education, 70*(3), 166–175. https://doi.org/10.2307/3211208.
Tulley, C. E. (2018). *How writing faculty write: strategies for process, product, and productivity*. Utah State University Press.
University of Cincinnati main campus. UC demographics & diversity report. *College Factual.* https://www.collegefactual.com/colleges/university-of-cincinnati-main-campus/student-life/diversity.
Vaughn, L. M. & Lohmueller, M. (2014). Calling all stakeholders: Group-level assessment (GLA)—A qualitative and participatory method for large groups. *Evaluation Review, 38*(4), 336–355. https://doi.org/10.1177/0193841X14544903.
Wallace, S. L., Moore, S. E., Wilson, L. L. & Hart, B. G. (2012). African American women in the academy. In G. Gutiérrez y Muhs, Y. F. Niemann, C. G. González, A. P. Harris (Eds.), *Presumed incompetent: The intersections of race and class for women in academia* (pp. 421–438). Utah State University Press.

APPENDIX A. RECRUITMENT EMAIL

Dear Colleagues,

As facilitators of faculty writing support initiatives at UC's main campus, we write to request your participation in a research study of writing support for faculty of color at UC.

Studies of retention rates among faculty of color have shown that "quality of experiences *once the individual arrives at an institution* have the greatest impact on retention" (Jayakumar et al. 2009, p. 550; our emphasis). If this holds, then impactful faculty support programs can be powerful tools in institutional culture change. In order to create a culture that welcomes and nurtures the needs of diverse faculty members, our study seeks to better understand how one aspect of culture change—writing support—can be keyed to the professional and personal circumstances of faculty of color.

If you self-identify as a nontenure track or tenure track faculty member of color, and you work at any UC campus where you are required to publish research or creative activity for reappointment, promotion, or tenure, then we invite you to take our survey. If you are interested in participating in a follow-up discussion about your experiences, you will have an opportunity to indicate your interest on the survey. This follow-up is completely optional. Likewise, if you wish to exit the survey at any time, you may do so. In that case, your data will not be saved.

Data from our study will be used for two purposes: 1) to propose supportive faculty writing programming at UC to partners around campus, and 2) to inform a book chapter we are writing about this topic.

The UC IRB determined this study to be exempt from review (#2021–0163). There are no known risks associated with the study. Participants will remain anonymous in our reporting process and will receive no compensation for participation in the study. If you have any questions or concerns before or while completing the survey, please feel free to contact us via email.

To access the online survey, please follow this link <<link redacted>>. We hope to receive your responses by May 10, 2021.

Thank you for considering this request.
Sincerely,
Dr. Laura Micciche
Professor of English Facilitator, Taft Faculty Write
Laura.micciche@uc.edu
Dr. Batsheva Guy
Program Director, Strategic Initiatives
CEAS Inclusive Excellence & Community Engagement
batsheva.guy@uc.eu

APPENDIX B. SURVEY QUESTIONS

Survey: Writing Support for Faculty of Color
DEMOGRAPHICS

Personal & Familial Characteristics:

1. What is your gender or gender identity? [man, woman, transgender, gender non-conforming, genderqueer, preferred response not listed (please specify)]
2. Please indicate the racial or ethnic groups with which you self-identify (check all that apply):

○ Asian/Asian American ○ Black/African American ○ Hispanic/Latinx
○ Middle Eastern/North African
○ Native American/Alaskan Native ○ Multiracial
○ White ○ Other

3. Were you born in the U.S.? y/n [if no: In which country were you born?] 4. Please indicate your generation status:
   ○ All of my grandparents and both of my parents were born in the U.S.
   ○ Both of my parents were born in the U.S.
   ○ One of my parents was born in the U.S.
   ○ Neither of my parents were born in the U.S.

4. Did your parents attend college, or are they currently? [yes, one parent; yes, both parents; no, neither; I don't know]

5. Did your parents earn college degrees? [yes, one parent; yes, both parents; no, neither; I don't know; direct to appropriate question below]
   What is the highest college degree earned by both of your parents?
   ○ Parent 1: Associates, Bachelor's, Master's degree in Arts & Sciences (MA, MS), Professional Master's degree (e.g., MBA, MPA, MSW, MSE, MSN, MPH, MFA, etc.), Doctorate + other
   ○ Parent 2: Associates, Bachelor's, Master's degree in Arts & Sciences (MA, MS), Professional Master's degree (e.g., MBA, MPA, MSW, MSE, MSN, MPH, MFA, etc. + other
   What is the highest college degree earned by one parent?
   ○ Associates, Bachelor's, Master's degree in Arts & Sciences (MA, MS), Professional Master's degree (e.g., MBA, MPA, MSW, MSE, MSN, MPH, MFA, etc.), Doctorate + other

6. In what industry did your parents spend the majority of their working lives? Select all that apply. [drop down]
   ○ Agriculture, Forestry, Fishing & Hunting ○ Utilities
   ○ Computer & Electronics Manufacturing ○ Wholesale
   ○ Transportation ○ Warehousing ○ Software
   ○ Broadcasting
   ○ Real Estate, Rental & Leasing
   ○ Primary/Secondary (K–12) Education ○ Health Care & Social Assistance
   ○ Hotel & Food Services ○ Legal Services
   ○ Homemaker ○ Religious
   ○ Mining
   ○ Construction ○ Manufacturing ○ Retail
   ○ Telecommunications

- Information Services & Data Processing ○ Finance & Insurance
- College, University & Adult Education ○ Other Education Industry
- Arts, Entertainment & Recreation
- Government & Public Administration ○ Scientific or Technical Services
- Military
- Other [add answer]

7. Do you have siblings? [yes, no, I don't know]

8. Did your sibling(s) attend college, or are they currently? [yes, one sibling; yes, more than one sibling; no siblings; I don't know]
    - [1 sib] What is the highest college degree earned by your sibling? [Associates, Bachelor's, Master's degree in Arts & Sciences (MA, MS), Professional Master's degree (e.g., MBA, MPA, MSW, MSE, MSN, MPH, MFA, etc.), Doctorate + other]
    - [more than one] Among your siblings, what is the highest college degree earned? Click all that apply. [Associates, Bachelor's, Master's degree in Arts & Sciences (MA, MS), Professional Master's degree (e.g., MBA, MPA, MSW, MSE, MSN, MPH, MFA, etc.), Doctorate + other]

Academic Identity:

1. What is the highest degree you have earned? [Associates, Bachelor's, Master's degree in Arts & Sciences (MA, MS), Professional Master's degree (e.g., MBA, MPA, MSW, MSE, MSN, MPH, MFA, etc.), Doctorate + other]
2. In what field did you earn your highest degree? [text box]
3. How long have you worked at UC? [drop down]
4. What is your college? [drop down + other]
5. What is your primary department? [drop down + other]
6. Do you serve in an administrative role? If so, what is your title and responsibility?
7. What is your current rank? [Nontenure track assistant professor, NTT associate professor, NTT full professor, Tenure track assistant professor, Tenured associate professor, Tenured full professor + other; answer will direct to appropriate questions in next section]

Writing Requirements for Reappointment, Promotion, and Tenure:
For nontenure track, all positions:

1. What genres of writing are required for reappointment and promotion in your department? Select all that apply. [article, book chapter, creative work, book, conference presentation, internal grant, external grant, not sure, + other]

2. How would you describe your attitude about your readiness to meet these requirements? Check all that apply. [confident, cautiously optimistic, worried, frustrated, angry, hopeless, +other]
3. Please briefly explain why you described your attitude as such.
4. What scholarly or creative projects have you worked on during the past two years? Click all that apply. [journal article, poem, story, novel, memoir, book chapter, book manuscript, grant proposal, research leave/sabbatical application, book proposal/prospectus, conference paper, book review, other]
5. Of those projects you've worked on, how many have you published, presented, or submitted? [1–5 + other]

For tenure track:

1. What genres of writing are required for reappointment and promotion in your department? [article, book chapter, creative work, book, conference presentation, internal grant, external grant, not sure, + other]
2. How would you describe your attitude about your readiness to meet these requirements? Check all that apply. [confident, cautiously optimistic, worried, frustrated, angry, hopeless, +other]
3. Please briefly explain why you described your attitude as such.
4. What scholarly or creative projects have you worked on during the past two years? Click all that apply. [journal article, poem, story, novel, memoir, book chapter, book manuscript, grant proposal, research leave/sabbatical application, book proposal/prospectus, conference paper, book review, other]
5. Of those projects you've worked on, how many have you published, presented, or submitted? [1–5 + other]

For tenured Associate professors:

1. What genres of writing are required for promotion from Associate to Full professor in your department? [article, book chapter, creative work, book, conference presentation, internal grant, external grant, not sure, + other]
2. How would you describe your attitude about your readiness to meet these requirements? Check all that apply. [confident, cautiously optimistic, worried, frustrated, angry, hopeless, +other]
3. Please briefly explain why you described your attitude as such.
4. What scholarly or creative projects have you worked on during the past two years? Click all that apply. [journal article, poem, story, novel, memoir, book chapter, book manuscript, grant proposal, research leave/sabbatical application, book proposal/prospectus, conference paper, book review, other]

5. Of those projects you've worked on, how many have you published, presented, or submitted? [1–5 + other]

For tenured full professors:
1. What year did you earn tenure?
2. How frequently have you published or presented your work since earning tenure? [drop down]
3. How would you describe your motivation to write and publish research and/or creative work? [highly motivated, motivated, not motivated, indifferent]
4. Please briefly explain why you described your motivation as such.
5. What scholarly or creative projects have you worked on during the past two years? Click all that apply. [journal article, poem, story, novel, memoir, book chapter, book manuscript, grant proposal, research leave/sabbatical application, book proposal/prospectus, conference paper, book review, other]
6. Of those projects you've worked on, how many have you published, presented, or submitted? [1–5 + other]

Background & Writing for Publication

Please indicate your level of agreement with each of the following statements: [strongly agree, agree, neither agree nor disagree, disagree, strongly disagree]

- My cultural background is important to the topics I write about.
- My educational background prepares me for the writing required for my success at UC.
- My family background prepares me for the social environment at UC.
- I have received direct instruction about how to write in my field.
- I learned how to write for my field by reading widely.
- I learned how to write for my field through trial and error.
- I am still learning how to write for my field.
- My home community has shaped my commitment to writing and research.
- When I write for professionals in my field, I worry that my work will not be taken seriously.
- I feel that I have to be more productive than my white counterparts in order to secure my position at UC.
- I often feel that I do not know the unspoken codes of academic writing and publishing.

- I feel confident that my voice and perspective are valued in my field.
- My community outside of academia is important to my writing productivity.

Writing Supports

Please indicate your level of agreement with each of the following statements: [strongly agree, agree, neither agree nor disagree, disagree, strongly disagree]

- I have allies in my department or at UC who support my writing goals.
- I have a regular writing group that helps me stay on task.
- My writing group includes faculty of color.
- I have allies at UC who share a similar cultural background and set of experiences.
- I have a mentor or set of mentors who support my writing goals.
- I have a family situation that supports my writing goals.
- I have applied for internal grants or fellowships to support my writing goals.
- I have received internal grants or fellowships to support my writing goals.
- My department allows a semester of leave for research.
- My department assigns value to my research.
- My department rewards my writing accomplishments on par with those of colleagues at the same rank.
- My department allows for a flexible teaching schedule to support my writing goals.
- My department assigns me to teach courses that align with my research.
- I feel like I belong in my department, which affects my writing productivity.
- I feel isolated in my department, which affects my writing productivity.

Writing Needs

Please complete the following statements by selecting all options that apply:

In order to achieve my writing goals, I need [blank] to be productive.

[blank] = a flexible teaching schedule, writing accountability partners, faculty of color affinity groups, writing groups, peer mentors, structured writing goals, access to grants/fellowships, work-life balance, formal mentorship, professional development opportunities, funding for my research, other

Optional: Please feel free to add any comments related to your writing needs that will help us understand what you see as factors supporting or inhibiting your productivity. [text box]

Optional: If you were able to give advice to new faculty of color about how to achieve their writing goals while at UC, what 1 or 2 pieces of advice would you offer?

Follow-Up

In order to better understand the challenges and rewards associated with writing productivity for faculty of color at UC, we will be conducting small group sessions for sharing ideas and resources. If you are willing to participate in such a session, please add your UC email address here:

CHAPTER 7.

WHAT PROFESSIONAL ACADEMIC WRITERS WANT FROM WRITING COACHING

Beth L. Hewett

Abstract: *I examine why professional academic writers seek external coaching to address writing and publication challenges, focusing on advanced scholars using Defend & Publish services. The study reveals that writers often turn to coaching when institutional support is insufficient, primarily for time management, project organization, and handling complex tasks. This chapter illustrates how coaching addresses specific gaps in academic support, offering vital assistance for writers struggling without institutional resources.*

Academic writers, particularly new ones such as those Tarabochia and Madden (2019) called "emerging scholars" (p. 423), may "struggle" (p. 424) to write and publish their ideas.[1] Emerging scholars generally include dissertation writers and early-stage academics. Studies that have considered some of the writing and publication issues encompassing this problem address the sheer challenge of writing as a difficult act (Tulley, 2018), the strategies needed to see academic writing as a practice of lifelong development (Tarabochia & Madden, 2019), first and other language interference (Sharma, 2018), and the challenges authors face from the COVID-19 pandemic (Cahusac de Caux, 2021).

To date, these studies have been conducted by interviewing and otherwise examining dissertation writers (Bloom, 1981; Chanock, 2007) and eminent academics in the writing studies field (Tulley, 2018). Others have considered established academic writers in comparison with graduate student writers (Tarabochia & Madden, 2019), international graduate students (Sharma, 2018), upcoming scholars in the nursing field (Steinert et al., 2008), and academics and faculty more generally (Boice & Jones, 1984; Geller & Eodice 2013; Wells & Söderlund, 2017). To add to the data these studies provide, I have examined the written requests of advanced, postgraduate scholars—also called *professional*

---

1   Since this article was written, Defend & Publish, LLC was sold and rebranded under the name Defend, Publish, and Lead, LLC. Now owned by Dr. Christine Tulley, the company has a broadened mission to support academic leadership.

academic writers—who sought specific coaching at Defend & Publish, LLC (D&P) to assist their writing and publication goals.[2]

One reason it is important to understand these scholars is because approximately 90 percent of postgraduate D&P clients, as evidenced anecdotally in our payment discussions, use their own funds rather than departmental or other grants for writing coaching. There is a seriousness of purpose involved in spending one's own (often sparse) resources to improve academic writing production and publication, which, as Tulley (2018) stated, is an investment in becoming prolific from which the university itself will gain as much as the academic writer. Tarabochia and Madden (2019) indicated that "relatively few universities offer sustained and systematic support for advanced writers," by which they seem to mean both graduate level and faculty writers (p. 424). In fact, to argue for such support would require some sense of what these academic writers state they need for help as well as what writing coaches discern they need through reading drafted text and talking with the writers.

RESEARCH QUESTIONS

To study these clients' needs systematically, I asked two research questions:

1. What stops academic writers from writing?
2. What support do they say they need to write productively for professional and personal purposes?

I theorized that these research questions might be answered in ways similar to the need of less experienced writers. *Fluency of content* as honed through a reading, writing, and revision process; *form* as determined rhetorically through audience-sensitive organization or persuasive arrangement; and *correctness* via editing are key features in much writing, as often attributed to Shaughnessy (1979), but these ideas are as old as the ancient rhetorical canon of invention, arrangement, and style central to Greek and Roman rhetorical education (see, for example, works by Cicero). These also are composing challenges of fluency and dysfluency that generally might resemble concerns of less experienced writers but that would increase in complexity as writers become professional academics and delve deeply into multifaceted intellectual and rhetorically sophisticated problems (Britton et al., 1975). And while writing failure can have important lessons for any writer (Brooke & Carr, 2015), I suspected that professional academic writers might minimally need assistance with fluency, form, and correctness to meet their goals.

---

2   Despite its new ownership and rebranding, the major mission of D&P remains sufficiently similar to D, P & L that I will refer to D&P in the present tense in this article.

Yet their very professional lives also seemed likely to affect their ability to begin and complete writing projects such that publication, if that was their goal, could be achieved. The need to engage with scholarly writing involves much investigation and research, processes that busy academics must build into their lives. Those with academic jobs theoretically have time built in although many are in overwork situations in which they must teach too many courses or their teaching is combined with heavy leadership or service workloads that preclude time for research and writing (see, for example, Association of Departments of English, 1992; Bourelle, et al., 2022). Thus, researching, writing (and rewriting), and publishing an article—several of which may be required to achieve job security—must be worked into an already-tight schedule. Books, which are more complex still, need to be shoehorned into one's schedule but also may be such an unfamiliar genre that the processes involved in creating a saleable book would seem daunting, indeed.

I decided to draw data from questionnaires required of all new D&P clients, involving only the postgraduate scholars whose projects include articles, books, and job-search and career-focused materials from 2019 to 2021. To report on patterns stemming from these academic writers' expressed needs, using these questionnaires alone enabled me to conduct an internal investigation without violating information stipulated as private in client contracts or overstepping ethical concerns (Bogdan & Bicklen, 1992).

The patterns I found strongly suggested an encompassing composing fluency and dysfluency problem in which all these clients' other writing needs reside or to which they are connected. Composition fluency regards people's ability to express orally and in writing the main point of the project—its thesis or argument—as well as its purpose as attendant to a particular audience (Ong, 1975; Porter, 1996). Many writers are unable to express themselves fluently at the inception of a project because they are still working out their ideas, something that social constructivists recognize as a process often aided by discussion and collaborative thinking (Bruffee, 1983, 1994). That's the practical reason for drafts but also for writing coaching overall. Writers often experience composition dysfluency when they are beginning to understand data or reasoning in terms of their research question(s), main points, or argumentative claim. In brief, I surmised that postgraduate clients may come to coaching because the broad view of projects with many moving parts and layers of argument is too complex for some writers to comprehend at once—particularly when time deprived—suggesting that peer-based coaching assistance can help. In fact, the results of this study's analysis strongly indicate that all the issues with which the writers in the study requested help were connected to an overarching sense of composition dysfluency that could be addressed only by grappling with various aspects of writing, attending to writing through attention to fluency, form, and correctness at its base. Writers could not finish struggling until they were finished writing, and they could not be finished writing until they had wrestled their thinking *and* writing from composition dysfluency to fluency. Albeit not writing per se, finding time for reading, thinking, writing, and building individually helpful writing habits also were key to fluency. Coaching supported all these outcomes.

COACHING SETTING

POSITIONALITY

I am a white scholar and the first and former owner of D&P (now D, P & L under owner Christine Tulley), which is an academic writing coaching company that for 20 years has provided writing support to graduate students writing articles and dissertations and to professional academic writers producing articles and books as well as promotion and tenure documents and other career-focused documents. Although I have worked at several institutions of higher education, I was not thus employed when I started D&P. Nonetheless, I consider myself to be a working academic scholar, not an "alt-ac," a term that demeans those without the increasingly less available traditional, full-time, tenure-line academic positions.

My goal in forming the company was to provide necessary academic support services to scholars who otherwise might not meet their goals of successfully writing and defending dissertations or publishing academic articles and books. My motivation was a strong desire to see struggling people—particularly those who had a later start in academics—succeed. In addition to having been successful in both these skills in my early forties, I had been a primary developer of the writing theory and practice for undergraduate online-based writing coaching at both Smarthinking and TutorVista, which are online tutoring programs. Yet I wanted to improve on those approaches (Hewett, 2015b), believing I could create a company that satisfied both coaches and clients, one that is constrained not by larger corporate goals but by goals that directly address individual writers' needs based on their personal situations and steeped in contemporary rhetoric and composition theory, particularly theory that considered the characteristics of online writing instruction (Hewett & Ehmann, 2004; Hewett, 2015a). D&P works remotely with adult writers from all disciplines. I chose to develop D&P as an online company that uses phone, video, email, text, shared text through software like Google Docs for asynchronous and synchronous interactions, and (rarely) onsite modalities (Hewett & Ehmann, 2004; Hewett et al., 2022; Selber, 2004). Online interactions increase potential accessibility for clients (Oswal, 2015; Oswal & Hewett,

2013) as well as useful professionalization in online instructional settings for coaches as (future) faculty (Hewett & Ehmann, 2004; Rice, 2015).

D&P Philosophy

The company's coaching philosophy is that writing is a skill that can be taught and learned. The general D&P goals are for clients to complete their desired projects successfully; to write with confidence; and to use their writing skills in varied settings, for different topics, and with multiple audiences. Although clients may return to D&P for additional support with new projects, the company's goals are to teach, mentor, and support writers toward a sense of independence and mastery.

D&P Coaches

Regardless of their other working circumstances, coaches in D&P are recognized as academic scholars who choose to individually coach their academic peers in a wide range of writing challenges. In hiring coaches, I sought a diverse pool of rhetoric and composition or other communication studies PhD holders who teach or had taught in higher education settings. It is critical to the company's mission that coaches be experienced *writing* instructors who can work collaboratively with those whom they coach. Unlike companies that hire psychologists, for example, to assist graduate students with emotional issues connected to dissertation writing, D&P coaches are published academic writers (many with books), seasoned instructors, and have successfully completed and defended their doctorates in writing or other closely related communication disciplines. As new coaches, they are mentored in addressing the emotional aspects of writing under pressure, *and* they teach the writing skills that their clients need, addressing but going beyond the psychology of writer's block, for example. To be hired, coaches need to be sufficiently steeped in rhetoric and composition theory and practice to be able to assist adult writers with a wide range of skill levels and expressed needs (CCCC, 2013, 2015). To that end, they need to be open to learning some adult education theory (Knowles et al., 1998; Marshak, 1983). Coaches also need sufficient educational flexibility to recognize when writers' expressed needs are not their actual needs at specific times in the writing process, and they must be able to approach and potentially convince adult writers—both novice and seasoned— that another direction might be fruitful. Finally, they need to understand something about reading in a digital age, because more often than they might originally think, the client's writing problem is one of reading for comprehension and the ability to analyze reading for their topic's purposes, synthesize it, and theorize from it (Hewett, 2015a; Hewett et al., 2022, see Chapter 6; Keller, 2014).

In the past, these requirements unfortunately produced a somewhat narrow coaching pool. Although I actively sought to hire coaches from minority sectors, not as many scholars of color or scholars from different cultures have applied as white scholars; nonetheless, all who so self-identified were at least interviewed and given the initial training tasks (CCCC, 2016a). Some people of any background have chosen not to continue training while others successfully completed the practicum. More bilingual speakers and intercultural candidates have applied than people of color (NextGen, n.d.). Similarly, more white women than men of any background have applied, although the company now boasts of a somewhat more balanced women to men ratio. The pipeline for diversity in rhetoric and composition is narrow, and these coaching demographics appear to match it (McClain & Murray, 2016).

To support hiring a strong coaching faculty, D&P offers four specific benefits to coaches. First, coaches are paid a high hourly wage for what is known as contract labor. For ethical reasons, their hourly wage far exceeds that of most coaches in the writing industry (see, for example, Smarthinking wages for PhD instructors, which from my anecdotal experience has been as low as $15.00 per hour with little chance for raises) and exceeds the payment that adjunct instructors receive for working with multiple courses (CCCC, 2016b; MLA, 2023a, 2023b). At the time this chapter was written, new D&P coaches started at $30 per hour with rapid incremental increases upward of $60 per hour to honor their skills and abilities. Some coaches have enough clients to live on their wages (Christine Tulley, personal conversation, 7 June 2023). Second, all coaches receive the same training in coaching skills relevant both to writing instruction and working with adult writers in online settings. Such training, taken from contemporary writing and online writing theory (CCCC, 2013, 2015; Hewett et al., 2022), involves:

1. close reading of draft writing for strengths and weaknesses;
2. articulating in writing both opinions about that writing and educated suggestions for revising it, which can be decidedly more difficult to do in writing than orally because such suggestions require mature, tactful approaches to little-known clients;
3. discerning, naming, and teaching strategies for fluency, which includes modeling revision and talking through client questions; and
4. determining when and how to teach time management and realistic expectations to overscheduled, often perfectionist writers.

For all these coaching concerns, new coaches are assigned a seasoned coach mentor to assist them with their first several clients. Third, once trained and mentored, coaches have a great deal of autonomy in when and how they coach their clients, reporting once monthly on their progress and client needs. This autonomy honors the skill level of PhD holders in rhetoric and composition while supporting them whenever they have questions or problems. Finally, D&P coaches have additional professional opportunities to develop and teach webinars, compose and publish writing blogs and podcasts, and participate collaboratively in other company work. All combined, D&P is a legitimate, theory-driven faculty development venue of as much value to coaches as to their clients.

D&P Clients

Clients come from a wide variety of demographics, including both novice academics and seasoned scholars of all ages. Although D&P does not collect such information as it is unnecessary to working individually with clients, clients have at times self-disclosed their ages, races, ethnicities, cultures, sexual preferences, and gender identities. Nonetheless, coach training does involve working with a diverse clientele (NCTE, 2020, 2023; Pimentel et al., 2017). D&P does query them about their language/s fluidity and learning challenges such as ADHD, dyslexia, and reading disabilities, which are central to assisting them (Franke et al., 2012). Clients come from both traditional and for-profit universities and colleges; dissertating students from the latter institutions often struggle from insufficient committee support, inexperienced dissertation chairs, or exceptionally rigid, lockstep dissertation instructions and requirements. Many clients succeed at their goals and return for additional support or recommend D&P by word of mouth. Others leave coaching before completing their work with the coach, but some later report they finished their writing successfully, occasionally crediting a D&P coach for the support that got them moving forward in a useful direction.

D&P has had clients who work with coaches for merely weeks and others who dig in with coaches for months and years on ongoing manuscripts of varying lengths, sometimes more than one at a time. A few clients have worked on revising dissertations into books and others have used coaching to develop books geared toward a popular audience. In my tenure leading and coaching at D&P, some clients stand out. One of my clients, a gay scholar of color, has completed and published five articles and one book regarding racial trauma; during these years, he has also worked with me on tenure and other job-focused documents, advancing from assistant to associate to full professor and serving two years as department chair. I found myself unable to assist one international client whose writing was so strong that I could not find appropriate ways to help her edit it to a briefer manuscript; she was deeply unhappy with me. Only one client, a busy school administrator, failed her dissertation attempt (mentored well under another coach) because the client was unable to bring herself to tighten her focus and make the document sufficiently her own; in other words, she could not see her occasional plagiarism of major documents, could not use advice about her apparent thesis, and ran out of time after apparent procrastination.[3] Only one unrepentant client had a contract terminated for services due to obvious plagiarism and his stated desire that I do the writing for him.

METHOD

To research what clients have requested as writing project support and why, I used a qualitative, grounded theory approach, allowing categories to emerge from the data (Creswell, 2014; Denzin & Lincoln, 2011). These categories often involved the same data viewed from differing perspectives. At times, the data was cross-referenced. The data came from 19 (of an original 20) randomly selected client questionnaires from 2019 to 2021, which means many former clients' needs were not captured in the study. These questionnaires were completed by postgraduate academic writers seeking coaching support primarily in scholarly articles and books, as well as job search materials.

Although they had many similar concerns regarding fluency and dysfluency, I eliminated dissertation writers from the pool of possible participants for this study, preferring to focus on professional academics. Dissertation writers certainly have needs beyond merely researching and writing: learning how to navigate their committees, meeting timelines for an extensive book-length monograph, presenting original material in dissertation defense and conference settings, and offering oral rebuttals and additional information to interested parties to these presentations. Presumably, however, the professional academic writers in the participant pool had navigated these more novice issues and were engaged with other concerns that affected their desired, new, or ongoing employment.

In addition to article and book writing, I included job search and career-focused documents for promotion and tenure because several clients specifically referenced these needs in their new client questionnaires. As part of D&P new client protocol, I also provided a 30-minute, no-cost, phone or video consultation to each of these clients. However, in the data collection and analysis, I used only their written questionnaire responses and not my contextualizing notes from the consultation; to the degree possible, I wanted to study the research questions from their own words and not from notes filtered through

---

3   She seems to be one of the rarer clients who, in retrospect, might have benefited more from a weekly onsite appointment that might have been harder to skip than an online meeting.

my understanding of the interaction (Creswell, 2014). Because D&P promises complete confidentiality to clients, which includes not revealing any personally identifying information and intellectual property, in this study I offer no personal or professional details that, while contextualizing, might breach clients' privacy. Additionally, I quote only the most generic of coaching requests as any more specific requests might leave clients open to identification.

All new clients complete a new client questionnaire to assist in a proprietary process that includes the Initial Reading Report. Questionnaires provide space for such information as (1) name; (2) institution; (3) degree-level desired or held; (4) discipline; (5) languages in which the client reads and writes; (6) learning challenges or accommodations needed; (7) project on which the client is working; (8) desired or required deadlines; (9) why the individual is seeking a writing coach; (9) writing, time management, or interpersonal concerns that are interfering with finishing the project; (10) types of help the client desires; and (11) any other information the client wishes to share.

Client needs typically do not fall into tidy categories despite the questionnaire's organized questions. Often, clients do not constrict themselves to the textboxes identified for each question; they might talk about first-language interference under more than one question, for example. For this study, I organized the data into two overarching categories of (1) the type/s of desired assistance in coaching, including actions the client wanted from a coach, and (2) the contextualizing concerns that may affect completing a project and the coaching interactions. After completing this categorization of the data, I then broke down the information into more discrete analyzable chunks. Finally, I synthesized all the data under the overarching category of challenges related to composing fluency and dysfluency (including strengthening writing and reading), as shown below.

Requested Coaching Actions for D&P Professional Academic Writers

- Overarching Challenges
  - Composing Fluency and Dysfluency
  - Strengthen Writing
  - Strengthen Reading
- Desired Coaching
  - Publishing Processes
  - Formula Development
  - Genre Transitions
  - Writing Processes
  - Time and Project Management

- Contextualizing Concerns
  - Original and Additional Languages
  - Disclosed Disabilities
  - Life-work Balance

Figure 7.1 conceptualizes the overarching *dysfluency to fluency* challenges with *writing* and *reading* as their primary concerns even when their words do not specifically articulate writing and reading as their issues in achieving fluency. I make this distinction through observation of hundreds of clients and thousands of student writers whose fluency problems emerge specifically in muddled writing and who often cannot describe, summarize, paraphrase, analyze, or synthesize what they had read to reach their thesis or main point, hence rendering them unable to cogently theorize for an audience (coaches or other readers) what sometimes seems clear in their minds. Although reading at higher levels of intellectual pursuit often is dismissed as unnecessary to teach or discuss, the differences between digital and traditional paper-based reading as well as increasingly more challenging material can interfere with fluency and compromise writing fluency (Hewett, 2015b). In Figure 7.1, this study's clients *desired coaching* and *contextualizing concerns* are nested within the overarching category of fluency from dysfluency. In this chapter's Data section, many of these stated concerns are subcategorized as well.

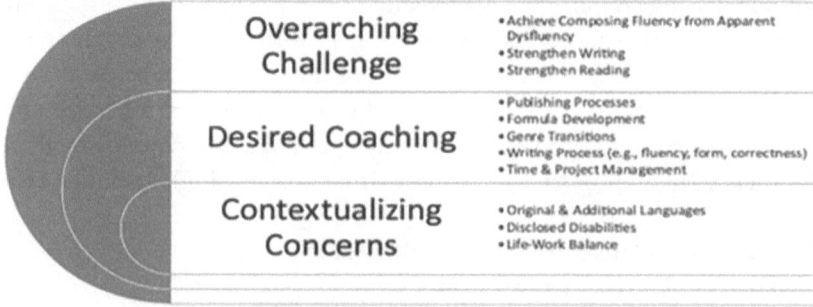

Figure 7.1. D&P Professional academic writers' reasons for seeking coaching

Demographics

I randomly selected 20 client questionnaires from D&P clients who entered coaching from 2019 to 2021 and were internally filed as working on scholarly articles and books specifically. I discarded one outlier, a client with an MS degree who sought entrance into a PhD program that required a published paper for admittance. The rest of these clients held PhDs and held or sought faculty positions. Clients identified themselves as being in humanities (e.g., writing studies, history, English literature), social sciences (e.g., nursing, psychology, social work, business management), and STEM (e.g., biology, chemistry) disciplines with some cross-disciplinary approaches. Of these, five were male and 14 were female. At the time of completing the questionnaire, all 19 either were part-time or full-time faculty or seeking a position in a postsecondary institution with ranks from assistant, associate, and full professor; a few clients indicated that they held academic leadership positions. Several clients with jobs in academia were seeking new jobs and considered themselves to be on the market or desiring to be on the market soon. Two clients identified themselves as working internationally and 17 worked in the United States.

DATA

Desired Assistance

The desired assistance that clients requested consisted of six overarching categories: fluency and dysfluency, publishing processes, formula development, genre transitions, writing processes, and time and project management. These categories tended to entail additional subcategories for understanding clients' needs, as I outline and describe below.

Composing Fluency and Dysfluency

I coded only clients who explicitly requested help with composing fluency and dysfluency under this category. Composition fluency is the ability to express one's ideas clearly and cogently both orally and in writing. This oral aspect holds the primacy of orality over writing, as Ong (2002) indicated, suggesting that although one might not be able to express an idea orally prior to writing, that expressive ability is part of a composing process in which orality and writing are intertwined. Composition dysfluency often occurs early in the project when writers are sorting through their ideas. With argumentation, a prominent scholarly genre, writers must understand their logical reasoning in the context of data from many sources, research question/s, main points, and argumentative claims, among other concerns. Clients may come to coaching because the broad view, so to speak, is far too large or the many competing points of a project appear to be floating in front of them much like disconnected clouds. These are issues of finding fluency in writing. Seven clients indicated a need for assistance from composing dysfluency to fluency.

This coaching request seemed implicit. None of the clients outright said, "Please help me become fluent with my topic and data." Instead, I discerned the need for composing fluency assistance primarily from the stated need for conversation with a coach about the project in process. One client specifically asked for "intelligent conversations" while another requested to "have productive, involved conversations about how to best move this piece forward." This second client also expressed a sense of being "capable" but "I really just need someone who can see the big picture of the piece." A third person similarly indicated needing to talk about the project, stating that it was essential to "verbalize to someone what I am trying to argue and what I'm thinking" and to receive "help with talking out arguments and chapters." The fourth client said: "I'd like to talk through my ideas with someone who can ask pointed questions."

Composing fluency is not only an issue of orality; dysfluency tends to underlie writing that appears to be disconnected or lacking cohesion. Other requests for fluency indicated a sense of being confused about the project's direction or endpoint rather than need for oral conversation. The fifth client in this category requested that the coach help with determining material that should and should not be kept within the project, expressing a sense of being "lost in the many ideas that research generates" making "writing them out very challenging because I keep understanding things differently." A sixth client expressed lack of "clarity in writing" while making a specific transition from one discipline's writing requirements to that of another discipline: "I really need help understanding why I'm not good at communicating my ideas in writing." Finally, the seventh client in this category expressed that the book project did not have a "throughline," insofar as "It takes me a long time to discover my argument. I get absorbed in analysis, in many possible directions." These three stated dysfluency issues seemed to indicate a sense of being perplexed about how to compose when ideas are not fully developed.

Publishing Processes

Publishing and the publication process is new to many clients who seek to understand what a manuscript should do, how to target a journal and/or its audience, and the steps one must take to write a potentially successful manuscript. These issues often occur for newer academics who have little to no experience with publishing but find themselves needing to publish either to secure an academic job or to keep it. Continuing contracts, tenure, and promotion often require journal publication in well-regarded, field-specific journals. However, more experienced academics also may request assistance with the revision process of a rejected or long-neglected "revise and resubmit" piece.

Seven clients asked for assistance with publishing or the publication process. One expressed a sense of being "overwhelmed and clueless" given insufficient "mentorship in my [graduate] program" and needing assistance from the "very basics." Like the first client, the second client asked for support in "preparing and reviewing the submission packet," a process that can eliminate authors who do not pay attention to the details. Similarly, the third client requested coaching to assist with "identify[ing] places I can publish and help me with the application." Another requested support with revising manuscripts that had received a revise-and-resubmit response from a journal; additionally, this client indicated that other manuscripts had been rejected outright, suggesting that the manuscript was unsound or that the selected journal hosted the wrong audience for its message or style. This client mentioned not knowing how to read and address reviewer feedback. A fifth client was employed in a position that required frequent publication of scholarly articles as well as successful grant writing. For this person, the article manuscripts and grant applications were "at different stages of preparations" with some in review and others due within two months. Finally, the sixth and seventh clients were interested in coaching for book publication, expressing needs for "help understanding the book publishing cycle, editor expectations, proposal-writing norms" and "help in the crafting of the book proposal/proposal process."

Formula Development

Writing studies professionals sense that writing is an organic process in which different projects develop uniquely. However, people from other disciplines may see writing as just another process in a series of professional processes that comprise a career. If writing is just a process consisting of steps A-Z, there logically should be some concrete steps one can take to circumvent difficulties and to make any project move forward more efficiently. Time is an issue in such cases as academics have competing tasks to which they can devote only so many hours. Therefore, one might consider it reasonable to fashion a specific formula for developing and completing a writing project.

Two clients specifically asked for assistance in cultivating formulas for writing more efficiently and effectively. In the first case, the client desired "some sort of formula, process, or technique" that would help in developing more than one scholarly article from a larger project. The client indicated that the formula would "hopefully" be useable "in the future, too." In the second case, the client was interested in "improving my writing productivity" through an increase of "the number of typed pages" to a specific "unit of writing time," a mathematical proposition for writing. Productivity was important to this client as this person experienced spending "too much time finishing the projects," estimating as many as six hours daily and five days per week. Specific parts of the writing process, such as "early drafts . . . [take] too long."

Genre Transitions

I use the term "Genre Transitions" here to include overarching project types. Specifically, clients expressed themselves as desiring support in moving the dissertation to articles, article writing generally, moving the dissertation to a book, book writing generally, and multiple genre requests. Such project types represent some of the major genres that academics attempt to write. Others, such as grant writing and job search and career documents, are not included here because these genres were not indicated as separate, major project goals, although they were mentioned in some client questionnaires as part of multiple projects in which the clients were involved. Furthermore, a different form of genre transitioning could occur when writers moved from the composing style and conventions of their home disciplines to that of another discipline; two clients mentioned this goal.

Dissertation to Article

In the first subcategory of "Genre Transitions," 6 of the 19 clients requested support with moving the dissertation to one or more articles. In this subcategory, the requests were remarkably similar in terms of the need to break down the larger project into smaller parts that, once separated, would comprise an argument. In this situation, the dissertation might have been completed recently or years earlier.

The first client requested help with "understanding where to put the lines in my existing project to break it down"; such actions of taking apart a larger project like a dissertation required knowing what data to include in which potential article/s, whether specific chapters could be taken wholesale to develop cogent articles, and "how do I know if I have done enough new writing?" This last issue suggests a need to understand what specifically comprises an article of the kind the client was envisioning (e.g., literature review? methods? discussion? theories?). The second client also needed assistance with deconstructing the "long dissertation chapters" to write "high impact journal articles" as well as determining where to publish them because of going on the job market within one academic year. Similarly, a third client asked for support with "develop[ing] an article from a broader piece such as a diss chapter" given that a dissertation often has or appears to have "multiple arguments" from which a "core thesis" or narrowed focus must be determined. Another client had tried already to publish an article from a dissertation chapter; the manuscript, which the writer had been crafting and recrafting for two years, was rejected and needed to be fully revised. The fifth client wanted to develop two articles from the dissertation and requested assistance with the entire journal manuscript process from determining "topics," to "deciding on potential journals," and learning "how to approach writing a journal article" as "a new process for me." Finally, the sixth client requested help with creating five articles from the dissertation, each of which would be developed from models that the writer found within the project's data. This client also saw potential for "possibly a few other ideas I see from my dissertation," which was an unusual number of articles overall to be imagined from a dissertation project that might, instead, have been a candidate for a book project.

Article Writing

Six clients requested assistance with article writing generally. These clients had been working on projects beyond the dissertation, and they were seeking support with various processes in developing articles. For example, the first client had been working on an article project for more than 18 months and expressed "need[ing] help getting it over the finish line." Among the tasks the client highlighted were the article's structure, the "right writing tasks for each part," "flow," editing, and developing a potentially successful "submission packet" for the completed manuscript. This client had a particular submission timeline in mind. The second client, a scientist, expressed a career need for constant publication. The requested assistance was: "To guide me through generative writing and organizing steps. To optimize my editing process." A third client, whose manuscript had received "lots of bad reviews," wanted help with "clarity" in revising the piece. The fourth client had a large item list for writing a publishable article from research that had occurred post-dissertation. This individual also indicated not "receiv[ing] support with publication in my PhD program" as teaching, not research, was its focus. A few years into a tenure-line program, this client had no publications and wanted assistance with "shaping" newly researched "ideas/data" into "a journal article in reasonable time." Concerns included the order in which one should write and how to narrow down or weed out a great deal of material. This client mentioned a future desire to develop one article from the dissertation but that the current project was newer and therefore more important to publish first. A fifth client sought to publish two articles by the end of the year as well as some "creative" writing. In particular, "Academic publications could be the ladder to begin finding a better job elsewhere." Finally, a sixth client was working on a specific article that this individual considered to be a "larger project" and had completed another "article-length manuscript" submitted for review at the discipline's premier journal.

Dissertation to Book

One client of 19 indicated a desire to create a book from the dissertation, a process that often requires a great deal of revision and reimagination of the project's audience and purpose. This client had been working on the revision from dissertation to book for more than five years, and a "goal for achieving publication of my book is tenure and career advancement." As a social-sciences scholar, this client was focusing the book to a humanities audience, which is a form of crossing genres and requested "help in the crafting of the book proposal/proposal process" particularly.[4]

Book Writing

Conceptualizing a book project that is not from a dissertation differs from proposing and completing a dissertation in form, audience, and purpose. Four clients specifically requested coaching with book projects. These request statements tended to be more about describing the overall project, but I discerned some specific writing-focused desires from them.

The first client expressed: "I need to [get] help conceptualizing my book project and keeping the theme consistent throughout the various chapters as well as assistance with editing." The second client was more verbal about the entire project's inception, research and data collection that had occurred over several years' time. This person indicated a personal desire to publish the material given promises made to study subjects. Requested support included how to manage a book project particularly within a heavy job "workload," how to find and articulate the most "valuable points," "honest" coach feedback, learning when new data is needed and when to let go of unnecessary information, and "understanding the book publishing cycle, editor expectations, proposal-writing norms." The issue of writing a book while working an academic job (as well as for the purposes of maintaining an academic job) emerged for one dean, the third client in this category, who requested "feedback on my writing. Revising with the readers' reviews in mind." Finally, the fourth client, who had been working on the manuscript for four years, wanted a coach to "to assist my tenure requirements" while also wanting "copy editing help" and "keeping the chapters connected with the overall book thesis," in addition to stated fluency-based opportunities to talk out ideas.

Multiple Projects in Different Genres

Three clients indicated that they were working on several genres at once, making it important for coaches to use the questionnaires to proffer a first understanding of their goal priority. The first client in this subcategory requested "coaching in article development" toward tenure, desiring "start to finish work" in using "explanatory detail and researched support," clarity of writing, revision, and editing. Beyond this project, the client waned to work on the tenure file to "deep-[en]" the "next draft for possible contract after review." The second client, a seasoned academic with multiple publications, sought coaching to develop stronger

---

[4] Another client sought to make such a disciplinary-based genre movement, this time from a science to a social science writing approach.

accountability for both article completion and a book, primarily from a desire to achieve promotion but also from a desire to clear the desk to focus on the book alone. A third client also desired coaching assistance with both articles and a book project to develop consistency of writing and progress on all the projects.

Writing Process

Many of the 19 writers in this study indicated a need for coaching with various writing processes. I categorized these discretely to better understand what these academic writers considered important for their projects. These processes—of which clients tended to request more than one—are content, organization, style and correctness, research, length, and drafting and revision. Readers may notice that some of these quoted statements have been used in support of other categories for client support requests as writing processes often are entangled with, for example, genre or fluency.

Content Generation

Thirteen clients either overtly or obliquely mentioned a need for content development or other content-focused assistance in coaching. Examples of overt requests regarding content generation include:

- "to guide me through generative writing"
- "narrowing the focus; determining core definitions; . . . determining a core thesis from multiple arguments"
- "also need to discuss narrowing my thesis and reframing my introduction"
- "deciding on topics"
- "coaching in article development, use of explanatory detail and researched support for argument"
- "help articulating the most valuable points, then drawing upon the findings to illustrate them"

Examples of content-focused comments that are more oblique may appear more mechanical in nature; however, underlying them is the ever-present need for content with which to work. These examples include:

- "how to research, write, and publish"
- "high-level academic writing"

Organization

Four clients made specific requests for assistance with the organization of their writing. Organization references might address how to arrange the overall project to section-, paragraph-, and sentence-level issues, but organization also included when to begin writing particular portions or sections of text. The first client asked for help with "set[ting] the right writing tasks for each part [of the structure]" along with advice on "flow and structure." The second client simply mentioned "organizing steps." The third client expressed a problem with organization relative to the article's disciplinary conventions for an argument:

> Order of information can be a challenge for me, as the [XYZ] I'm writing about is a minor work by a major [XYZ], so I'm never sure how much summary to provide or where to place it. Most critical essays I've read on this piece open with a summary of the [XYZ], but this necessarily delays the thesis by at least a paragraph. Need help managing how much of which information should be here and in what order.

The client's understanding of the disciplinary conventions required specific coaching feedback for various ways this writer might construct the written argument. Finally, the fourth client requested "guidance in what order to write things," which, in the context of the questionnaire, seemed to indicate not where something would appear in the text necessarily but more likely the process of when to write particular parts of the text.

Style and Correctness

Issues of style and correctness occurred in 10, or nearly half, of the clients' questionnaire requests. Three clients asked more for support with style insofar as they sought concision, sentence structure assistance, and clearer writing: "concise writing, sentence structure," "clarity in writing [in the context of communicating ideas better]," and "advising on flow and structure." Regarding style in a more mechanical sense—but one that is important for publishing—one client requested coaching assistance with "citation styles for particular journals" and moving from the previously familiar style (e.g., MLA) to a newer one for that person (e.g., APA). Six clients specifically asked for assistance with editing their finished work. One of those six requested support in "writing clearly, revising, and editing," which suggests a concurrent interest in style. Other requests for editing were brief:

- "helping to edit"
- "to optimize my editing process"
- "editing"
- "assistance with editing"
- "I also could use some copy-editing help"

Research

Two clients asked for coaching support with issues of research for larger projects. They seemed to want assistance with finding how researched data and published literature fit within a larger project. The first client asked for "help knowing whether to gather new data, help letting go of some of the findings for now so I can focus on this project." The second client sought to talk about research and research methods with a coach in order to start a new project well: "I'm in a bit of a lull as I start to search through a series of interconnected ideas and plans to consider, what next I should focus on, and how I should proceed (research methods)." Because of the COVID-19 pandemic, something I touch upon later, the client expressed a need to "talk through research methods with someone" because, despite "a general familiarity with a variety of research methods," the pandemic had caused functional challenges with "travel and human subjects research" that needed to be surmounted.

Length

Issues of article length emerged for only two clients. The first client indicated a generalized "need to trim down and refocus the article," while the second took that need further into decision making: "I need someone to help me make decisions about what to keep and what to do."

Drafting and Revision

It can be difficult to separate the often-concurrent processes of drafting and revising those drafts. In general, clients tended to see drafting as a process of writing new text, taking text apart, and putting it together. They most often discussed revision as a process required by journals or editors before publication would be possible. One client indicated that drafting, particularly the early drafting process, was a tedious practice that simply "takes too long" to finish. Two other clients focused on the breaking apart of earlier text as in taking a dissertation and dismantling it into chapters (i.e., "Can any chapters be stand-alone publications?") and the putting together of apparently fragmented text (i.e., "It looks more like a set of articles than a cohesive book with a focused argument"). All clients who specifically mentioned revision or intimated a need for it did so in the context of reviewer feedback and whether and how they were revising with feedback in mind:

- "Please let me know if . . . I frame the narrative in the revision according to the feedback."
- "revising R&R and not accepted article ms, to include addressing reviewer feedback"

- "revise and publish a previously rejected article draft"
- "lots of bad reviews"
- "approaching reviewer feedback and making necessary alterations"

Time and Project Management

Time management is intimately connected to project management—sometimes seemingly inseparable—and together they are the final subcategory in this overarching category of desired assistance and coaching actions. Time and project management were such major issues that 15 of the 19 clients in this study raised it as at least a partial reason for seeking a writing coach. Client requests for coaching assistance with time management tended to fall into three primary categories: (1) how to find time for writing within heavy workloads, (2) how to schedule writing profitably, and (3) how to balance cognitive work with other life demands. Requests for coaching support toward project management tended to involve (1) the size or number of projects and (2) being held accountable to someone outside of oneself.

Finding Writing Time

Finding the time to write challenged nine clients with a heavy or especially varied workload. For the first client in this subcategory, a varied workload looked like applying for jobs, beginning "a post doc in one month," "teaching online" daily, and developing a new media forum for dispersing some of the research. These tasks were combined with a desire to publish two to three articles within eight months. Altogether, the desired series of tasks may have seemed insurmountable for clients and, likely, were an unsustainable goal for a short time even for an employed and established academic. The second client indicated a potentially more doable scenario because of having "set aside the summer with no teaching to work on this project as much as possible," yet admitting to "juggling a lot in a little amount of time"; having "been working on the book for 4 years," this person wanted to submit "first draft of manuscript to publisher by" a date that was less than six months out. A third client indicated having "a heavy teaching load," and this individual planned to "make time for this [writing] work but [I] need that time to be purposeful and productive because there is simply not much extra to go around." Coaching, therefore, could not be an adjunct to the academic work but a core part of its success. Other client indicators of a heavy or varied workload included

- "associate professor chairing 2 university committees, global pandemic . . . , teaching and on a job hiring committee"

- "full time job; academic job, kids"
- "challenging workload (4/4), parent to a preschooler"

Three more clients requested coaching help to improve their general productivity by seeking to make bigger projects more doable in the time available. One declared a need for: "Help creating bite-sized chunks of writing to do that push the work forward more formally than research memos do"; such "bite-sizes need to fit in short enough time blocks that I can realistically make progress on them during a normal working week. 2-hrs-ish chunks would be logical. Smaller bites too." A fifth client with a similar need expressed a desire for coaching in "developing a more detailed and structured writing practice and schedule. I would like help developing a consistent writing practice, self-accountability, deadlines, and writing toward specific journals." Finally, a sixth client, a self-described "productive writer," requested that the coach "help me make some decisions about how I might concentrate my energies in a productive way...."

Scheduling Writing Time

Scheduling writing time takes "finding time" a step further; placing writing time on a calendar and prioritizing it as having value beyond the many must-dos that can knock it off the calendar is something five clients wanted. The first client in this group indicated having worked on the manuscript for more than a year and a half and "need[ed] help getting it over the finish line." This client had "blocked out" five weekdays on the calendar and was "asking for coaching to get me to a place where I have manuscript ready for submission by the end of that week." To meet that goal of honoring the scheduled time required not only that the client honor the internal deadline but also that the coach be able to offer moment- and point-of-need assistance when requested by the client. A second client indicated a narrow window of time during which this person experienced "mental acuity" and for writing in conjunction with the physical energy expended daily workouts and the need for good sleep, resulting in the exclamation: "I need a schedule!" A third client similarly found a need "to set my goals—timewise." This client also had what might appear to be an ambitious schedule for writing production: completing a "cv and cover letter overhaul" by the end of July that year, finishing "two articles for publication" by the end of November and concluding an unnamed number of "creative writing" projects by December. Therefore, "time management once we resume teaching in September" was a stated scheduling desire. For two other clients, scheduling of writing was a requested concern. One, on sabbatical with "large stretches of time available to me," wanted to complete "a second article-length manuscript by January." A second client admitted to having "a large backlog of work I committed to and cannot face this on my own; and the semester is starting. Time management: I teach and have various administrative duties. Time management is generally a problem."

Balancing Cognitive Work with Other Demands

Any of the clients already considered in this subcategory of time and project management might be considered to have unstated issues related to balancing the highly focused intellectual work of academic disciplines with a wide variety of other demands. Working on more than one paper at a time could cause dysfluency, for example, whenever one switches from one project to another. In this grouping, two clients specifically mentioned that intellectually focused cognitive work could be derailed by other demands. The first client noted mental interference particularly: "I could be distracted by teaching responsibilities when fall semester starts, especially that we still don't know how it is going to be managed with the current [pandemic] situation." The second client, who worked at a particularly stressful public university, mentioned that "the teaching and service responsibilities can crowd research and writing time into a tiny corner unless I insist otherwise."

Despite expressing being deeply connected to the study this person had developed and carried through, at the level of writing the book, "I struggle to put this work first." And, regardless of having "improved my time management by using a modified Pomodoro method starting several years ago," the client's "heavy load at my job includes teaching [four courses] and interim directing a writing center." This individual recognized "hav[ing] let other work creep into my writing group time, but I now plan to reserve at least one 3-hr block per week (with my group) for the book project." This expression of renewed purposeful engagement was not unusual among the clients in this study.

Working with Large or Multiple Projects

Academics may work on more than one project at a time, and often one of those writing projects is larger than the others. Therefore, setting priorities for work in terms of personal energy and time can be challenging. Seven of the 19 clients indicated they were attempting either a large writing project—typically a book or major grant application—or multiple projects at a time—sometimes including career-focused materials like CVs, application letters, and tenure files. Clients referenced these projects in ways already noted, such as the client described above who claimed that working from inspiration and deadlines do not always coincide. For the second client in this group, it had "been some time since I've taken on a project of this size," suggesting that the dissertation might have been the largest project before this book-in-progress. Such projects, as the third client indicated, required a coach's help "to set the right writing tasks for each part." The fourth client described the problem of working on a book in greater detail:

> I honestly don't know what's realistic for completing the whole manuscript. I therefore need external drivers. I have no successful experience since the dissertation of handling a long form manuscript. . . . Insights about managing a book manuscript and prioritizing writing, given my existing workload.

The fifth client declared that this individual was working both on a journal article and a book—at least mentally sorting them out—and finding that "help [was] definitely needed in taking all these ideas/data and shaping them into a journal article in reasonable time," with the pandemic having "amplified my need for support." The sixth client in this grouping commented on constant publication needs, leading to a number of pieces in the hopper: "My job requires me to constantly publish and submit grants. At this point, I have one paper in review. Two more that are at different stages of preparations. Two grants under review. Two grant deadline[s] in the next two months." Such a vast number of intellectual projects at any one time suggested a "need to improve my writing productivity" because other life aspects seemed to be ignored. Finally, the seventh client expressed a desire for a formulaic approach to get at "multiple distinct articles from my project," a process that might be useful "in the future too."

Being Held Accountable

Accountability concerns knowing that it matters when a project is not completed, is not completed in a timely manner (especially for the topic and data), or is not completed on time, such as for a requested revise-and-resubmit deadline or other promised date. After academics complete the PhD—and even before for people in programs with lackadaisical attitudes toward degree completion—there are few people who will care what that scholar does or when. When individuals are job seeking or desiring tenure or promotion, they often turn up the heat and reprioritize their writing projects. Therefore, it was not surprising that six clients indicated a desire for coaching support with self- and other-based accountability. The first client had sought to build in accountability through a writing retreat, but the COVID-19 pandemic led to its being cancelled: "Trying to get myself through the process has not been effective." The second client in this grouping indicated that time and "inspiration" affected accountability, or "deadlines." Particularly, working "40+ hours a week" was challenging for both time and energy; therefore, "I have often worked on inspiration or deadlines. The lack of deadlines has been really hard because inspiration isn't always there." External deadlines appear to have more sticking power than internal ones, as this client and others revealed:

185

- "Looking for someone to hold me accountable and have productive, involved conversations about how to best move this piece forward."
- "Accountability with regular meetings and 'homework' between so I can make progress with an interested witness."
- "Possibly some accountability and use as sounding board if anxiety creeps in."
- "Accountability, work on issues of perfectionism/procrastinations, goal setting, etc."

Contextualizing Concerns

All the writing-focused issues described under Desired Assistance are deeply interrelated, as readers can see from the repetition of some clients' words in various categories. That said, no writing-focused issues existed for these clients outside of the contexts of their lives. The D&P questionnaire asked specifically about such individual backgrounds as language, disabilities, or other challenges as well as miscellaneous information to provide coaching with potentially deeper and more immediate understanding of clients' needs, allowing them to work together more quickly and effectively. Efficiency is no small goal either, given that clients pay for the coaches' services. Therefore, this section offers three categories of contextualizing material: clients' original and additional languages, disclosed disabilities, and life-balance issues.

Original and Additional Languages

The questionnaire was written to learn something about potential language interference if such might exist, given that many clients are international and/or otherwise multilingual scholars whether they live abroad or in the United States. The clients in this study tended to offer simple statements regarding the languages they speak, read, and write. Eight of 19 clients indicated they had multilingual backgrounds. First languages included French, Neapolitan, Farsi, Italian, Arabic, Hindi, and German. Other languages besides English included Swedish, Spanish, Russian, and Latin. Of language interference, one client stated, "Farsi is my native language. I think my speaking abilities are symmetrically better than my writing skills." Given the general propensity of orality in a language to be learned earlier than reading and writing skills (per Walter Ong), this statement was not surprising. Another client, whose "first language is Arabic," claimed to "read and write mostly in English," also not surprising for an international academic. A third client possessed reading skills in "English, French, Spanish, and Russian" but wrote primarily in English. Finally, a fourth client who expressed speaking, reading, and writing fluency in both their native German and in English, reads in French, Italian, and Latin. However, this individual's sense of language interference is that having these many languages "slows me down. My style is a bit pedestrian and not very interesting. I write better in German."

Disclosed Disabilities

In the questionnaire, there is a textbox for clients who choose to do so to disclose disabilities that may require accommodation on the coaches' parts. Although this textbox can be left blank if desired, two clients in the study were frank about having what might be called learning disabilities or challenges. They provided little information beyond that, however, insofar as they did not suggest what accommodation they found helpful. One client indicated a diagnosis of a "visual processing disorder learning disability that often results in typos." The second client merely stated, "I have ADHD and have trouble sticking to deadlines!"

Interestingly, nine clients noted that they or family members had mental health challenges that affected their writing. The most frequently cited of these was anxiety, as referenced by five of the clients. Additional diagnoses they indicated were depression, bipolar "habits" that could lead to either "euphoria" or "complete loss of hope," and perfectionism that in combination with anxiety led to procrastination. The final client in this group expressed experiencing "some sort of mental, psychological block that deters me from proceeding ahead that emerged in complacency towards doing anything academic." One client mentioned a depressed spouse and another noted feeling "dispirited" by a denied promotion.

Life-Work Balance

Finally, there were several contextualizing client concerns that were categorizable as life-work balance issues, ones that could delay or completely derail a writing project. 13 of the 19 clients in the study referenced concerns that challenged their ability to balance life and work, particularly completing writing projects. Three clients directly mentioned or alluded to the lockdown and online/onsite teaching challenges wrought by the COVID-19 pandemic. Their ability to complete writing projects was therefore compromised: "The pandemic has amplified my need for support," "I could be distracted by teaching responsibilities when fall semester starts, especially that we still don't know how it is going to be managed with the current [pandemic] situation," and "but I'm struggling to think about what might be quickly available and possible given difficulties with travel and human subjects research during a pandemic."

Children were often mentioned as a challenge in balancing life and work. Among these responses was the challenge of pandemic-based homeschooling in conjunction with potty training: "I also have younger children who are at home with me a few days a week. Reading/writing while also teaching second grade and potty training hasn't been the easiest thing." Other children-focused responses included making space for work among small children: having a "20-month-old toddler," being "parent to a preschooler," and being "the co-parent of a toddler. We share childcare evenly and have an extra 12 hours of coverage a week from a grandparent." Older and multiple children, too, were cited as challenging the life-work balance: "I have a heavy teaching load, 3 teenagers, and have not completed a journal article before" and "I am stuck. Full time job; academic job, kids, confidence." Living with a "a partner and his children in my life that requires attention to family" also indicated a need to balance life and work. Not to be outdone, there was the next phase of parenting: "I'll be a new grandma . . . which may shift my attention a bit." Finally, there was the challenge of the "8-month-old puppy." Teaching, being on a job hiring committee or chairing other committees, seeking tenure or other promotion, working as an associate professor or assistant dean, and being on the job market seemed to present additional challenges that contextualized the lives of these clients in the study.

DISCUSSION

Academic life brings with it many challenges, not the least of which is the rapidly shifting ground in any day or week from wearing the different hats of a scholar, teacher, or service provider to the institution. Research remains an important factor in contemporary academia, and its production and publication can lead to new or different jobs and a solid career; the lack of published research and the development of other essential writing can make a career difficult to maintain even in a primarily teaching institution. Therefore, it is important to understand lived experiences in the writing lives of academics who seek coaching or other support with their writing projects. For this chapter, I have analyzed information from the entrance questionnaires for 19 D&P clients to discern what they expressed they wanted and needed in coaching. Their needs fell into two specific major categories of the assistance and coaching actions they desired and the other concerns that contextualize their writing lives.

Here, let's pause as I switch genre conventions. I don't want to bore you with repeating the results you've just read for yourself. So far, this chapter has been traditionally composed of data from studying 19 D&P clients' initial questionnaires to get at their lived experiences of stalled writing projects. Your next expectation might be that I'll contextualize this data with contemporary published literature. But I'm not going to do that. Instead, I'm going to rely here on my many years of experience with both novice and experienced academic writers to hazard an educated guess as to what's happening in these scholars' writing lives. To be sure, as I transition from the more comfortable scholarly genre to this less frequently used (for me, at least) speculative approach, I've been struggling with how to express what I think—what I speculate—connects all these expressed needs from the writers in this study. This struggle has caused me to hesitate, feel frustrated, talk out, start and stop writing by hand to move to the computer, scratch out and delete text, take many more hours than I'd planned (and more hours than I really have time for) to write this piece, and feel like I'm working with a foreign language. In short, my need to express my thoughts differently from what I originally planned has caused me to struggle deeply with fluency and dysfluency just like the scholars who were the study's subjects. I'll begin again.

This study suggests multiple ways that academic writers can go off track and that coaching can help them. However, even though only 7 of the 19 clients directly indicated a need to address factors of *composition fluency and dysfluency*, I believe all the clients' needs are connected by a single thread: the struggle for composition fluency in the context of the many factors that might cause genuine dysfluency, or a lack of ability to express the message.

Fluency is the ability to talk and write about the ideas that are fighting to get out of one's head. A nice analogy for fluency is that of telling a joke, a humor genre that is formulaic and offers structure, much like the *formula development* some of the clients sought. The first time I try to tell a new joke, it tends to fall flat, and listeners are not sure what to laugh at, if anything. By the third or fourth time I tell that joke, I am better at it, and listeners usually laugh. After I have gotten the hang of telling that joke, I begin to add a few new elements of tone, register, or words and the joke has become my own to tell. I am in control of the joke. People laugh. Fluency of a joke—an oral form—is then compromised when I then try to write out the joke. How can I convey in words alone the tone and register necessary to make it laugh-worthy? Once again, I'm dysfluent. Becoming fluent in the written joke, an altogether new process, also takes my time and effort. It also takes understanding and developing the language of laughter.

When I provide workshops to educators, I share that each course students take as undergraduates and graduates requires them to grapple with new ideas. Each subject stresses them cognitively as they try to figure out what they are learning and to assimilate information into knowledge. In postsecondary settings particularly, students are in three to five courses a term, meaning they must convert information into knowledge in all those courses. Many teachers ask students to demonstrate knowledge through written papers, sometimes multiple papers a term. That is a lot of information conversion! The very process of writing, as writing studies professionals know, is one in which writers can take unfamiliar material and transform it into something familiar, which is one reason we teach students about *drafting and revision*. This writing process enables writers to discover their ideas and work with them more deeply; eventually—if time, life, and thinking allow—writers become able to express what they really think or want to say with some degree of confidence and clarity.

Therefore, I share with educators, if students only write one draft, their writing will seem to be fuzzy and their point unclear simply because the ideas *are* fuzzy and the point *is* unclear. Time and (re)working of the ideas are needed for composition fluency to emerge. Anything less is dysfluent. When students are writing multiple papers a term on multiple new and intellectually challenging topics, they may, by the end of the term, merely begin to become truly fluent with just a few of the ideas they have been struggling with. When they begin with new material in the next term, students genuinely need to seek fluency with new ideas, information, and knowledge. That is one reason professors of other disciplines complain that students apparently were not taught to write in their writing courses; those professors simply do not understand the serious cognitive and writing work that transforms composition dysfluency to fluency in every single course and for every single topic covered in each of those courses! Postsecondary education is a lot about composition fluency and the necessary dysfluency that precedes it.

So, too, with dissertating writers. They not only are attempting to produce "new" and "original" knowledge, but they are doing so in an unknown, often untaught, and high-stakes genre—the dissertation—that they will never use again. Dissertation writing, which I do not address in this chapter, harbors its own major challenges with fluency stemming from the genre itself, its high-stakes nature, and often unrealistic expectations. Then, when the dissertation is complete (or sometimes as part of the dissertation itself), academia expects publishable scholarly papers from it; these papers also necessarily must pass through phases of composition dysfluency to reach fluency and potential for publication. The expectation for learning *publishing processes* makes these papers high stakes, too. The *genre transitions* from dissertation to articles and/or books or from new research to articles or books again force writers to learn new high-stakes genres. This work requires what one of the clients cited in the study above called a "throughline," again necessitating that writers make fluent arguments. The academy complicates these high-stakes knowledge and genre concerns with the need to make insightful or so-called "original" arguments, the requirement to contextualize any new ideas within the discipline's tradition of using others' published scholarship, and the necessity of being crystal clear—well, composition dysfluency reigns for quite a few drafts and deep revisions.

Writing processes that emerge in seeking composition fluency certainly include *content generation, organization* with frequent attempts at rearrangement of content, and *style and correctness* preceded by a great deal of *drafting and revision*. For example, academic writers who think they only need "editing" may not realize that by "editing" they mean deep revision, often guided by astute coaches or mentors as readers. Of course, when, where, and how to *research* typically is early work in the search for how to delineate and then express one's own ideas, but the "re" in "research" calls upon scholars to search again and again over the course of a project's development. *Length* commonly is a genre issue, but it is also an issue of being clear, as composition fluency may require a divergence or two from the main idea to fully clarify that main idea—first for the writer and then for the readers.

There can be no question that issues of *time and project management* interfere with academic writers' abilities to meet their project goals. Academic writers, whether they have part-time or full-time positions, tend to have ample concerns regarding *finding writing time* amidst multiple work tasks and family needs. For that, some really benefit from *being held accountable* by coaches who care about their success. Although I nested *life-work balance* within the major category of *contextualizing concerns* in this study, these clients' own words revealed that children, teaching, and pandemic adjustments certainly impacted their writing. The inability to keep up strenuous intellectual work daily when combined with other serious endeavors—like families, *mental health concerns*, and self-care (which was addressed only by one client who insisted on physical workouts, revealing by its absence elsewhere in the responses that lack of attention to self-care is another reason academics may suffer when writing)—strongly indicates that scholarly writing requires some *scheduled writing time*. Not finding writing time or having scheduled is part of the need to *balance cognitive work with other demands* and, in combination, these suggest that composition fluency again is at risk in academic writers' lives.

Cognitive work may be enjoyable—it certainly is for me—but it is hard work that can be exhausting. Particularly using larger chunks of time to get into flow work, one's mind and body may become tired; moving on to another cognitively challenging task like teaching becomes harder over time (or is that age?), requiring more rest and balance of life and work demands. It is crucial to the academic "life of the mind" that it also must be a life of the body and the heart. Otherwise, burnout and lack of productivity are the inevitable results. People who are *working with large or multiple projects* may find themselves especially taxed because their cognition is being challenged in multiple areas. There can be no question that finding and keeping a sense of composition fluency is affected when one is pulled from one intellectual task to another; returning to one of those tasks on another day means beginning in a state of dysfluency while, minimally, reminding oneself of the previous session's work and discovered meaning in the drafted writing. Those with learning or other cognitively experienced *disabilities* may struggle even more to recover earlier fluency and to stay on task with it in a new session.

Finally, the issue of *original and additional languages* arises. Many writers are linguistically fluent in speaking, reading, and writing multiple languages. It is challenging enough to find linguistic fluency in a single language like English; to be a native writer in a different language means that one likely is a native thinker and speaker in that language. Such multilingual capability necessarily interferes to some degree with finding clarity in English, an issue of composition dysfluency even for those who know exactly what they want to say should they be able to say or write it in the native language (CCCC, 2020; Lu & Horner, 2016). One coach told me that we are all nonnative speakers in the language of writing. Of course. Orality is primary; reading and writing are secondary and tertiary (Ong, 2002). Undoubtedly, matters of original and additional languages create composition fluency challenges for many academic writers.

CONCLUSION

Given my premise that challenges with composition fluency and dysfluency are common to all the writers in this study, additional research would be helpful in seeing how coaches support them. Such research into these or other academic writing coaching clients would usefully involve data from consultations, interviews, coach perspectives, and the writing itself. Additionally, viewing this study data through the lenses of my colleagues' ideas expressed in this book also would yield new understanding of professional academic writers' needs.

That said, it would be especially helpful for coaches, mentors, editors, and reviewers to bring to their reading of unpublished academic scholarship and their interactions with academic writers a variety of strategies for identifying how other conditions and contexts might lead to composition dysfluency. Editors and reviewers especially might support writers with good ideas by offering a response that encourages those ideas and supports them with specific suggestions for revision. Among their suggestions might be to access a mentor or professional writing coach who can assist with finding the keys to fluency for the piece. Writers who seek publication have something to say and may need support in bringing that message to the forefront. Those who assist academic writers can help them by understanding what is interfering with composition fluency and then working with the writers to eliminate the roadblocks they can, map ways to circumvent the roadblocks they cannot eliminate, and build new roads to writing with clarity.

REFERENCES

Association of Departments of English. (1992). ADE guidelines for class size and workload. *Association of Departments of English.* https://tinyurl.com/38db57b5.

Bloom, L. Z. (1981). Why graduate students can't write: Implications of research on writing anxiety for graduate education. *Journal of Advanced Composition 2*(1–2), 103–17.

Bogdan, R. & Biklen, S. (1992). *Qualitative research for education: An introduction to theory and methods.* Allyn and Bacon.

Boice, R. & Jones, F. (1984). Why academicians don't write. *Journal of Higher Education 55*(5), 567–582.

Bourelle, T., Hewett, B. L. & Warnock, S. (2022). *Administering writing programs in the 21st century.* Modern Language Association.

Britton, J., Burgess, T., Martin, N., McLeod, A. & Rosen, H. (1975). *The development of writing abilities (11–18).* Macmillan Education.

Brooke, C. & Carr, A. (2015). Failure can be an important part of writing development. In L. Adler-Kassner & E. Wardle (Eds.), *Naming what we know: Threshold concepts of writing studies* (pp. 62–63). Utah State University Press.

Bruffee, K. A. (1984). Collaborative learning and the "conversation of mankind." *College English, 46,* 635–653. https://doi.org/10.2307/376924.

Bruffee, K. A. (1993). *Collaborative learning: Higher education, interdependence, and the authority of knowledge.* Johns Hopkins University Press.

Cahusac de Caux, B. (2021). Doctoral candidates' academic writing output and strategies: Navigating the challenges of academic writing during a global health crisis. *International Journal of Doctoral Studies, 16,* 291–317. https://doi.org/10.28945/4755.

Chanock, K. (2007). Helping thesis writers to think about genre: What is prescribed, what may be possible. *WAC Journal, 18,* 32–41. https://doi.org/10.37514/WAC-J.2007.18.1.03.

Cicero. (1988). *Cicero II: De invention, De optimo genere oratorum, Topica* (E. W. Sutton & H. Rackham, Trans.). Harvard University Press.

Conference on College Composition and Communication (CCCC). (2013). A position statement of principles and example effective practices for online writing instruction. Committee for Effective Practices in Online Writing Instruction. https://cdn.ncte.org/nctefiles/groups/cccc/owiprinciples.pdf.

Conference on College Composition and Communication (CCCC). (2015). Principles for the postsecondary teaching of writing. National Council of Teachers of English. https://ncte.org/statement/postsecondarywriting.

Conference on College Composition and Communication (CCCC). (2016a). CCCC statement of best practices in faculty hiring for tenure-track and non-tenure-track positions in rhetoric and composition/writing studies. National Council of Teachers of English. https://cccc.ncte.org/cccc/resources/positions/faculty-hiring.

Conference on College Composition and Communication (CCCC). (2016b). CCCC statement on working conditions for non-tenure-track writing faculty. National

Council of Teachers of English. https://cccc.ncte.org/cccc/resources/positions/working-conditions-ntt.
Conference on College Composition and Communication (CCCC). (2020). Disability studies in composition: Position statement on policy and best practices. National Council of Teachers of English. https://cccc.ncte.org/cccc/resources/positions/disabilitypolicy.
Creswell, J. W. (2014). *Research design: Qualitative, quantitative, and mixed methods approaches.* Sage.
Denizen, N. K. & Lincoln, Y. S. (2011). *The Sage handbook of qualitative research.* Sage.
Franke, A. H., Bérubé, M. F., Neil, R. M. et al. (2012). Accommodating faculty members who have disabilities. *Academe, 98*(4), 1–13.
Geller, A. E. & Eodice, M. (Eds.). (2013). *Working with faculty writers.* Utah State University Press.
Hewett, B. L. (2015a). *Reading to learn and writing to teach: Literacy strategies for online writing instruction.* Bedford/St. Martin's Press.
Hewett, B. L. (2015b). *The online writing conference: A guide for teachers and tutors.* Bedford/St. Martin's.
Hewett, B. L., Bourelle, T. & Warnock, S. (2022). *Teaching writing in the 21st century.* Modern Language Association.
Hewett, B. L. & Ehmann, C. (2004). *Preparing educators for online writing instruction: Principles and processes.* National Council of Teachers of English.
Keller, D. (2014). *Chasing literacy: Reading and writing in an age of acceleration.* Utah State University Press.
Knowles, M. S., Holton III, E. F. & Swanson, R. A. (1998). *The adult learner: The definitive classic in adult education and human resource development* (5th ed.). Gulf Publishing.
Lu, M. Z. & Horner, B. (2016). Translingual work. *College English, 78*(3), 207–218.
Marshak, R. (1983). What's between pedagogy and andragogy? *Training and Development Journal (October),* 80–81.
McClain, K. & Murray, J. (2016). An analysis of job listings on rhetmap.org for junior scholars: Academic years spanning 2013–2014, 2014–2015, and 2015–2016. http://rhetmap.org/doc/2013to2016rhetmapreport.pdf.
Modern Language Association (MLA). (2023a). MLA recommendation on a minimum salary for full-time entry-level faculty members. Modern Language Association. https://tinyurl.com/4tf6m379.
Modern Language Association (MLA). (2023b). MLA recommendation on minimum per-course compensation for part-time faculty members. Modern Language Association. https://tinyurl.com/54nx2uzk.
National Council of Teachers of English (NCTE). (2020). NCTE position paper on the role of English teachers in educating English language learners (ELLs). National Council of Teachers of English. https://ncte.org/statement/teaching-english-ells.
National Council of Teachers of English (NCTE). (2023). Culturally and historically responsive education. National Council of Teachers of English. https://tinyurl.com/3vkdrdhs.

NextGen. (n.d.). *International scholars anti-discrimination (ISAD) open letter. Google Drive.* https://drive.google.com/file/d/11WB6alGV9nZoX7DnAcP-FFa69Myh-HE8/view.
Ong, W. J. (1975). The writer's audience is always a fiction. *PMLA 90*, 9–21.
Ong, W. (2002). *Orality and literacy: The technologizing of the word.* Routledge.
Oswal, S. K. (2015). Physical and learning disabilities in OWI. In B. L. Hewett & K. E. DePew (Eds.) *Foundational practices of online writing instruction* (pp. 253–289). The WAC Clearinghouse; Parlor Press. https://doi.org/10.37514/PER-B.2015.0650.2.08.
Oswal, S. & Hewett, B. L. (2013). Accessibility challenges for visually impaired students and their online writing instructors." In L. Meloncon (Ed.), *Rhetorical accessibility: At the intersection of technical education and disability studies* (pp. 135–155). Baywood.
Pimentel, O., Pimentel, C. & Dean, J. (2017). The myth of the colorblind writing classroom: White instructors confront white privilege in their classrooms. In F. Condon & V. A. Young (Eds.), *Performing antiracist pedagogy in rhetoric, writing, and communication.* (pp. 109–122). The WAC Clearinghouse; University Press of Colorado. https://doi.org/10.37514/ATD-B.2016.0933.2.05.
Porter, J. E. (1996). Audience. In T. Enos (Ed.) *Encyclopedia of rhetoric and composition: Communication from ancient times to the information age* (pp. 42–49). Garland.
Rice, R. (2015). Faculty professionalization for OWI. In B. L. Hewett and K. DePew (Eds.) *Foundational practices of online writing instruction* (pp. 389–410). The WAC Clearinghouse; Parlor Press. https://doi.org/10.37514/PER-B.2015.0650.2.12.
Selber, S. A. (2004). *Multiliteracies for a digital age.* Southern Illinois University Press.
Sharma, S. (2018). *Writing support for international graduate students: Enhancing transition and success.* Routledge. https://doi.org/10.4324/9781351054980.
Shaughnessy, M. P. (1979). *Errors and expectations: A guide for the teacher of basic writing.* Oxford University Press.
Steinert, Y., McLeod, P. J., Liben, S. & Snell, L. (2008). Writing for publication in medical education: The benefits of a faculty development workshop and peer writing group. *Medical Teacher, 30*(8), 280–285. https://doi.org/10.1080/01421590802337120.
Tarabochia, S. & Madden, S. (2019). In transition: Researching the writing development of doctoral students and faculty. *Writing & Pedagogy, 10*(3), 423–452. https://doi.org/10.1558/wap.34576.
Tulley, C. (2018). *How writing faculty write: Strategies for process, product, productivity.* Utah State University Press.
Wells, J. M. & Söderlund, L. (2017). Preparing graduate students for academic publishing: Results from a study of published rhetoric and composition scholars. *Pedagogy: Critical Approaches to Teaching Literature, Language, Composition, and Culture, 18*(1), 131–156. https://doi.org/10.1215/15314200-4216994.

CHAPTER 8.

INTENTIONAL INSTITUTIONAL SUPPORT FOR FUTURE FACULTY: A FOCUS ON GRANT AND PROFESSIONAL WRITING

Charmian Lam
Indiana University

Abstract: *This chapter examines the role of institutional support for doctoral students and early-career faculty, emphasizing grant writing and professional materials. Using grounded theory, I connect the development of academic identity with targeted writing support, showing that external training in faculty skills significantly aids students' sense of belonging and professional success.*

Authors in writing and composition studies have declared a need to examine how graduate students transition into academia (Yancey, 2013) and to critically address increasing racial diversity in the field (Carter-Tod, 2019; Mueller & Ruiz, 2017). Writing studies is also uniquely situated because the practice of writing is involved in so many stages of beginning and maintaining an academic career and because writing is often inseparable from one's identity. Yancey's (2013) special issue on the profession in *College Composition and Communication* called for an examination into how graduate students transition into academia and showed "a variegated portrait of the profession" (p. 8). However, few studies leveraged knowledge about inclusive graduate student development as future faculty to address why individuals with minoritized identities are not joining the professoriate. Thus, I use the literature in higher education about graduate student belonging as future faculty to inform the existing, inclusive efforts across writing and composition studies.

Given the well-studied topics of graduate student teaching and second language development pertaining to graduate student development as faculty, I endeavor to show how intentional writing development has implications for graduate students' sense of belonging within their academic and professional communities in the humanities and social sciences. First, a review of the research on graduate student writing development and sense of belonging is provided, with close attention to the experiences of students with minoritized identities. Then, I present and discuss a study that used a grounded approach and thematically analyzed six semi-structured interviews with doctoral students in the humanities and social sciences at a public, predominately white, R1 institution. In the results, I featured my participants' suggestions and advice to fellow graduate students, faculty mentors, and program administrators. Exploration into this area is important to stakeholders who are invested in improving the experience of graduate students who are developing into faculty and increasing opportunities for their success. This chapter addresses the implications of minoritized graduate student writing development on students' senses of belonging within their disciplines, with focus on these questions:

1. What are the required, yet implicit skills graduate students must learn as future faculty writers?
2. Where and how do graduate students learn to become faculty writers?
3. How have training experiences in faculty writing affected participants' sense of belonging in academia and within their respective disciplines?

LITERATURE REVIEW

Professional development (PD) is the experience of "multidimensional growth" engendered by traditional academic experiences, mentoring, peer relations, introspection, training, and supervision (Ducheny et al., 1997). Teaching and research skills are the most common purposes and topics of PD and are overwhelmingly represented among studies about formal graduate student development (Brill et al., 2014; Rizzolo et al., 2016). However, graduate student definitions and expectations of PD extend beyond teaching and research. Ducheny et al. (1997), in a study of 604 psychology graduate students' definitions of PD, found that PD was not perceived as discrete, event-based skills training. Instead, they found that PD is a complex process of incorporating "personal and professional experiences, profession-based and individual values, skills and areas of expertise, educational background, and the establishment of professional relationships"(p. 89). Given the individualistic definition of PD according to graduate students, further research is needed that examines how graduate students obtain writing skills that prepare them as faculty, such as the writing of grant applications and job letters.

Of all the topics of PD, writing development beyond the disciplines (e.g., job materials and grant writing) is least represented in the literature and is one of the most high-stakes and personal topics addressed (Austin & McDaniels,

2006; Mitic & Okahana, 2021). As used in this chapter, the term *academic* writing differs from *professional* writing in that the former refers to skills situated within disciplinary conventions in research, teaching, or other scholarly work. This study is concerned with professional writing, which describes transferable writing skills, ranging from grant applications and writing for the job market or career advancement. In most institutions, writing training for graduate students entails mentorship with faculty advisors on the topics of academic writing, research, and teaching (Austin & McDaniels, 2006; Rose, 2012).

But the role of faculty also includes writing in administrative contexts, such as securing research funding (Austin & McDaniels, 2006) and preparing job materials (Dadas, 2013). Shortcomings in training have implications for a lower sense of belonging in academia, especially for those with minoritized identities (Strayhorn, 2019).

Why Belonging Matters

Several authors have defined a sense of belonging, but most of the studies have done so with undergraduate students. Sense of belonging is a context-dependent feeling associated with being a valued and supported member of one or more communities at an institution (Goodenow & Grady, 1993; Hausmann et al., 2007; Strayhorn, 2019). Hurtado and Carter (1997), in a foundational study of belonging, argued that belonging is not integration or assimilation, as such a model implies that minoritized individuals must normalize by adhering to the dominant cultures within an institution. Belonging matters particularly for students with minoritized identities because it is associated with academic persistence (Strayhorn, 2019) and is fostered through identity-affirming cultures (Hurtado & Carter, 1997) and positive and authentic relationships with peers and faculty (Meeuwisse et al., 2010). There have been relatively fewer studies of how graduate students experience belonging and the implications of it on outcomes. Some studies suggest that belonging is "markedly different" for graduate students (Gardner & Barnes, 2007, p. 369), giving impetus for this study, since writing professional materials is one of the ways that graduate students gain acceptance into their discipline.

This chapter focuses on the minoritized identities pertaining to ethnicity, race, and international student status, because these identity markers are referred to when calls to diversify the writing discipline are made (Carter-Tod, 2019; Mueller & Ruiz, 2017). Belonging helps those with minoritized identities feel like they are valued members of their discipline, especially when others in the discipline are white (Ore et al., 2021; Strayhorn, 2019). The topic of race in the field has long been a focus for many scholars, such as Victor Villanueva

(1993) and Asao Inoue (2019). But few scholars have considered how learning professional writing skills may influence graduate students belonging in their disciplines. Writing professional materials are often not formally taught (i.e., in a course) and lack of skill composing them can be a bottleneck for entry into and belonging in academia.

For whom and to what extent is belonging an issue? There are few national, longitudinal studies on graduate student transition into professional academia. In a 10-year longitudinal study, the National Center for Education Statistics reported that 23.3 percent of those who enrolled in a doctoral degree program between 1993 and 2003 were "no longer enrolled and had not obtained a degree" 10 years later (Nevill et al., 2007, p. vi). Nevill et al. showed that many factors are related to graduate persistence, but "these relationships may reflect more complexity among multiple factors" and are worth pursuing further (p. 55). The relatively lower rates of completion are often linked to the recurring theme of a feeling of isolation for graduate students (Strayhorn, 2019) or lack of institutional support in the form of peer and faculty mentorship (Mitic & Okahana, 2021). More intentional institutional support is needed given the implications for graduate student belonging, especially for students with minoritized identities.

Professional Writing and Minoritized Graduate Students

The Council of Graduate Schools' report on the value, timing, and participation in PhD professional development (PD, n=4,370) found career preparation and grant writing to be among the most important skills according to graduate students (Mitic & Okahana, 2021). Job market preparation and grant writing are two areas that are commonly addressed as missing (Heflinger & Doykos, 2016). Compared to other similarly valued skills, 70 percent of respondents noted that opportunities for training in grant writing were either not offered or respondents were unaware of them (Mitic & Okahana, 2021). Indeed, international professional organizations, such as the Consortium on Graduate Communication, provide help to members in at least 27 countries. However, help remains behind a paywall and is an extra step for industrious or well-connected graduate students.

Academic perseverance and professional identity development have been linked with mentorship and support (Brill et al., 2014). Graduate students are motivated to seek training and development because they desire to develop a professional identity within an academic community (Austin & McDaniels, 2006; Ducheny et al., 1997). Strayhorn (2019), in a mixed methods study of 360 graduate students at 15 different institutions, found formal and informal socialization, defined as meaningful engagement and exposure to peers and faculty, a critical aspect of a sense of belonging. Additionally, having a sense of belonging contributes to students' performance, satisfaction, and success in doctoral programs (Curtin et al., 2013; Strayhorn, 2019). Pascale (2018) found that graduate students experienced belonging through perceived peer support, perceived faculty support, class comfort, perceived isolation, and empathetic faculty understanding. Pascale also found that graduate students, dissimilar to undergraduates, valued balancing school with life when forming a sense of belonging. This suggests that institutional initiatives for graduate student belonging should consider incorporating students' families to some extent.

The existing studies on positive graduate student belonging point to two major influences: mentorship with faculty and socialization within the academic community, especially for students with minoritized identities (Le et al., 2016; Curtin et al., 2013). Minority and international students often experience additional labor for social adjustment including, but not limited to: (a) language difficulties and cultural differences; (b) unfamiliar patterns of classroom interactions, academic norms, and conventions; (c) inadequate learning support; (d) difficulties in making friends with domestic students; and (e) lack of sense of belonging (Le et al., 2016). Curtin et al. (2013) compared the experiences of belonging and academic self-concept for 841domestic and international students and concluded that international students are less likely to cite belonging as an important factor to their research and academic success.

On the other hand, domestic minority graduate students value belonging and, compared to their majority counterparts, are statistically less likely to find faculty mentors with similar cultural backgrounds because of the shortage of minority faculty in higher education for the majority of disciplines. But those who find supportive faculty mentors give effusive credit for their openness and flexibility (Le et al., 2016). Using ANCOVA, Curtin et al. (2013) found within-group differences in how domestic and international students experienced advisor support (p. 108). Support, defined as professional and socializing advice and emotional support, was found to directly improve students' sense of belonging and academic self-concept.

Filling the Gaps in Faculty Mentorship

The importance of faculty mentorship on graduate student belonging and success cannot be emphasized enough, as reviewed in the previous section. While this practice is highly individualized, the quality of the writing training also depends on graduate students' working relationship with their mentor, which makes for uneven training. In general, minority and international students rely on a mixture of strategies to receive training, including self-development among peers and on-campus resources (Holley & Caldwell, 2012; Le et al., 2016). Nonetheless, many students turn to institutional resources for self-development because of a perceived lack of expertise from faculty (Austin & McDaniels, 2006; Heflinger & Doykos, 2016). Faculty tend to train on matters immediately relevant to students' academic roles (e.g., teaching and research assistant), but teaching and research are only a part of the responsibility associated with faculty positions (Austin & McDaniels, 2006). Indeed, Dadas's (2013) study on job market preparedness among 57 scholars in rhetoric and composition showed how not all graduate students were adequately trained to write as faculty. Some students seek additional help in centers for professional development, such as centers of teaching and learning or career centers (Rose, 2012).

In a mixed methods study of 688 doctoral students at a mid-sized Southeastern U.S. university, Heflinger and Doykos (2016) found many notable gaps in training regarding leading research teams, supervising others, teaching, and grant writing. Many students suggested the creation of structured, cross-discipline collaborative mentorships to better prepare students and reduce disciplinary "siloing" (Heflinger & Doykos, 2016, pp. 351–352). Along those lines, Austin and McDaniels (2016) add that grant-making skills are "important for future faculty members to start to develop while in graduate school" (p. 425).

When present, grant writing workshops have been helpful in the professional development of graduate students. In one quantitative case study of a grant writing preparation workshop for communications graduate students, respondents had "overwhelmingly positive experiences" (Mackert et al., 2017, p. 246). Respondents felt the program provided great value, improved their writing skills, gave them skills to pursue funding in the future, and helped them secure tenure-track faculty positions. Their program is designed to train future health communication scholars in finding funding and submitting applications as faculty and researchers. Research on PD and senses of belonging for graduate students suggests that such a well-received program may have had a positive effect on the professional identity of the participants (Curtin et al., 2013; Posselt, 2021; Strayhorn, 2019). Mackert et al. (2016) did not extend the scope of the study to determine whether their programming had any farther-reaching effects, such as sense of belonging.

In summation, professional development is imperative for engendering a sense of belonging within the academic and professional community for graduate students. A sense of belonging has been linked with perseverance in students and, by extension, the subsequent job candidate (Curtin et al., 2013; Strayhorn, 2019). While factors such as financial support aid in creating a sense of

Intentional Institutional Support for Future Faculty

belonging, budgets are often out of the control of faculty. Institutions and faculty can use existing programming and mentorships to develop doctoral students' skills and grant and professional writing to increase their senses of belonging.

METHOD

This study was conducted with respondents from a large, Midwestern, doctoral degree-granting public institution classified with "very high research activity." According to institutional data, the majority (65.4%) of doctoral degrees are conferred through the business school, college of arts and sciences, school of public and environmental affairs, law school, school of engineering, and school of education. All interviews were recorded and kept following IRB-compliant procedures.

SAMPLE

Six respondents (Table 8.1) were recruited via email to participate in semi-structured interviews about their experiences pertaining to professional development resources and the opportunities available to them. Each interview lasted approximately 30 minutes. The respondents were either doctoral students (n=2), doctoral candidates (n=2), or alumni with recent successful job placements (n=2). Respondents were either enrolled in or had just graduated from programs in the humanities or social sciences. Additionally, all participants experienced the entirety of their doctoral program at the same institution.

Table 8.1 Demographics of Respondents

Respondent	Gender	Race / Ethnicity	Educational Status	Discipline	Residency Status
Moira	Female	Black	Doc Student	Counseling Psychology	International
Fernando	Male	Latino	Doc Student	Spanish and Portuguese	International
Kel	Female	White	Doc Candidate	English	Domestic
Jackie	Female	Black	Doc Candidate	Higher Education	Domestic
Su Hyun	Female	Asian	Alumni	Literacy Studies	International
Christine	Female	White	Alumni	English	Domestic

Note: All names have been changed.

DATA COLLECTION AND ANALYSIS

Data collection and analysis followed the practices common to grounded theory (Charmaz, 2014). Created by Barney G. Glaser and Anselm L. Strauss in the mid–1960s, grounded theory is a qualitative, inductive approach where researchers develop categories and theories about a phenomenon, rather than test a hypothesis. Constructivist grounded theory is an ideal tool for interpreting trends in research participants' lives because of its main principles: interpretation without preconceived theories, a deeper read of data through an iterative analytical process, and the understanding that social phenomena are interpreted through researchers' subjectivity (Charmaz, 2014). In essence, researchers who use grounded theory see a phenomenon and build questions that extract both the context and the interviewee's experiences and meanings. In this case, the research questions and interview questions (Appendix A) were formed after I was made aware of the experiences of alienation from a perceived lack of writing training in my position in graduate student development at my institution.

The interview data for each participant were closely read for markers of meaning from the interviewees, such as conversational cues and choice of words to describe their experiences. Researcher reflections and analysis of the interviews were recorded in a memo. Next, codes that emerged from each interview served as points of comparison for the next person's interview, and so on. The codes and data then helped the researcher form additional areas to explore in subsequent interviews (Charmaz, 2014). From there, researcher reflections in memos defined preliminary analytic categories of experiences for the respondents.

POSITIONALITY

Researchers are the primary interpretive instruments that are shaped by their larger social and cultural context; thus, a positionality statement places known biases at the forefront. I embody a diversity of identities and understand that the intersection of my dominant and nondominant identities shapes my worldview. At the time of this study, I was a graduate student in the work of graduate student professional development; as such, this topic is professionally and personally meaningful. My interpretations, as a result, reflect my perspective. To mitigate that, and to share some of the power in meaning making, the voices and experiences of students are featured as much as possible. Additionally, I consciously chose not to compare students to straight, white, cisgender, heterosexual men, who are often overrepresented in study samples, because doing so implicitly holds them as the ideal, comparative standard, thus reinforcing existing hierarchical structures of power. It is my intention to add complexity and authenticity to the portrayal of those studied, disrupting the common monolithic portrayal of underrepresented and minoritized students.

RESULTS

Emergent codes included graduate students' experiences of professional development across the humanities and social sciences within one institution, a separation between preparation for academic and administrative/professional writing, and how graduate students addressed the perceived shortcomings in their writing training.

Graduate Perceptions of Professional Development and Belonging

Starting questions in grounded theory are often the "what" and "how," aimed at eliciting participants' experiences (Charmaz, 2014). Though coding general experiences was rather straightforward, it is nonetheless helpful to establish a starting point for comparison. Participants revealed how their perspectives and expectations of receiving PD changed as they progressed through their graduate careers. Many described a "growing up" or adopting a realistic perspective of the outcome of a PhD colored by job prospects. Others expressed frustration at the lack of training throughout their years in their programs. Ultimately, experiences vary, and training is highly dependent on the mentorship style and availability of the faculty advisor.

At the beginning of their respective doctoral programs, respondents either did not think about professional development for the job market or trusted their programs to help them identify and develop the necessary skills. Christine (white, domestic, alumni in English) noted that, at the beginning of her program, she was "naive about the importance of job market training." Fernando (Latino, international doctoral student in Spanish and Portuguese) chastised himself for thinking that a doctoral program was just "more undergraduate college, taking classes and writing papers." He said that, while he did think about his career, he did not think about the details, and thought the department would prepare him. Kel (white, domestic, doctoral candidate in English) remarked that she expected her department to function as a directory, or "hub," to external resources for professional development.

On the other hand, Jackie (Black, domestic, doctoral candidate in Education) and Su Hyun (Asian, international, alumni in Literacy Studies) were very cognizant of the need to tie their graduate experiences to their future careers "from day one." Both recall attending departmental and external professional development workshops even as a first-year student. Jackie admits to being very career-driven and stated, "When I decided to go back to school, I knew that I had to bother people and make the most of everything because I didn't want to be stuck in a job again!" Su Hyun was also particularly career-focused, expressing high stakes as an international student pursuing a doctoral degree for her career: "My whole family relies on me. So, I'm meeting everyone and attending all different workshops and webinars."

Across all disciplines, race/ethnicity, nationality, and levels of career drive, minority identity, and discipline, respondents' expectations about professional development were largely not met within their departments and schools. Many, such as Moira and Kel, expressed frustration. Moira is an international Black doctoral student in counseling psychology, a department within the school of education. She said, "I'm not from here. I just want an understanding of how things work." When asked about how much training she received about writing, she said, "Grants? Umm, zero. That's the thing. Even as the support for the program is teaching us how to write articles, even quals and writing articles for journals, there is no structural support that you get. They just expect that you're going to do it." Kel acknowledged that grants were important to her graduate career and perhaps to her future faculty life, but her department did not provide any training. Conversely, Su Hyun only had positive things to say about her faculty advisor: "If he didn't know [the answer], he knew someone who knew." Fernando said that his experiences were mixed, "[his faculty advisor] was very helpful with getting papers published. It's like wow, you're giving comments at 10pm? Thank you!" But he was disappointed in the amount of help he received in securing grants for research. Fernando recalled struggling to know "what was right" when starting to draft grant proposals for his dissertation research and didn't know where to turn for help.

Ultimately, Moira provided a great explanation of the variation in graduate experiences of professional development: "It's at the level of the individual faculty rather than a structural component in the program to help people." Kel added, "The degree and quality of training really varies and is dependent on advisors."

TRAINED AND UNTRAINED WRITING

Though respondents spoke about writing as a monolithic skill, three types of writing emerged in the coding: (a) job materials; (b) administrative, professional writing; and (c) grant applications. Across all three types, students who participated in workshops or collaborated with faculty members to obtain skills described themselves as having been trained. Conversely, students who completed such writing tasks without training described it as "untrained writing." When respondents, especially minoritized students, experienced a lack of training, they expressed self-doubt about their academic progress or viability on the job market. Quality training in professional writing helped international students' confidence as job candidates and their sense of belonging in the discipline and department. Su Hyun explained that professional writing was difficult at times because she was uncomfortable with the "braggy" tone in job materials for American positions. Her department did not train her, but her advisor helped edit her materials. Not all training is equal; a messy writing workshop appeared to have deleterious effects on belonging. Fernando described his professional seminar, a required class for doctoral students in his department, as "chaotic." The instructor used too many student-led lessons that resulted in a confused cohort. He stated, "I found the training to be alienating, especially because I am international, and less and less like I belonged in the field." Christine felt similarly to Fernando, despite having a different discipline. She remembers thinking, "Oh I've done everything wrong" in terms of applying for future jobs. Christine noted that the workshop "was very R1 oriented and in terms of support." The training consisted of reading samples individually, drafting without instruction, and graduate student peer editing. She summed up: "There was no discussion of genre. No discussion of what it does and what should it do and what it does well."

Two respondents from social sciences also felt unprepared in their field practicum experiences due to a perceived insufficiency in their training for administrative writing. Moira, an international Black counseling psychology doctoral student, remarked about the gap between what she learned in the classroom and what was expected in her counseling practicum: "The department did teach us some assessments, but what was a little bit of letdown is that they thought we should learn in practicum. And practicum expected me to know them already." She trained herself in administrative writing for her practicum by reading her supervisor's previous reports to learn the professional genre. Su Hyun agreed regarding classroom practicum, stating that she had to learn how to write and give feedback to her students in her first year of teaching by herself, not from her classes or her advisor.

Grant writing was largely untrained. In some cases, grant writing was part of a required academic benchmark, such as qualifying exams. Moira stated, "There's been no real training in that regard. [The program expects] us to pick it up explicitly in program experience, but no one teaches it." In a similar vein, Jackie reflects on her department's common usage of a grant proposal as a prompt for qualifying exams, though she did not receive any training in her coursework for such a task. She asked emphatically and rhetorically, "Now where was I supposed to know this from?" She said that her experience made her question her future in the program and in the discipline. Jackie stated, "We didn't talk about grants at all in our classes. I get that they're trying to help us to apply later but writing it first for quals put a bad taste in my mouth" for future grant applications. Fernando echoed Jackie's sentiments when he sought grant funding for his travels to Spain to collect data for his dissertation. He added, "Honestly? I Googled a lot to find examples, wrote something, and my advisor ended up revising all of it. I felt so stupid. Like, I can't do this." For Christine, knowledge of grant writing was more important to her professional roles than her role as a student. As part of her employment as a writing tutor during her doctoral studies, she attended the grant workshops facilitated by the institution's graduate school but did not hear about them from her department. Otherwise, she would not have known about the training.

Three types of professional writing emerged in the code when respondents described their experience in receiving writing training. Respondents described how either the lack of training or the "trial by fire" method of training instilled a low sense of belonging within the discipline and in their department. It appeared that many students either created or joined training external to their departments and schools, as explained in this next section.

Individually Bridging the Gap

The participants described mixed training experiences in professional writing and job preparation from their departments. Some said that they "felt" the departmental training was insufficient when comparing perceived skills required for faculty positions. Others knew the training was not enough because the departments "had no idea what [they] were doing" when drafting job materials. As such, most respondents experienced disappointment or insecurity about their academic belonging. Respondents sought to supplement perceived shortcomings in professional development with help external to their department, either by asking others for writing help and/or searching for new opportunities to gain skills.

Christine was in a lucky position because she could ask a newly hired faculty member about professional materials in their field, except for a diversity statement, as the faculty member did not prepare one. When Christine found her departmental workshops insufficient, she turned to her institution's center for teaching and learning. She said, "I went to [center for teaching] and learned a lot about writing a diversity statement and pedagogy. [A newly hired faculty member] didn't have to write a diversity statement I think, so he couldn't help me." Others were not as fortunate to have a new hire; however, cold calling and informational interviews seemed to help.

By her second year, Jackie wanted to get more experience before she was on the job market. She recalls, "The squeaky wheel gets oiled or uhh the loud mouth gets fed you know? I kept asking like can I join you on this research project? Can I be your TA? It worked. And I feel like I got training for writing articles I wouldn't have if I didn't ask." Jackie feels much more prepared for future roles as a teaching and research faculty because of her "cold calling" departmental instructors and institutional administrators. Christine was already on the job market and also did some "cold calling" about jobs, rather than focusing on writing skills. She felt that her departmental workshop on professional writing was not equipping her with the skills that she thought would be helpful. She recalled that all but one of the faculty members in her department "got jobs before diversity statements were a thing." Fernando joined an article-writing group coordinated by the university's writing center. He identified his advisor's greater interest in helping him edit articles rather than start them.

Moira and Kel criticized the need to seek external sources for professional development. They both mentioned how there is never enough time. Moira says she felt as if she was "taking on external experience to gain experience to use and being torn in 1 million directions to meet requirements for the department and job." If her counseling psychology classes trained her in the administrative genre conventions of her profession, she would not have to add more responsibilities to her already overbooked schedule. Graduate students in Kel's English department tried to start up a regular "brown bag [session]" during which different faculty would discuss job preparation, but it fell through from a lack of time. Kel shared that she was "already working two and more jobs; [there's] too much to do and not enough time and not enough money" as a graduate student. There was a strong implication that the department failed when a graduate student had to organize PD for everyone. Overall, participants filled the gaps in their writing training over the course of several steps: observations of necessary skills as future practitioners and faculty, self-assessment of abilities, and reaching out to their social and professional networks to help them secure training not provided by their departments.

LIMITATIONS

Conducting research faithfully requires acknowledgment of the limitations of this study. This study is limited by qualities common to all studies with small samples at one institution. First, case studies are one snapshot of a status quo for some at a singular point in time. The small sample size makes it impractical to generalize findings; however, the strength of case studies resides in in-depth analysis, and description rather than generalizability. This study aimed to examine the professional development of graduate students as future faculty and how their sense of belonging may have been connected. The findings are limited to graduate students in the humanities and social sciences by design, as many graduate students in STEM, for example, receive training in grant writing through their co-curricular lab placements (Thiry et al., 2011). Second, not all identities, or aspects of identities, are represented in the sample. It is possible that, with different students, other salient themes and topics would have subsequently emerged. Lastly, this study only shows the view of students who would voluntarily give their time and perspective. Given the topic of the study, engagement in professional development and belonging, an analysis of the students who are inclined toward diligence may allow for loose deductions to the rest of the population. We may never know the experiences and belongingness of students who do not participate in research.

DISCUSSION AND FUTURE DIRECTIONS

Findings suggest that graduate students in the humanities and social sciences need more intentional institutional support for writing skills that they will need as faculty members—namely, on-job materials and grant writing. Considering the variety of contexts in which graduate students write, intentionality requires a direct and purposeful drive when providing writing development for graduate students. Supportive writing development requires sustained effort and mindful timing to fit the busy schedules of graduate students and their faculty mentors. The creation of supportive, intentional writing training is an accessible practice because it negates the need for graduate students to find their own training or supplement training provided by their faculty mentors.

Contrary to Ducheny et al. (1997), this study's respondents spoke of PD as individual events. The respondents also implied that an *ending* point existed in PD as a graduate student, delineated by perceived self-confidence in completing academic and professional tasks. The contradiction may be due to some students' desires to compensate for the alienation felt in their departments. For example, much of Kel's training in professional writing was external to her department and occurred because of her job as a writing tutor, making her feel a sense of belonging with her workplace colleagues. Kel's experiences corroborate the findings in Phillips (2012), which presented graduate writing groups and writing centers as a community of practice for future academics (see Lave & Wenger, 1991). Though Kel received training in professional writing through her job, her department in the humanities did not provide support that engendered a sense of belonging in the department: "My experiences [in professional development] have negatively impacted my sense of belonging in the program and discipline." Su Hyun, on the other hand, had a positive experience. When asked why she thinks so, she said, "I already learned so much culture and writing coming here. [Learning administrative writing] is just the same." Additionally, her sense of belonging was positive, like the findings in Le et al. (2016) of other international Asian women.

Respondents unanimously report that job materials, administrative/professional writing (e.g., assessment reports, teaching observations), and grant applications are the required and implicit genres that graduate students must learn, for which they were provided with mixed levels of writing training at the institutional level. Lack of confidence in these genres was often associated with a low professional self-concept or sense of belonging among the participants. They regularly spoke of these three writing contexts having enough variations in tones, audiences, and purpose as to cause uncertainty and confusion for the writer. To prepare future faculty, graduate student development must include professional writing training in the discipline-specific contexts that extend beyond research. For example, writing reports and teaching reviews were only important to Moira and Su Hyun, respectively. Moira, a doctoral student in counseling psychology, taught herself to communicate as a future faculty member by decoding her supervisor's reports—a common strategy in writing studies. If formal training in this genre was available, it is likely that Moira would not feel alone and discouraged in the field. There is evidence that professional development in writing must distinguish between subgenres and offer discipline-specific content and guidance for positive influence on sense of belonging.

Lastly, graduate students gain external training by operationalizing institutional knowledge or cultural capital about academia. Individuals whose department prefers to do things "in house," as Christine said, often do not receive advertisements and callouts to institutionally organized workshops from departmental administrators. Instead, Christine had to be connected enough or be on the right email list to become aware of specific offerings for writing training. Fernando, similarly, had to find his own examples of the types of writing his advisor wanted him to do. Others, like Su Hyun, benefitted from knowledge shared by their advisors, who functioned as a signpost to institutional offices. Still others, like Jackie and Christine, who "cold called" administrators and instructors for opportunities, used their cultural and social capital to effectively communicate for employment and informational interviews. The respondents all thought that the responsibility of making students aware of PD opportunities resided with their departments and advisors.

IMPLICATIONS FOR GRADUATE STUDENTS

A few study participants noted the lack of time to engage in PD and other activities as graduate students. Su Hyun would like to remind graduate students that the same time challenges are true for their advisors; "Everyone is overworked and guards their time." Participants in this study were most satisfied with help that was external to their department as a starting place for skill development in professional writing. Institutions vary, but most have a center of teaching, a career center, and/or an office of graduate study that may offer assistance in the form of workshops or webinars. These events are attended by fellow graduate students in similar situations and experts in writing job materials and grant writing. While socialization is not the same as feeling a sense of belonging (Soto, 2002), it can be a start.

Writing training for graduate students that is external to their disciplines can help identify and edit the discipline-specific idiosyncrasies that may be a detriment when writing to audiences outside of their field. As Christine noted,

> Attending grant and instructor training at [the center for teaching] was instrumental to my development as a professor because it helps me see what sorts of things are specific to my field and what things cross my field. When on the job market, you're going to be talking about things not necessarily in your field.

With each new position, one must start relearning and building capital again. These types of training would benefit from the teaching practices from writing studies—decoding the genre in Moira's case or, in Fernando's case, gaining familiarity in types of writing by finding examples.

Implications for Educators

When asked for changes they could make to the education they received in their department, participants in this study gave conservative suggestions while keeping in mind the limitations of resources. Overall, their comments echoed those found by Rose: "The top recommendation is to prioritize professional skills training for graduate students in ways that will ensure the mobilization of their knowledge and skills . . . in a variety of workplace settings" (2012, p. 28).

For job materials, departments should collaborate with centers of teaching to deliver presentations that cover the basics, freeing time for advisors to give discipline-specific training. As Christine so bluntly stated, "Some faculty in my department, especially if they've been out of the market for a while, just aren't equipped to teach people how to write these materials." Outsourcing some of the job material writing development allows graduate students to benefit from center consultants' ongoing research about the genre. Faculty advisors, especially those who were newly hired, can supply the disciplinary culture and expertise.

A PD workshop could be housed within an office of graduate studies. Moira suggested a "formal class or workshop to learn grant writing or intro to article writing because faculty vary in expertise, and you can be sure you are picking up all the skills that are important." To this, I am reminded of Fernando criticizing his workshops for being too messy because they were student-led. In that instance, his cohort was a group of "clueless people desperate for a job leading other clueless people." Future studies should examine whether training opportunities external to departments are useful for graduate students. And, given the discipline-specific needs and time demands of graduate students, it may be worth testing the utility in different formats of the course: as a standalone training course or training sprinkled throughout all courses within a graduate program. What is most important for the success of the workshop is attention to the three subgenres and providing structure for graduate students to continue to grow and improve.

CONCLUSION

Writing studies scholars have called for a re-examination of how graduate students transition to academic roles (Yancey, 2013), a re-examination of race and labor in the discipline (Inoue, 2019; Osorio et al., 2021) and a diversification of the discipline (de Mueller & Ruiz, 2017; Ore et al., 2021). And writing is simultaneously interwoven with identity and a means for graduate students to enter academia. Writing training has been linked with graduate students' sense of belonging, especially for students from historically underrepresented minority groups (Pascale, 2018; Strayhorn, 2019). A sense of belonging has a direct effect on students' persistence; thus, professional development contributes toward student success (Strayhorn, 2019). Therefore, writing training in professional materials has direct implications for graduate students with minoritized identities to feel a sense of belonging in their disciplines and in academia. Professional writing has distinct subgenres that require their own focus in graduate student professional development, such as writing for job materials and developing grant proposals. By including opportunities for aspiring faculty and professionals to develop appropriate writing skills beyond research, institutions are promoting a sense of belonging while preparing them with the competencies they need to fulfill all aspects of their work.

REFERENCES

Austin, A. E. & McDaniels, M. (2006). Preparing the professoriate of the future: Graduate student socialization for faculty roles. In J. C. Smart (Ed.), *Higher education: Handbook of theory and research, vol 21* (pp. 397–456). Springer. https://doi.org/10.1007/1-4020-4512-3_8.

Brill, J. L., Balcanoff, K. K., Land, D., Gogarty, M. & Turner, F. (2014). Best practices in doctoral retention: Mentoring. *Higher Learning Research Communications, 4*(2), 26. https://doi.org/10.18870/hlrc.v4i2.186.

Carter-Tod, S. (2019). Reflecting, expanding, and challenging: A bibliographic exploration of race, gender, ability, language diversity, and sexual orientation and writing program administration. *WPA: Writing Program Administration, 42*(3), 97–106. https://www.wpacouncil.org/aws/CWPA/asset_manager/get_file/382251?ver=25.

Charmaz, K. (2014). *Constructing grounded theory.* Sage. https://doi.org/10.4135/9781526402276.

Curtin, N., Stewart, A. J. & Ostrove, J. M. (2013). Fostering academic self-concept. *American Educational Research Journal, 50*(1), 108–137. https://doi.org/10.3102/0002831212446662.

Dadas, C. (2013). Reaching the profession: The locations of the rhetoric and composition job market. *College Composition and Communication, Special Issue: The Profession, 65*(1), 67–89. https://doi.org/10.2307/43490807.

Ducheny, K., Alletzhauser, H. L., Crandell, D. & Schneider, T. R. (1997). Graduate student professional development. *Professional Psychology: Research and Practice, 28*(1), 87–91. https://doi.org/10.1037/0735-7028.28.1.87.

Gardner, S. K. & Barnes, B. J. (2007). Graduate student involvement: Socialization for the professional role. *Journal of College Student Development, 48*(4), 369–387. https://doi.org/10.1353/csd.2007.0036.

Goodenow, C. & Grady, K. E. (1993). The relationship of school belonging and friends' values to academic motivation among urban adolescent students. *Journal of Experimental Education, 62*(1), 60–71. https://psycnet.apa.org/record/1994-35250-001.

Hausmann, L. R. M., Schofield, J. W. & Woods, R. L. (2007). Sense of belonging as a predictor of intentions to persist among African American and White first-year college students. *Research in Higher Education, 48*(7), 803–839. https://doi.org/10.1007/s11162-007- 9052-9.

Heflinger, C. & Doykos, B. (2016). *Paving the pathway: Exploring student perceptions of professional development preparation in doctoral education.* Innovative Higher Education, 41, 343–358. https://doi.org/10.1007/s10755-016-9356-9.

Holley, K. A. & Caldwell, M. L. (2012). The challenges of designing and implementing a doctoral student mentoring program. *Innovative Higher Education, 37*(3), 243–253.

Hurtado, S. & Carter, D. F. (1997). Effects of college transition and perceptions of the campus racial climate on Latino college students' sense of belonging. *Sociology of Education 70*(4), 324–345. https://doi.org/10.2307/2673270.

Inoue, A. B. (2019). How do we language so people stop killing each other, or what do we do about white language supremacy. *College Composition and Communication, 71*(2), 352–369.

Lave, J. & Wenger, E. (1991). *Situated learning: Legitimate peripheral participation*. Cambridge University Press. https://doi.org/10.1017/CBO9780511815355.

Le, A. T., LaCost, B. Y. & Wismer, M. (2016). International female graduate students' experience at a midwestern university: Sense of belonging and identity development. *Journal of International Students, 6*(1), 128–152. https://doi.org/10.32674/jis.v6i1.569.

Mackert, M., Donovan, E. E. & Bernhardt, J. M. (2017). Applied grant writing training for future health communication researchers: The health communication scholars program. *Health Communication, 32*(2), 247-252. https://doi.org/10.1080/10410236.2015.1113485.

de Mueller, G. G. & Ruiz, I. (2017). Race, silence, and writing program administration: A qualitative study of US college writing programs. *WPA: Writing Program Administration, 40*(2), 19–39.

Meeuwisse, M., Severiens, S. E. & Born, M. P. (2010). Learning environment, interaction, sense of belonging and study success in ethnically diverse student groups. *Research in Higher Education, 51*(6), 528–545. https://doi.org/10.1007/s11162-010-9168-1.

Mitic, R. R. & Okahana, H. (2021). Don't count them out: PhD skills development and careers in industry. *Studies in Graduate and Postdoctoral Education, 12*(2), 206–229. https://doi.org/10.1108/SGPE-03-2020-0019.

Nevill, S. C., Chen, X. & Carroll, C. D. (2007). The path through graduate school: A longitudinal examination 10 years after bachelor's degree (pp. 1–119). National Center for Education Statistics. https://doi.org/10.1080/00221546.2011.11777209.

Ore, E., Wieser, K. & Cedillo, C. (2021). Diversity is not justice: Working toward radical transformation and racial equity in the discipline. *College Composition and Communication, 72*(4), 601–620.

Osorio, R., Hutchinson, A., Primeau, S., Ubbesen, M. E. & Champoux-Crowley, A. (2021). The laborious reality vs. the imagined ideal of graduate student instructors of writing. *WPA: Writing Program Administration, 45*(1), 131–152.

Pascale, A. B. (2018). "Co-existing lives": Understanding and facilitating graduate student sense of belonging. *Journal of Student Affairs Research and Practice, 55*(4), 399–411. https://doi.org/10.1080/19496591.2018.1474758.

Phillips, T. (2012). Graduate writing groups: Shaping writing and writers from student to scholar. *Praxis: A Writing Center Journal, 10*(1). https://www.praxisuwc.com/phillips-101.

Posselt, J. R. (2021). *Promoting graduate student wellbeing: Cultural, organizational, and environmental factors in the academy*. Council of Graduate Schools. https://cgsnet.org/wp-content/uploads/2022/01/CGS_Well-being-ConsultPaper-Posselt.pdf.

Rizzolo, S., DeForest, A. R., DeCino, D. A., Strear, M. & Landram, S. (2016). Graduate student perceptions and experiences of professional development activities. *Journal of Career Development, 43*(3), 195–210. https://doi.org/10.1177/0894845315587967.

Rose, M. (2012). *Graduate student professional development: A survey with recommendations*. The Canadian Association for Graduate Studies. https://tinyurl.com/56dbsabp.

Soto, A. J. (2002). Reexamining doctoral student socialization and professional development: Moving beyond the congruence and assimilation orientation. In J. C. Smart & W. G. Tierney (Eds.), *Higher education: Handbook of theory and research, vol 17*. Springer. https://doi.org/10.1007/978-94-010-0245-5_8.

Strayhorn, T. L. (2019). *College students' sense of belonging: A key to educational success for all students* (2nd ed.). Taylor & Francis. https://doi.org/10.4324/9781315297293.

Thiry, H., Laursen, S. L. & Hunter, A. B. (2011). What experiences help students become scientists? A comparative study of research and other sources of personal and professional gains for STEM undergraduates. *The Journal of Higher Education, 82*(4). https://doi.org/10.1080/00221546.2011.11777209.

Yancey, K.B. (2013). From the editor: About the profession. *College Composition and Communication, Special Issue: The Profession, 65*(1), 5–12.

Villanueva, V., Jr. (1993). *Bootstraps: From an American academic of color* (1st ed.). National Council of Teachers of English.

APPENDIX A. LIST OF INTERVIEW QUESTIONS

- What expectations did you have about how the institution would prepare you professionally when you first entered your program?
    - How were those expectations met or not met?
- How important is/was receiving professional/job training in a doc program to sense of belonging?
- In your opinion or experience, what are the required, yet implicit, professional skills that graduate students must learn as future faculty?
- What training did you receive about applying for funding ops (grants/fellowships) and future jobs?
    - What training do/did you wish you had?
- Anything else you would like to add about institutional support for doctoral students' professional development?

APPENDIX B. CODE CHART

Theme	Codes	Sub-codes
1. Graduate Perceptions of Professional Development and Belonging	1.1 Professional development	1.1.1 Faculty mentorship experiences
		1.1.2 Impact of mentorship on career development
		1.1.3 Writing skill development
	1.2 Sense of belonging	1.2.1 Departmental community
		1.2.2 Peer belonging
		1.2.3 Belonging in discipline
2. Trained and Untrained Writing	2.1 Job materials	2.1.1 Sources of training
		2.1.2 Formal training insufficient
	2.2 Administrative, professional writing	2.2.1 Sources of training
	2.3 Grant applications	2.3.1 No training
3. Individually Bridging the Gap	3.1 Self- and peer-assessment	3.1.1 Seeking training in the moment
		3.1.2 Peers' writing feedback
	3.2 Experiential advice	3.2.1 New hires, recent alumni, informational interviews

CHAPTER 9.

MOVING BEYOND "A BASKET OF SKILLS AND A BUNCH OF PUBLICATIONS": DEVELOPING A WRITERLY IDENTITY THROUGH FACILITATING FACULTY WRITING GROUPS

Kristin Messuri and Elizabeth Sharp
Texas Tech University

Abstract. *We explore how facilitating writing groups impacts faculty identity, particularly for women faculty members. Drawing on data from a large women's writing program, the chapter discusses how facilitators balance the dual role of participant and leader, and how these experiences help resist competitive pressures in academia.*

Writing is central to the tenure and promotion processes of faculty from all disciplines, yet few faculty members self-identify as writers, instead understanding themselves as teachers, professors, or researchers (Banks & Flinchbaugh, 2013; Elbow & Sorcinelli, 2006). Writing, for most faculty, is an activity in service of their professional identity—something they must do, and do well, but not an integral part of their identities. This limited understanding of writing is at odds with the field of writing studies, which understands writing as a means of developing and expressing professional identity. As Estrem (2015) has explained, "Writing—as a means of thinking, a form of inquiry and research, and a means for communication within a discipline—plays a critical role in . . . identity transformation and expansion" (p. 55). The subject of developing professional identities through writing is common in scholarship about graduate writers (Curry, 2016; Martinez, 2016; Pemberton, 2019). However, there is a tacit assumption that faculty have done this complex identity work and now have fairly static, fully formed professional identities, an assumption that belies the shifting, contingent, evolving nature of identity and the developmental processes faculty continue to experience.

DOI: https://doi.org/10.37514/PER-B.2025.2555.2.09

The centrality of writing to the development of professional identity is just as important for faculty as it is for student writers, yet little research addresses faculty writerly identity. This gap in the research is unsurprising, given the dearth of research on faculty writers in general, which this collection seeks to bolster. Tarabochia (2020) and Werder (2013) have argued that the intrapersonal dimension, which Werder (2013) describes as "how one views one's sense of identity" (p. 281), is central to faculty writers' development, understanding identity as part of the more comprehensive construct of self-authorship. Tarabochia and Madden (2018) found professional identity to be a concern of early-career faculty across disciplines as they try to establish themselves as scholars in their chosen fields. Writerly identity, or what Williams (2018) called "literate identity," has implications for writers' agency, "the perception, drawn from experiences and dispositions, that the individual can, in a given social context, act, make a decision, and make meaning" (p. 10). Although Williams studied student writers, the interconnectedness of writerly identity and agency can be extended to faculty writers. Moreover, there is evidence that writing programs geared toward enhancing faculty writing productivity are more effective when faculty understand themselves as writers (Banks & Flinchbaugh, 2013). Wells and Söderlund (2018) and Tulley (2018) have performed important empirical inquiries into rhetoric and composition faculty's experiences with writing for publication. However, more research is needed to explore the formation, expression, and development of professional and writerly identities for faculty across disciplines. In addition, further inquiry is needed to examine writing support structures that could enhance the development of faculty's professional and writerly identities.

Lee and Boud (2003) found evidence suggesting institutionally embedded multidisciplinary faculty writing groups could support this growth. They described writing groups as local sites of practice where academic identities were developed, as they "reposition participants as active scholarly writers within a peer-learning framework" (p. 198). Their investigation focused on faculty writing groups centered on peer feedback. Although this structure is the most common described in the literature, many models exist with varying membership, purposes, activities, and other dimensions (Haas, 2014). Further work is needed to investigate whether other writing group structures, such as "write-on-site" groups where participants meet to work independently, may serve faculty in similar capacities.

Most of the existing literature focusing on writing groups and professional identities is not based on empirical research; instead, it relies heavily upon the authors' personal experiences in a group, primarily as participants but also as writing program administrators or faculty development specialists engaged in faculty support. Little research provides perspectives other than the authors'; a notable exception is work by Tarabochia and Madden (2018). Research using qualitative methodologies has the potential to increase the perspectives involved in the research beyond the authors' personal experiences and increase the diversity of the writing group participants under study.

WRITING PROGRAM BACKGROUND

This study explored a large-scale writing program developed at an institution during its transition to Carnegie Tier 1 status. We describe the group as women-centered because it is designed to support faculty who identify as women, and conversations and materials often focus on this population. However, the program is open to faculty of all genders and academic appointment types. The women-centered nature of the group is significant because of gender disparities in tenure and promotion found throughout academia (Misra et al., 2011), including among faculty in language fields as found in a survey of MLA members (Modern Language Association, 2009). The MLA report indicated that tenured women faculty dedicated two fewer hours per week to research compared to men; conversely, they dedicated more time to course preparation (1.8 hours per week) and grading or providing feedback on student work (1.6 hours per week). Although these disparities may seem small, "over the years the accumulation of these microdifferences may add up to the major inequity that is the substantial difference in time between men and women attaining the rank of professor" (p. 2). Considering gendered differences in time spent on research, writing programs have the potential to help address the larger structural issues that affect women faculty.

The program in this study currently serves approximately 100 faculty members from 11 colleges and more than 30 departments. The largest user group is assistant professors, but faculty of all ranks, including those who are not tenure eligible, are represented. The program's primary activity is meeting weekly for write-on-site groups; therefore, for the purposes of this study, we refer to the "writing program" when considering the administrative or holistic qualities of the program and "writing groups" when referring specifically to activities that occur in the virtual and physical writing group spaces. Other program activities include writing retreats, professional development events, and networking events. The program is structured such that faculty members are divided into approximately 10 writing groups, each of which is led by a faculty facilitator. Each group meets for three hours each week: 15–30 minutes of discussion time, usually centered on a brief reading or discussion topic, followed by independent writing time. Faculty commit to participate in one semester at a time, but the majority stay in the program for multiple semesters, and many continue to participate for much longer; about half of current members have been in the group for more than two years. The authors offer a detailed description of the group's structure and benefits, as well as its women-centered focus on feminist principles in other publications (Sharp & Messuri, 2023).

Over the course of the program's history, 20 faculty have served as facilitators (typically 10 to 11 serve in a given semester). They are recruited by the program co-directors based on their past experiences as strong participants in the group. Only one facilitator was invited to lead a group without prior participation because her history of winning grants made her a logical fit for a grant writing group being developed at that time. Program co-directors intentionally recruit facilitators from diverse personal backgrounds and from various departments and ranks, though they are typically already tenured to protect junior faculty from dedicating time to an additional service commitment. Most facilitators serve for multiple semesters; several have chosen to continue in this role for several years.

Prior to the beginning of each fall or spring semester, faculty facilitators are assigned to one writing group with 6 to 15 faculty members; most groups have 10 to 12 members. Each week, facilitators are responsible for leading 30-minute discussions at the beginning of the writing session as well as maintaining regular communication among group members and assisting in the administration of the group (e.g., building a "syllabus" of readings used during meetings, planning writing retreats, administering surveys to participants, and writing reports to program sponsors). To recognize their labor, facilitators receive a modest stipend of $500 per semester, compensation that was enabled by recently established permanent funding from the provost's office and the research office.

METHODS

Study Design

In the present study (IRB 2019–60), we examined faculty facilitators' experiences and identities linked to their role as leaders in a women faculty writing program. Because facilitators take leadership roles in these writing groups and dedicate their intellectual and emotional labor to sustaining the program, they are a particularly rich group to study when considering the effects of writing groups on faculty's writerly identities. During the focus groups, participants were asked questions about their experiences facilitating a group as well as how those experiences influenced their professional identities as faculty members and writers. The focus groups, which were conducted virtually, were recorded and transcripts were created.

Participants

Within a span of a month, we conducted four virtual focus groups with three participants in each group (total participants = 12). Participants were from a wide variety of disciplines, including English (n=2), education (n=2), STEM (n=1), law (n=2), history (n=2), anthropology (n=1), Russian (n=1), and communication studies (n=1). Participants included five full professors, five associate professors, one assistant professor, and one retired associate professor. Three of the participants also served as administrators (i.e., department chair, associate department chair, associate vice president of research, interim vice provost) during a portion of the time they were facilitators. One-fourth of the sample identified as women of color. Most of the sample had facilitated four or more semesters, two participants had facilitated during one semester, and two had facilitated three or fewer semesters. Seven of the participants had facilitated in both the face-to-face groups and virtual groups; four facilitated face-to-face groups only and one facilitated virtual groups only. At the time of participating in the research, half of the participants no longer served as facilitators. One facilitator took a position at another university, several became administrators, and one (the assistant professor) was asked by her department to stop facilitating because she had too much service outside of her department. Some facilitators led general writing groups that were open to all writing program members, while others led groups dedicated to women faculty of color, faculty writing grant and fellowship applications, and parents of young children. All but one had been involved in the writing groups as participants before becoming facilitators.

Analysis

We watched the focus group video recordings and read the transcripts from the focus groups multiple times. As we engaged with the data, we kept running notes of the ideas and concepts emerging from the data. We drew on the constant comparative method (Glaser, 1965), whereby each relevant idea in the data was compared to previous ideas and either integrated within a previously noted idea or added as new idea/concept. Then, we threaded together the ideas to develop broader themes.

Positionality

Our analyses and interpretations were necessarily influenced by our identities and experiences. Both of us are white, cisgender women from the United States, identities which are especially important to consider in the context of a women-centered group with members (including the study participants) who have diverse intersecting identities. As program co-directors, we hoped to create space for facilitators with different racial, ethnic, linguistic, and national backgrounds. That diversity is reflected in our participants, who were from that pool of facilitators. As authors, we recognize the limitations of our personal perspectives, and, in response, we have intentionally highlighted the voices of our participants through our extensive use of direct quotations.

Our institutional appointments and disciplinary backgrounds are also reflected in this research project. Kristin is the Managing Director of the Writing Centers (a staff position at her institution) with a research background in writing studies. Elizabeth is Director of the Women and Gender Studies Program and Professor of Human Development and Family Studies. As co-founders, former facilitators, and current participants in the group, we came to this project with personal experiences of the writing program as well as existing relationships with study participants. We needed to consider how our own personal and professional investment in the program might influence our interpretations of our findings. Therefore, in writing this chapter, we critically and recursively reflected on how our perspectives related to the focus group data with the intention of mitigating potential bias.

FINDINGS

Writing group facilitators indicated that participating in the writing group, whether in the role of member or facilitator, strongly affected their writing practices, resulting in significant changes in their understandings of themselves and others as writers. Facilitators described joining the writing group, and specifically forming a writing community and learning more about others' writing practices, as "transformative" and a "paradigm shift." Throughout the focus groups, there was a sense that the act of joining the group caused the most significant shifts in both writing practices and scholarly or writerly identities. However, facilitators noted that taking on the leadership role of facilitator enhanced their identities as scholars and writers. The significance placed on the role of facilitator versus member was most pronounced in those who had facilitated for several years versus those who only facilitated for a semester or two.

Group Identity

Facilitators felt a very strong sense of identification with the writing program. In the context of a question about professional identity, a facilitator said that "being part of the program is part of your professional identity . . . whether you're a participant or facilitator." Another called it "a big part of my identity as a faculty member" at our institution. For one person who has participated since the group's inception and facilitated for one year, identification with the writing program superseded identification with her department, which is typically a faculty member's strongest affiliation:

> I don't have a very strong connection to my department at all, but I feel very connected to people across the university because we've been in writing group together, and I've always said the writing group . . . [is] my [home].

This affinity with the writing group led some facilitators to take on the leadership role because they felt a desire to contribute to the group. One facilitator said, "I feel like it was kind of my duty to . . . give back to the program what I thought it had given me." Another noted that this sense of identification with the group is common to many program participants and could motivate others to act in a leadership capacity as needed: "I have the sense that any of us would do it . . . if a group needs to be led by somebody, then we step in, and we do it."

Several facilitators, especially those who served in that role for several years, said their sense of identification with the program grew stronger when they moved from program participant to facilitator, in terms of both how they understood themselves and how they were viewed by others. Several noted that after they became facilitators, they were more likely to promote the writing group to others, especially faculty in their departments and faculty who were new to the university. One called herself "the champion for" the program to others in her department; another said she had become "an ambassador of the program." Facilitators also indicated that acting in this leadership role enriched their connections with other group members as they developed stronger one-on-one relationships beyond what members typically develop with one another. Several spoke about their emotional investment in their group members' writing, enthusiastically recounting members' accomplishments that felt like personal victories. One facilitator's enthusiasm was palpable as she talked about her group member's recent book coming out: "I was so excited, and I . . . bought the book, and . . . it arrived, and I was just, like, *so excited* . . . because, you know, we had been in group together for years, and I had sort of been with her on that journey." She went on to explain that, in general,

> I feel like I spend more of my professional time thinking about what other people are doing and just being more . . . emotionally wrapped up in that experience, and I think that's been a really good thing, I think that there's . . . kind of a solidarity that comes from that, and also

just a lot of professional satisfaction in seeing other people succeed.

Some facilitators commented that they were specifically motivated by promoting the success of other women. As one explained,

> I love this program, I'm committed to this program, I believe in what we're doing, and I'm excited to be a part of . . . the people who are trying to push it forward even further . . . I find that work really rewarding . . . particularly in this [context] because I felt like I was helping . . . women in particular, and it was making the university a better place.

Here, the women-centered focus of the group contributed to the facilitator's identification with the group as well as her sense of satisfaction.

Professional Identity: Mentors, Leaders, and Administrators

When asked about how leading the writing groups influenced their professional identities, facilitators offered a variety of answers, including seeing themselves and others seeing them as mentors, leaders, and administrators. They considered how the program helped them reflect on their identities as leaders and (possible) administrators in the future.

Mentors

One of the central features of the writing program is the bi-directional mentoring that occurs within the groups. Women faculty of different ranks and different disciplinary backgrounds are intentionally placed in each group to encourage mentoring. Among facilitators who discussed their identity as mentors within and beyond the writing groups, there was an overarching sense that they found value in both mentoring and learning from other women faculty in the writing groups. Almost all facilitators indicated they had acquired new writing techniques as well as time and energy management advice from women in their groups. For example, several facilitators discussed learning to set smaller writing goals and developing more effective goal setting strategies in general. One facilitator told us that she learned from other women the "aggressive use of the Outlook calendar to block out time when no one can schedule a meeting" as one way to get more of her writing completed.

In addition to learning from other women faculty, the facilitators enjoyed the opportunity to mentor and contribute to the success of women faculty members. In the words of one facilitator, being a facilitator "augments the part of my professional identity that speaks to mentoring and supporting other colleagues" and "supplements" other mentoring roles she has.

In the context of the mentoring aspect of their professional identities, several facilitators indicated that the multidisciplinary nature of the groups made their work especially rewarding. One facilitator explained that she liked "mentoring" and "helping . . . other faculty . . . not just in my department or discipline or college or anything like that." Similarly, another facilitator felt that as writing group facilitators, we are "providing a real contribution to advance scholarship . . . all across departments. That feels pretty good."

A few facilitators specified that they especially appreciated the opportunity to mentor junior colleagues. In particular, those who were further along in their careers saw it as an opportunity to share wisdom with junior faculty. One explained, "I had been experiencing ageism and sort of a dismissal within my home department" and was gratified to find that group members found her "seasoned advice actually useful." Another said the mentoring role has "allowed me or given me the space to start embracing the fact that I'm an elder professor and being okay with that, and that does have some value." She found this perspective especially rewarding in the context of working with more junior faculty, saying,

> I'm humbled. . . . They're amazing. They're doing such wonderful work that it's like, God, I wish I was that smart when I was in their place, you know? . . . We women are doing so much good and such amazing research that we really are contributing to the university, to the knowledge base, to the web of knowledge, and I just think everybody should know about it.

Leaders

Facilitators felt that this leadership role empowered them to shape the writing program. One commented, "I appreciate the fact that I was now at the decision-making table, at the big kids' table" and helping to make decisions about the syllabus, reports to sponsors, and other matters that affected the entire program. Others said they felt "empowered" to take care of issues they had noticed, ranging from "creature comforts," such as snacks and room temperature, to managing the conversations at the beginning of each session. One facilitator felt empowered because she was able to enhance what the program had previously offered her as a member. For example, she was able to get her group members parking passes, and she provided snacks at every session.

With this leadership identity, many facilitators felt an increased sense of responsibility, which some found stressful or anxiety-provoking, but others found rewarding. One facilitator said she possessed a "hostess" mentality in which she felt obligated to ensure everyone was okay and getting what they needed. Because of the hostess role, some of the facilitators indicated that they were able to get more research done when they were members than when they were facilitators. A related theme was the sense of obligation to model productive writing practices to the group, often based on the readings and discussions shared with group members. Common examples facilitators noted included planning their writing sessions, focusing on writing during group meetings, completing the assigned readings, and identifying additional writing times during the week. Many facilitators talked about the challenges of managing discussions at the beginning of each session, especially ensuring that participants did not steer the conversation in an unproductive, negative direction; interrupt others; or dominate the discussion. These dominators, or "super talkers," were mentioned in every focus group and were considered disruptive because they "hijacked" conversations, silencing other voices and causing discussions to run long, impinging upon dedicated writing time. Some facilitators found managing such situations challenging because, as one explained, "I am just a peer . . . it's not like when you're teaching a class." They shared techniques they found successful, such as setting a timer or inviting other members to contribute to the conversation.

Acting in the role of facilitator caused some to inhabit leadership roles, even when they were not otherwise inclined to do so. One noted, "I don't necessarily see myself as an authority figure, but sometimes the facilitator situation requires, like, a little bit of 'authoritating.'" Another said she does not typically see herself as a leader, but this group challenged her to take on a leadership role outside of her comfort zone: "I'm not a leader in any sense, in any way, and so it is pulling me out of . . . my natural introvert, reticent, 'I'm going to sit in the back row'" means of interacting. Taken together, these themes suggest that performing the facilitator role in and of itself is a form of leadership development.

Administrators

As facilitators self-identified with the writing program, so, too, did their colleagues, department chairs, and other administrators identify them with this work, especially as it applies to faculty development and diversity, equity, and inclusion. One facilitator noted that this recognition has created "more service opportunities for better and for worse," an experience shared by several in the focus group. One facilitator was asked to facilitate a similar writing group for faculty of all genders in her department. However, she declined the request to facilitate because she believed the group would replicate gendered dynamics that occur elsewhere (e.g., women being expected to contribute food, conversations centering on competition instead of collaboration). Another said she became known as the "gender mentorship writing person" and was asked to chair a gender equity task force. She later moved to a different institution and was nominated to be the Associate Dean for Faculty Development within her first three months. She commented that her involvement in the writing program "created a lot of opportunities quickly" in her new setting. This identification of facilitators with the writing group benefited the program as well, as when two facilitators leveraged their positions as administrators to assist the program in gaining permanent funding from the institution's upper administration.

Several of the facilitators held administrative positions in their departments or in upper administration, either during or after their time as facilitators in the writing group. One facilitator identified "synergies" with her role in the research office, as it allowed her to encourage writing group members and especially junior faculty to apply for funding they may not have known about otherwise. However, several of these women who were no longer facilitators left due to time constraints related to these administrative responsibilities, an example of one downside of facilitators gaining the leadership skills needed to succeed as administrators. Women faculty (these facilitators included) already have disproportionate service loads, and adopting new administrative roles may leave them with little time for writing.

In a few cases, facilitating the groups helped create an identity perceived by others that suggested the facilitators were capable administrators. As previously mentioned, one facilitator was nominated for an administrative role just a few months into her position at a new institution. Another facilitator started warming up to the idea of being an administrator—something she had avoided for most of her career.

TRANSLATING WRITING PRACTICES TO OTHER CONTEXTS

Facilitators also translated their experiences with the writing group to other contexts. As one facilitator explained, "I found several levels of using my facilitating skills and applied them to my other duties." The experience of facilitating enhanced facilitators' domain knowledge related to writing, as well as their mentoring, leadership, and administrative skills, allowing them to translate that knowledge to other contexts.

Facilitators took their administrative knowledge of the writing groups and used them as the basis for similarly structured groups for other faculty in a facilitator's department, for faculty at another institution (after a facilitator suggested it to a friend), and, most commonly, for the graduate students they advise. For example, one facilitator who described a writing group she started for her doctoral students emphasized the way the group helps them to develop their scholarly identities.

Others reflected on how facilitating the writing group enhanced their work with graduate students regardless of whether they adopted the structure of a writing group. One noted that the leadership and mentoring aspects of the facilitator role had "transferred . . . into the way that I approach writing processes and working with my graduate students. There are some things that I was doing, but others that . . . just through facilitating the group, that I incorporated into the writing processes with them, not just as they're working for degree completion but also in collaborative projects." She went on to describe how she shared insight from her own writing practices as well as those of other writing group members when a graduate student was having trouble with a collaborative writing project.

The writing group also translated into making facilitators more effective in other administrative roles. For example, one facilitator of a grant writing group who later became an interim department chair explained, "Being a facilitator has helped me figure out some of the things that I now, as a department chair, need to impart on my junior faculty that are in my department and just starting out with grant writing." In this way, the writing groups functioned as informal training that facilitators carried into other professional contexts.

WRITERLY IDENTITY

Participants indicated that being a facilitator and a participant in the writing groups enhanced their scholarly identities. For example, one participant reflected on how her understanding of herself as a scholar and writer changed through her participation in the writing groups:

> When I first got a tenure-track job . . . I viewed [publications] at first as that many disconnected hoops I had to jump through. So, I would jump through this hoop, and then I would jump through the next hoop, and this hoop, and this hoop, and they were unconnected to each other. But being part of the group has helped me coalesce all those hoops into an important part of my job and an important part of my identity, and had I not been in the group I wouldn't think of myself in the same way that I do now that I have a body of work that is united and cohesive and I have developed an expertise on a specific subject. I think, without the support of other women doing the same thing and creating an identity,

> I . . . would just be a person with a basket of skills and a bunch of publications, but I wouldn't understand them all as one important part of my job.

Within the groups, interacting with group members and engaging in regular conversations about research and writing enabled facilitators to develop and express scholarly and writerly identities.

Scholarly Identity vs. Writerly Identity

Although many facilitators identified ways the writing program enhanced their scholarly identities, several of their responses indicated tensions between their identities as scholars and their identities as writers. For example, one participant questioned, "Do I think of myself [as writer]? I think of myself as an academic, and part of that is writing." Another said, "I don't see myself as a writer, I see myself as a scholar, and I want to claim that as my identity as a scholar . . . I communicate through the writing." One facilitator of a writing group focused on grant writing noted that facilitating "reaffirmed my . . . identity, I think, as a grant writer. I've never thought of myself that way but, you know . . . I have to live and die by it. If I don't have it, I'm not successful according to the world that we live in."

Disciplinary background played a strong role in determining whether facilitators felt that the writing program enhanced their writerly identity. Prior to joining the writing groups, facilitators who were not English faculty tended to identify as scholars with writing as one task that contributes to their scholarly identity rather than constituting a central part of their identity. After leading the groups and being part of them, several were more comfortable with viewing themselves as writers.

Both English faculty members who were part of the focus groups indicated that they had previously thought of themselves as writers and understood writing as a significant aspect of their identities. One shared:

> English is about writing . . . [a writerly identity] was something that I already had. . . . This is part of . . . who you are as a professional in English . . . you think of yourself as someone who writes . . . but the thing that has changed a little bit for me . . . I look back at the things that I've accomplished, the work I've done in my career, and I think, "you know what—I'm actually okay at this."

This experience of gaining confidence in one's scholarly work and writing abilities was a common theme among facilitators. However, many felt it was difficult to tease out the identity shifts resulting from progressing in their careers from those caused by participating in and facilitating the writing groups. One said that around the time she became a facilitator, she was getting publications into stronger journals, "and that was really empowering, and so I felt like . . . dedicating more time into writing . . . and it wasn't this thing I was trying to squeeze in between putting kids down for naps or grading or whatever else." This theme of increasing the quantity and quality of publications emerged from several facilitators' responses, though most could not attribute it specifically to the facilitator role. For example, another facilitator noted, "The positive support within the group has helped my confidence, but I think some of that would have happened anyways, it's just to a greater degree. It's like the group is a multiplier."

Understanding Other Writers' Experiences

In the context of gaining confidence as a scholar/writer and enhancing writing skills and productivity, many facilitators identified hearing about others' challenges with research and writing as pivotal to their own professional growth. Many facilitators similarly reflected on how group conversations about writing challenges normalized their own struggles with writing, resulting in changes in how they experienced writing and understood themselves as scholars and writers. As one explained, "Because I have watched so many other people struggling the same way that I am struggling [it] has turned my struggle into something that is perfectly normal and part of a process." This understanding resulted in a shift in writerly identity for at least one facilitator. The facilitator who had self-identified as a writer since graduate school went on to explain that gaining an understanding of the experiences of other writers, specifically their struggles, caused this shift in her writerly identity: "That's been kind of empowering to realize . . . yeah, it is a struggle, it's not that it's not hard, it's not that it's not frustrating and, you know, you want to pull your hair out, but I've actually done well." Another believes that this experience is common among participants in the groups beyond facilitators. She described how, before the writing group formed, "we were all on our little islands, and . . . you kind of have this idea that there's [sic] these people who are out there who are just, like, tearing through everything, and it's easy for them, and to find out that . . . maybe those people exist, but most of us are just—it's hard, it's hard, writing is hard." One facilitator reflected on how the writing group disrupted the academic culture of perfectionism, explaining,

> Academia is kind of like social media in a way, where we see everybody's successes and we don't necessarily see the shadow CV with all the failures, but to meet with people on a weekly

> basis, and they're like, "I just had nothing in my tank this week, I got nothing done," or "I got two rejections on the same day, and I'm just . . . really down," that has kind of helped me distance myself emotionally from some of the things I put out, and I think I'm more willing to put out things now because, if it comes back to me, so what? It's going to come back with suggestions, and I can make it better, and I can try again.

Group conversations functioned to demystify individuals' writing processes and experiences, including the challenges members face, thereby altering facilitator understanding of their own writing processes and scholarly or writerly identities. It is important to note there that some of the facilitators mentioned that the women-centered aspect of the writing program offers a safer space to share vulnerabilities. Additionally, one facilitator said that the program "has really been super instrumental in professionalizing women across campus and empowering them . . . we were in silos before and now we can address the issues that everybody's having . . . and have a united front" for issues affecting women. In other research projects from the writing program, we share in detail about the value of the women-centered space (Sharp & Messuri, 2023).

Others reflected on how they came to understand that different writers have different needs and processes, realizing that there is not a single way to be productive. One facilitator began to "see certain things that work for me don't work for other people," coming to a stronger understanding of the diversity of writing practices. Another explained, "It's interesting to see everybody struggling with the same stuff and to see in what ways we are struggling all the same way and in what ways we're struggling in unique ways." She went on to discuss how she believes that, for her,

> the best practices have floated to the top, and they are the obvious ones that I know I need to follow to be successful: carving out the time, touching the project frequently and in smaller groups rather than waiting for some magical window in two weeks when I will have nothing else going on in my life and I'll be wildly productive.

Facilitators found that developing practices that work for them as well as "forgiving" themselves when they did not meet writing goals were important shifts in how they experienced writing and understood themselves as writers. At the same time, they recognized and respected that other writers have different practices and needs.

Facilitators also reported stronger positive emotions associated with writing due to normalizing struggles, developing consistent and effective writing practices, and writing as part of a community. One facilitator shared,

> There were moments before joining this group that when I would put my hands on the keyboard I'd literally almost be shaking, like there would be that much anxiety. And so, when I say it was transformative, [it] really shifted in a deeply psychological level. . . . It's hard for me now not to be writing and enjoy writing.

Others expressed that they also enjoyed writing more than they had prior to joining the group, as they had reframed the way they understood writing.

DISCUSSION

Although most universities are concerned with faculty development and growth, there are few initiatives that are effective for women faculty (Cardel et al., 2020). The present study focused on leaders within a women faculty writing program. The findings indicated that the faculty writing groups had important implications for women faculty success and encouraged women faculty to think deeply about multiple types of identities: group identity, professional identity (especially as related to identities as mentors, leaders, and administrators), and writerly identity. The study follows Aitchison and Lee (2006) in understanding the "notion of community" as an "intrinsic element" of research writing groups that allows "identification" among group members (pp. 271–272). The strong sense of group identity found in the writing groups in the present study is aligned with other accounts of faculty writing groups, such as that described by Fajt et al. (2013), who reflected on how "collaboration helps us resist becoming needlessly isolated in our specialized academic disciplines" and how the women-centered space created by that group provided "common ground," much like the group discussed in this study (p. 173). Moreover, facilitators indicated that participating in the writing groups and taking on leadership roles enhanced their sense of themselves as mentors, leaders, current/future administrators, and scholars, thereby demonstrating growth in multiple, interrelated aspects of professional identity. The emphasis facilitators outside of the English department placed on professional or scholarly identities rather than writerly identities is in keeping with previous research indicating that faculty typically do not identify as writers (Banks & Flinchbaugh, 2013; Elbow & Sorcinelli, 2006). However, upon further inquiry, the data indicated that facilitators did develop writerly identities, some self-identifying as writers for the first time, reflecting both new understandings of themselves and enhanced understandings of writing as an evolving, recursive, individualized, contextual, contingent process.

Facilitators' experiences with the writing program enabled them to support others in forming, re-thinking, and cultivating writerly identities. The data indicates that facilitators transferred their knowledge and experiences to help their group members, students, junior faculty, and others find resources, experiment with new strategies, develop and join writing groups, and enhance their writerly identity development. It is worth noting that facilitators came to understand that different writers have different practices, though they also identified some common strategies that they and others have adapted to their own needs and circumstances. While their reflections on writing practices often noted the day-to-day behavioral advice of the sort featured in writing advice manuals, they understood these practices as part of long-term, individualized, evolving processes rather than discreet, one-size-fits-all tips and tricks devoid of context. This emphasis on adapting writing practices, as well as the specific practices facilitators found effective, is in keeping with Tulley's (2018) finding that prominent writing studies faculty "adapt similar practices in widely diverse ways to local employment contexts, career stages, family circumstances, and individual preferences" (p. 146). That the current study included faculty from multiple disciplines suggests that, while writerly identity may be influenced by disciplinary background, sustained discussions about writing among a diverse community of writers may enhance faculty's understanding of writing practices and processes.

The communal setting, which facilitators consistently associated with supportive, candid discussions about writing, added an important dimension (and, often, challenge) to straightforward productive writing advice favored by writing advice manuals and articles. In this way, the writing groups under study may, to some degree, use the communal forum to circumvent focusing too heavily on behavioral strategies at the expense of understanding writing as a complex emotional, intellectual, rhetorical process, concerns about typical writing advice manuals articulated by scholars such as Johnson (2017), Tarabochia (2020), and Werder (2013). Future writing group discussions could engage more fully in discussions and events that "combine behavioral goals with a focus on inquiry and intellectual complexity," as Johnson (2017, p. 67) suggests.

Pleasure in writing was also identified by Lee and Boud (2003) as central to the experiences of writing group participants, especially those who participated over the course of multiple years, as they gained facility with writing and publication: "Pleasure . . . has to be substantially located within the processes of 'doing' the writing groups. The fact that the writing groups have been deeply satisfying to all participants is clearly a major factor in their success" (p. 198). Moreover, the pleasure in writing facilitators felt aligns with the experiences in the women-only writing group described by Bosanquet et al. (2014), who state, "Writing circles for women offer a pleasurable and productive social space that can ameliorate" the structural academic and social challenges women face in the academy (p. 375). In the present study, the sense of joy surrounding writing as well as the satisfaction in contributing to a community of writers were revelations to many facilitators and important factors in enhancing their writing productivity and professional activities and identities.

In summary, the communities created by the writing program encouraged intellectual engagement, candid interactions, and emotional connections that helped facilitators develop more robust professional practices and writerly identities as well as experience pleasure in writing. These outcomes allowed facilitators to cultivate more complex, holistic mentoring practices that surpassed the simplistic behavioral advice common in many faculty writing advice books.

LIMITATIONS AND IMPLICATIONS FOR FURTHER RESEARCH

Although our study offers several important insights, we could have improved the design of the study by composing more homogeneous focus groups on some important dimensions such as length of time as a facilitator and whether the groups were face-to-face or virtual. For example, one of the focus groups included a facilitator who had only been a facilitator one time and the other facilitators who had been leaders in the program for 10 times or more. Another focus group had two facilitators who had only conducted face-to-face groups, while the other member had conducted in both face-to-face and virtual modalities. In the future, we think it would be instructive to have a focus group limited to facilitators who are also administrators, because they contend with high service loads that place significant constraints on their time—conditions the groups are designed to mitigate. Future work could also analyze facilitators' experiences in the context of other identities, particularly race, as the need for mentorship as well as the disproportionate service and mentoring loads experienced by faculty of color are well documented. Additionally, future research should consider conducting a study examining members' reflections and experiences with facilitators. For example, which facilitator practices and personalities tend to be especially helpful for members?

CONCLUSION

The present study adds to the small but growing scholarship on the importance of faculty writing programs, especially at large universities, and the crucial contributions they can make to faculty success (Sharp & Messuri, 2023). These findings have implications for writing program administrators who are developing faculty writing support and others who are implementing faculty success programs, especially as they consider the value of involving faculty in leadership roles within those programs. Our findings underscored the value of the writing program for the development of faculty facilitators' identities, especially as the facilitators are encouraged to think of themselves as writers, mentors, and leaders. Overall, there was a strong sense of generativity from most of the facilitators as they expressed their desires and joys of supporting other women's writing and career growth. The writing program helped the facilitators engage more deeply with their identities as writers and accomplish their own writing goals, and served as an outlet to "give back" to the program and to other women.

ACKNOWLEDGMENT

We wish to thank the facilitators who participated in our focus group for being generous with their insights, time, and labor not only in this study but also in serving the women faculty who participate in the Women Faculty Writing Program at our institution.

REFERENCES

Aitchison, C. & Lee, A. (2006). Research writing: Problems and pedagogies. *Teaching in Higher Education, 11*(3), 265–278. https://doi.org/10.1080/13562510600680574.

Banks, W. P. & Flinchbaugh, K. P. (2013). Experiencing ourselves as writers: An exploration of how faculty writers move from dispositions to identities." In A. E. Geller & M. Eodice (Eds.), *Working with faculty writers* (pp. 228–245). Utah State University Press.

Bosanquet, A., Cahir, J., Huber, E., Jacenyik-Trawöger, C. & McNeill, M. (2014). An intimate circle: Reflections on writing as women in higher education. In C. Aitchison & C. Guerin (Eds.), *Writing groups for doctoral education and beyond: Innovations in practice and theory* (pp. 374–98). Routledge. https://doi.org/10.4324/9780203498811.

Cardel, M. I., Dhurandhar, E., Yarar-Fisher, C., Foster, M., Hidalgo, B., McClure, L. A., Pagoto, S., Brown, N., Pekmezi, D., Sharafeldin, N., Willig, A. L. & Angelini, C. (2020). Turning chutes into ladders for women faculty: A review and roadmap for equity in academia. *Journal of Women's Health, 29*(5), 721–733. https://doi.org/0.1089/jwh.2019.8027.

Curry, M. J. (2016). More than language: Graduate student writing as "disciplinary becoming." In S. Simpson, N. A. Caplan, M. Cox & T. Phillips (Eds.), *Supporting graduate student writers: Research, curriculum, and program design* (pp. 78–96). University of Michigan Press.

Elbow, P. & Sorcinelli, M. (2006). The faculty writing place: A room of our own. *Change Learning, 28*(7), 17–22. https://doi.org/10.3200/CHNG.38.6.17-22.

Estrem, H. (2015). Disciplinary and professional identities are constructed through writing. In L. Adler-Kassner & E. Wardle (Eds.), *Naming what we know: Threshold concepts of writing studies* (pp. 55–56). Utah State University Press.

Fajt, V., Gelwick, F. I., Loureiro-Rodríguez, V., Merton, P., Moore, G., Moyna, M. I. & Zarestky, J. (2013). Feedback and fellowship: Stories from a successful writing group. In A. E. Geller & M. Eodice (Eds.), *Working with faculty writers* (pp. 163–174). Utah State University Press.

Glaser, B. G. (1965). The constant comparative method of qualitative analysis. *Social Problems, 12*(4), 436–445. https://doi.org/10.2307/798843.

Haas, S. (2014). Pick-n-mix: A typology of writers' groups in use. In C. Aitchison & C. Guerin (Eds.), *Writing groups for doctoral education and beyond: Innovations in practice and theory* (pp. 30–48). Routledge.

Johnson, K. (2017). Writing by the book, writing beyond the book. *Composition Studies, 45*(2), 55–72.

Lee, A. & Boud, D. (2003). Writing groups, change and academic identity: Research development as local practice. *Studies in Higher Education, 28*(2), 187–200. https://doi.org/10.1080/0307507032000058109.

Martinez, A. Y. (2016). Alejandra writes a book: A critical race counterstory about writing, identity, and being Chicanx in the academy. *Praxis: A Writing Center Journal, 14*(1). https://doi.org/10.15781/T2FF3MG5V .

Misra, J., Lundquist, J. H., Holmes, E. & Agiomavritis, S. (2011, January–February). The ivory ceiling of service work. *Academe, 9*(1). https://www.aaup.org/article/ivory-ceiling-service-work.

Modern Language Association. (2009, April 27). *Standing still: The associate professor survey; Report of the committee on the status of women in the profession.* Modern Language Association. https://tinyurl.com/29xrnv9k.

Pemberton, M. A. (2019). Rethinking the WAC/writing center/graduate student connection. In S. Lawrence & T. M. Zawacki (Eds.), *Re/Writing the center: Approaches to supporting graduate students in the writing center* (pp. 29–48). Utah State University Press. https://doi.org/10.7330/9781607327516.c001.

Sharp. E. A. & Messuri, K. (2023). A reprieve from academia's chilly climate and misogyny: The power of feminist, women-centered faculty writing program. *Gender, Work & Organization, 30*(4), 1236–1253. https://doi.org/10.1111/gwao.12967.

Tarabochia, S. L. (2020). Self-authorship and faculty writers' trajectories of becoming. *Composition Studies, 48*(1), 16–33. https://doi.org/10.37514/DBH-J.2020.48.1.02.

Tarabochia, S. & Madden, S. (2018). In transition: Researching the writing development of doctoral students and faculty. *Writing & Pedagogy, 10*(3), 423–452.

Tulley, C. E. (2018). *How writing faculty write: Strategies for process, product, and productivity.* Utah State University Press.

Wells, J. M. & Söderlund, L. (2018). Preparing graduate students for academic publishing: Results from a study of published rhetoric and composition scholars. *Pedagogy, 18*(1), 131–156. https://doi.org/10.1215/15314200-4216994.

Werder, C. (2013). The promise of self-authorship as an integrative framework for supporting faculty writers. In A. E. Geller & M. Eodice (Eds.), *Working with faculty writers* (pp. 279–292). Utah State University Press.

Williams, B. T. (2018). *Literacy practices and perceptions of agency: Composing identities.* Routledge.

CHAPTER 10.
LEADING FACULTY WRITING ACADEMIES: A CASE STUDY OF WRITERLY IDENTITY

J. Michael Rifenburg and Rebecca Johnston
University of North Georgia

Abstract. *This chapter examines faculty facilitators of writing academies, focusing on their role in fostering supportive environments that counter neoliberal imperatives in academia. Through interviews, the chapter highlights how collaborative writing groups foster community and resilience, offering a reprieve from academia's often competitive climate.*

In the Netflix show *Song Exploder*, rock band R.E.M. breaks down their 1991 Grammy-winning single "Losing My Religion." *Song Exploder*, based on the popular podcast of the same name, invites musicians to detail how they created their hit song. During this episode, the host interviews R.E.M.'s lead vocalist, Michael Stipe. The host asks for Stipe's permission to play aloud Stipe's isolated vocal performance from their hit song. Stipe cautiously agrees.

R.E.M., like most bands, records songs in pieces; each instrument and vocal performance is recorded separately and then mixed at the end. When the *Song Exploder* host plays Stipe's isolated vocals, Stipe uncomfortably listens. He sticks his tongue out and moans *ugh*. He closes his eyes, wrinkles jutting across his temples, his brow furrowed. He shakes his head back and forth, and, with his eyes still closed, turns his head up to the left. He looks pained as he listens to himself.

"It's still hard to hear," he remarks. "It's so naked, so raw; it's so unsupported."

Stipe cringes when he recognizes his "unsupported" singing because his singing was never intended to be unsupported. He recorded his vocals in anticipation of layering his vocals alongside the instruments his bandmates recorded. He recorded solo in anticipation and expectation of community.

Writing, like music, is communal. Scholarship on supporting faculty writers tells us again and again the importance of community for sustained and

DOI: https://doi.org/10.37514/PER-B.2025.2555.2.10

productive scholarly careers. In this chapter, we highlight work we undertake to bring faculty writers into community. We specifically listen to the lead vocalists, to continue our musical metaphor, of these writing communities: faculty facilitators of scholarly writing groups.

We first locate ourselves, our work, and the Write Now Academy (WNA), an application-based faculty and staff semester-long academy designed to support faculty writers. We then present our methodology and methods and position ourselves within this ongoing exploratory case study. Next, we take readers into our data—stories gathered from three faculty facilitators of the WNA. We conclude by engaging more fully with the idea of faculty writing groups, like the WNA, as a tool for dismantling neoliberal imperatives such as speed and competition. To do this dismantling, we lean on Mulya's (2019) argument focused on how faculty developers can push against neoliberalism. We extend Mulya's argument to our context of working with faculty writers at a teaching-intensive university in the southeastern part of the U.S. Ultimately, we argue that leading faculty writing groups supports faculty amid pressures to push more, and counters speed and competition by creating a community of practice among all faculty participants.

OUR CONTEXT AND EXIGENCE

We work at the University of North Georgia (UNG), a multi-campus institution that arose through the consolidation of two campuses and the addition of three. For many faculty, consolidation brought increased scholarship expectations in revised promotion and tenure guidelines. But the common course load for faculty remained 4/4. An exigence for the Write Now Academy (WNA), then, was the challenge of supporting faculty scholarship at a teaching-intensive university where all faculty members were primarily undergraduate teaching faculty first.

Our positionality is central, in ways we recognize and ways we may never recognize, to how we developed, implemented, and reported this study. Michael, as a tenured, white, male associate professor whose disciplinary home is writing studies, seeks to design qualitative studies that provide research participants space to speak and have their narratives and life experiences represented through the study. Rebecca is a tenured professor who was an instructor of music education for many years but turned to work in faculty development in 2015. She currently serves as the Associate Director of the Center for Teaching, Learning and Leadership. In that role, she helps to design and provide faculty development opportunities to assist faculty in building and maintaining scholarly productivity. Both Rebecca and Michael have a vested interest in cultivating a community of scholar-teachers.

The WNA is a semester-long, application-based academy open to full-time faculty and teaching staff. Led by faculty members who have previously completed the academy, participants work through Belcher's (2009) *Writing Your Journal Article in 12 Weeks*, meeting together on Zoom four times during the Academy to share progress. Faculty facilitators make use of a shared Google doc where participants respond to prompts based on the Belcher book. Successful completion of the academy is contingent upon participants submitting an article for publication by the end of the following semester. The WNA is housed in UNG's Center for Teaching, Learning, and Leadership, a faculty development center designed to support teaching, research, and leadership through a variety of programming options.

Two bodies of research shaped this academy. First, the WNA draws on the community of practice model as articulated by Wenger, McDermott, and Snyder (2002). The co-authors described communities of practice wherein participants "don't necessarily work together every day," but "share a concern, a set of problems, or a passion about a topic, and who deepen their knowledge and expertise in this area by interacting on an ongoing basis" (p. 2). In the Academy we share knowledge, set goals and deadlines, create a peer community, and foster a sense of self-efficacy.

Second, the WNA draws on research regarding how to support faculty writers; this research often arises from the foundational work of Boice (1985), an early advocate of faculty writers and writing. He and subsequent researchers (e.g., Eodice & Cramer, 2001; Tulley, 2018) provide faculty developers concrete steps for coaching faculty writers as they build sustained scholarly productivity. Most applicable to our work is scholarship specifically on how teaching and learning centers have an important role in supporting faculty writers (Gray, Madson & Jackson, 2018). We particularly draw from Cox and Brunjes's (2013) research on building support for faculty writers at teaching-intensive schools.

OUR METHODOLOGY AND METHODS

As decolonial researchers and theorists like Smith (2012) and Tuck and Yang (2014) remind us, we undertake qualitative research through our privileged position as white tenured faculty members who share a vested interest in cultivating an active community of scholar-teachers; therefore, we proceed with caution and a stated commitment to building knowledge collaboratively with our participants that benefits not just us, as researchers, but also the participants. Our methodology and methods grow out of our local context, grow out of our work with our research participants, and grow out of the kind of knowledge we and our participants want to build and circulate.

We designed a single-bounded exploratory case study because of the nature of our in-progress research; this chapter is the result of a larger project that studied supporting faculty writers at our home institution. We bounded our study spatially (at UNG) and temporally (Spring, 2020). The question we investigated was: *how does leading a faculty writing academy shape one's writerly identity?* In undertaking an exploratory case study on the effects on a faculty writing retreat on faculty well-being and productivity, Brantmeier, Molloy, and Byrne (2017) wrote that such research designs allow for researchers to "parse important themes and clarify the direction of related future projects" (n.p.). We continue an ongoing investigation of the effectiveness of our academy for participants and faculty facilitators and peek into our early data in this chapter.

Participants

We invited all faculty facilitators to participate in this study through an IRB-approved email invitation. They did not receive compensation for participation. We used semi-structured interviews in which we pre-designed a list of questions that helped us investigate our research question: *how does leading a faculty writing academy shape one's writerly identity?* After receiving consent, we audio-recorded the conversations. All three participants read over our draft to ensure we captured their words and experiences accurately. We use pseudonyms.

We interviewed:

- Todd, a tenure-track assistant professor of communication
- Madison, a tenured professor of psychological sciences
- Phillips, a tenure-track assistant professor of English

Stories as Analysis

We offer stories of faculty describing how serving as faculty facilitators for the WNA shapes their writerly identity. Our analysis, then, is one of story. In doing this work of story as analysis, we take guidance from Patel (2019) who, in "Turning Away from Logarithms to Return to Story," explained:

> In my own work, which is never my own but linked to many people, it has never been enough to ask an interview question, record it, code it, and report what I perceive to be the meaning underneath what is said. That sequence should smack of individualized hubris; it does to me. (p. 272)

Patel disagreed with the assumed value of objectivity and systematicity that stand as hallmarks of euro-centric academic research. Taking a story approach to qualitative research, then, asks that we do more than detail the mechanics of research, what Patel terms "logarithms." We offer these mechanics: who we interviewed, how, for how long. But we emphasize story as analysis by adopting what Stornaiuolo, Smith, and Philips (2017) called an "inquiry stance" in which researchers account for their own role in "unfolding activity" and "routinely question their own assumptions and positionalities while remaining sensitive and open to multiple interpretations" (p. 76). We draw particular attention to how Stornaiuolo, Smith, and Philips used *question, sensitive,* and *open* because these terms help us remain invested in story as analysis. Instead of chopping the words of our interview participants into pithy quotes that are then tucked tidily into charts and columns, we provide lengthy interview quotes, try to represent the ebb and flow of conversation as participants think through responding aloud to challenging questions about their writerly identity, and allow for contradictions to arise within individual stories, because exploratory case studies do not offer firm findings but in-the-moment reflections of people struggling with the challenging process of speaking aloud about writerly identity.

Through these three stories—one story for each research participant—we toggle between summarizing their experience and quoting them directly.

Stories of Faculty Facilitating the Write Now Academy

Todd

Todd serves in a tenure-track role in the School of Communication, Film & Theatre at UNG. His most recent publication, taken from his dissertation, found a home in the *Journal of Transformative Learning*. Even with a recent publication and smoothly progressing toward tenure and promotion, Todd said he emphasizes his writing struggles when leading the WNA:

> I tried to be honest with my colleagues saying that "I'm trying to help you guys be better writers, but remember, this is where I'm coming from. I come to the table with my own hang-ups. I'm not like this someone who produces and writes, and I'm not a prolific writer, and, and so, you know, I'm a flawed writer." But I like to work with my colleagues.

Todd first went through the WNA as a participant before he shifted to leading his colleagues through this Academy. Michael led the WNA when Todd completed it. Todd began his story by reflecting on what he learned as a faculty participant and then shifting to why he elected to serve as a faculty facilitator:

> I think my participation, as a faculty member, you know, working with [Michael], I remember that first semester that we got to know each other, that it was just so meaningful, for me, you know, to work with my colleagues, and to kind of realize my strengths in terms of writing. I benefited so much from that, it was just such a meaningful experience for me that, when I had the chance to lead the group, it just resonated so strongly that I thought, "I want to continue that, and maybe others can kind of feel what I felt."

He described the community that is built through the WNA:

> It's a safe space, you know, where colleagues can kind of get together, where they can self-disclose some of their fears about some of their limitations, demands on their time, and how all those things kind of impact writing. And I think it provides that nice structure within the community that we can kind of work together to say, "Okay, well, yeah, we've got these challenges; we've got teaching, we've got advising, we've got all these other things, but, but we also have to kind of, you know, set aside some time for ourselves, and work towards enhancing our own scholarship." And, so I think in that it just provides that nice sense of structure and a way to kind of connect with each other. That's very supportive and encouraging. And I think that's building that sense of community kind of helps us. It's empowering. And, you know, it makes us feel like, "Yeah, I can do this."

When his story shifted to how leading an WNA shaped his writerly identity, he described dispositions formed through WNA that support sustained scholarly productivity:

> [Leading the Academy] kept reminding me the very things that I learned initially when was taking the [WNA], not leading it, but just taking it in, and I fall sometimes into my own bad habits when I'm out of that community. Then I have to kind of remind myself like, "Okay, yeah, I have a writing goal. So, let's go back to what we learned about the basics from the Write Now Academy that I have to set aside some time." I tried to be honest with the colleagues that I was leading, I kind of reminded them that in many ways I'm leading this but I'm also learning as well. And I may give you some advice,

but I'm also looking to you for advice and, and motivation and structure to help me, because it's easy for me to fall into bad habits.

He brought these lessons on structure and discipline to bear on a then-current writing project:

> I am in the process of doing some writing right now. I saw a call from one journal, and they want the submission of essays about lessons we learned teaching online during COVID. And it just really resonated with me, right? So, I have been very, trying to be very structured, even though I'm busy with my teaching responsibilities and so forth. I try to set some time, like each morning. It's almost like depositing some money, like, before I pay all my other bills, I pay myself a little bit. So, I need to put some in my savings. And so, I need to work on me, and my goals first. I set aside maybe an hour every day, and I do a little bit of writing up, do some research thinking about my article that's due on August 31st. Then I think, "Okay, now I got that taken care of. So no, I don't have to feel, you know, stressed out or frustrated, because I'm not doing what I need to do." And then I think, "Okay, I feel some accomplishment. I've got some writing. Now, let me, let me check my emails. Now, let me start working on class prep, grading, and so forth. I've got the rest of the afternoon now to work on that." But I've already got my writing out of the way. I think that Write Now Academy helped me structure all that.

As he continued his story, Todd stressed the importance of helpful dispositions as a key to his writerly identity and what he saw as integral to supporting his writing:

> I think [serving as a faculty facilitator] definitely enhanced my own self efficacy as a writer. Prior to getting involved in the Write Now Academy, I didn't really think about writing and making that a part of my scholarship. Prior to my working with the Write Now Academy, I felt like I wasted some time. When I joined the Write Now Academy, it kind of set up, that, yes, I can do this. I think it enhanced my writing because, out of that, I actually had an article that was published. . . . That was so tremendously satisfying. I think the Academy kind of contributed to my being able to do

> that. Having this structure, having kind of being accountable to my colleagues that I needed to stay productive and, and generate things because I felt like I would lose face a little bit if I came to a meeting, and I said, "Well, you know, I didn't do anything." That wouldn't look very good for me, and so it kind of gave me accountability and motivation.

He concluded his story by pointing to concrete changes in his writing practice resultant of serving as a faculty facilitator:

> In terms of just my way of practicing writing, prior to my involvement in the Write Now Academy, either as a participant or as a facilitator, I used to always think that I needed huge blocks of time, and I think that kind of contributed to my lack of productivity. I learned that small steps kind of result in big outcomes. So, it's sort of my involvement that taught me to set aside some time in the morning and, and even if I'm doing just a short amount of writing, if it's 15 minutes, if it's a half hour, by the end of the week, that's cumulative, I can look back and I can say, "Okay, well, look at what I've achieved." And that kind of motivates me. These small, little steps that result in big rewards. I think that came across in facilitating the group. If we take these small steps, if we just write for 15 minutes or so, by the end of the week, we've got something sizable. If you write a paragraph or so, by the end of the week you see some tangible results that motivates you. I don't know if it improved the way I wrote, but I think, if anything, it just gave me a structure in which to write and be more disciplined and to motivate myself to sit down and begin. I think that was the greatest thing that I took away from my time in the Write Now Academy. So maybe it's more of a process thing, like how to sit down and write.

Madison

Madison serves in a tenured position within the Department of Psychological Sciences where she researches the impact of prenatal exposure to known toxicants and how this impacts later development and processes of learning and memory. She most recently published in the journal *Neurotoxicology and Teratology*.

Like Todd, Madison told a similar story about why she elected to serve as a faculty facilitator of the WNA. She wanted to help her colleagues:

> It's this type of service for the university that I actually really liked. Most of the stuff that I do, some of it is just like, 'Oh, you're on this committee, you do this thing.' But this seemed to be really impactful. And having gone to the Write Now Academy, I wanted to help those who are coming through it again, or going through it after me with the experiences that I had gained when I did it, and I just felt like I had a lot to contribute to it. And it was a way of fulfilling that goal, while also getting rewarded to the service aspect of it.

Madison, like Todd, articulated how leading a WNA has shaped her writing and how she thinks about herself as a writer:

> Okay, so my writing has changed after being a part of the [WNA], especially regarding contacting the editors and knowing that process a little bit better. So, when I had to lead the [WNA], I felt a lot more that I had to lead by example, more so than when I did the [WNA]. To lead by example, I would actively do the skills that the book [*Writing Your Journal Article in Twelve Weeks*] was talking about . . . it made me more conscientious about my writing. [Leading the WNA] made me more understanding that the work I'm doing isn't just for publication; it's to help my fellow people with their struggle. My struggle with writing and my accomplishments in writing can help them. I felt more conscientious or more aware of my writing process because I had to lead them.

She continued by reflecting more on how she views herself as a writer:

> I obviously struggle with writing; that's why I [participated in] the Write Now Academy. Sometimes it feels like, since I struggle with writing, I shouldn't be the one who's telling others how to go about writing . . . I would say that when it comes to writing, it's not always my favorite part. Writing itself can be a daunting task at times, right? And the fear of rejection from an editor is intimidating a lot of the times. But, when I'm in it, I dive into it. And one thing that I think really stuck with me, and I shared with the [WNA], is one of the tenets of research ethics is that when you have data to share that you should share. You need to publish because it's just something you're supposed to do. You need to be getting your knowledge out there for the world to know. When I feel less than

motivated, I realize it's something I need to be doing. It's an ethical thing.

Madison articulated benefits she has derived from leading the WNA and connects these benefit to a current writing project that finds her co-authoring with a colleague and writing in a genre in which she does not have experience:

> Leading the [WNA] allows me to better understand and see examples of different kinds of writing. We get so embedded in our specific form of writing within our department. So, you know, I do empirical studies, I write empirical reports; you know, purpose, methods, results, conclusions, that kind of thing. And literature reviews or meta-analyses or things like that are outside of my ballpark in a way. And so leading [WNA] allows me to have a better chance to have a true discussion with people about that kind of style of writing. That's benefited me now because I'm doing a collaborative research study with some colleagues in my department, and it's a review paper, which is very different than what I'm used to. But having gone through this kind of thing I've seen concrete examples of what this should look like. And we also talked about the process of writing that paper. So that helps me. That part has really helped me a lot with this specific collaborative study.

Madison concluded her story by reflecting on a writerly identity supportive of sustained scholarly productivity:

> Having to lead the [WNA], in a way, forces you to feel more confident with it. And you end up realizing how much you know that you didn't know you knew. And a little bit of that whole fake it 'til you make it kind of thing. Or it's like, "I'm not very confident in my writing, but I'm going to exude the confidence needed to run this academy." And then you feel more confident because of it. I think that that was probably the biggest benefit of how it helps me in my approach to writing. It's changing your whole dynamic of how you think about yourself as a researcher, and approach writing and feeling confident and your skills that you kind of underplay sometimes.

Phillips

Phillips, a tenure-track assistant professor in the Department of English, has published three single-authored books and is currently working on a fourth. In his words, he researches "the interplay of science fiction, horror, and especially folk tales and folk beliefs." Even though his CV suggests that he is an experienced writer, he expressed surprise when Michael invited him to lead an Academy:

> Well, to be honest, it definitely took me by surprise. You know, my career trajectory has been really interesting. And I had a lot of publications before I was even on the tenure track. So, you know, I never thought about myself as being in a position to mentor other people on the publication process and taking their academic writing to publication. So, my initial reaction was surprise and it kind of made me reflect on some of the things that I had accomplished with all of their challenges, pitfalls, a lot of those especially early, and I guess I just thought, if I could help people just getting to navigate those, it would be a nice thing to do.

When our conversation turned to how leading the WNA shapes one's writerly identity, Phillips paused. He said,

> Interesting. It's gonna be hard to articulate. Let me think through that. This fourth book is the only one that I didn't write . . . which, as I reflect on it, I don't think writing a book from introduction to you know, chapter six, seven, conclusion, whatever, front to back is the best way to do it. But that's what I essentially did with books one through three. I might have waited for the introduction on book three, just a little bit. But [book four], I have written completely out of order. And so that part's easy to articulate. *Why* is more difficult. I think it has to do with, well, partly it had to do with the fact that I was really trying to find the core of the argument that I was trying to make. And I think it probably has to do with discussions [in the WNA] about really identifying the stakes of your argument. Maybe being, even though it was more difficult, but being better at recognizing what those are. But if there was anything that sort of changed me in terms of my practice, it might be that.

THEMES IN THE STORIES

We approach these excerpted stories through our research question: How does facilitating the WNA shape one's writerly identity? These stories emphasize how serving as faculty facilitators for the WNA helps Todd, Madison, and Phillips with their own writing projects. In their stories, Phillips points to changes in his writing processes, while Madison and Todd reflect on dispositions that help with their current writing projects. Phillips is working on his fourth single-authored book. In his story, he describes how, for the first three books, he largely wrote linearly: introduction, chapters in order, and then the conclusion. With this book, however, he finds himself writing it "completely out of order." He points to leading the WNA as a reason for taking on a new approach to writing an academic book after successfully writing three books. Phillips says the repeated attention to "really identifying the stakes of your argument" pushes him into a new writing process: writing a book completely out of order in a quest to find that central argument. Todd and Madison are currently working on writing projects, too. Madison is co-authoring what she calls a "review paper" with a colleague in her home department of psychological science. While she is an expert on the content, she is new to the review paper genre. She points to serving as faculty facilitator of the WNA as central to helping her "have true discussions with people" about different genres of writing. These conversations are informing her current work. She admits she has read review papers, but "reading isn't the same as talking about the process of writing [which] has really helped me a lot with this specific collaborative study." Finally, Todd is writing in response to a call for papers. He finds that the WNA helped him with discipline, motivation, structure, and accountability. His story kept returning to these four terms. He describes how he wanted to lead by example and was concerned he would "lose face a little bit" if he came to a WNA meeting without working on his own writing. He tries to set time aside each morning to write a response for the call for papers and describes this time as "depositing some money . . . I pay myself a little bit" before moving onto teaching responsibilities. All three faculty facilitators readily provide examples of how serving as faculty facilitators shapes their writing practices by pointing to their current writing projects and skills or dispositions honed through the WNA that they are leveraging to complete these projects.

Todd and Madison also focus their stories on self-confidence. Both admit to struggling with writing and feeling a bit hesitant to lead a writing group. Todd says that he is open with his colleagues about coming "to the table with my own hang-ups . . . I'm a flawed writer." He says that prior to his involvement in the WNA, he "didn't really think about writing and making that part of my scholarship." Madison states she initially joined the WNA as a participant because "I obviously struggle with writing . . . writing itself can be a daunting task." Both point to how leading the WNA increased their self-confidence as writers. Todd says doing so "definitely enhanced my own self-efficacy as a writer." Madison offers that "having to lead the [WNA], in a way, forces you to feel more confident with it. And you end up realizing how much you know that you didn't know you knew . . . I think that was probably the biggest benefit of how it helps me in my approach to writing." While Phillips's story did not focus on struggles with writing, he did mention that, like Madison, he ended up realizing he knows more about academic writing and the publication process than he previously thought. When Michael asked Phillips to serve as a faculty facilitator, Phillips said he began to "reflect on some of the things that I had accomplished with all of their challenges and pitfalls . . . I thought that if I could help people navigate those, it would be a nice thing to do." Here, we note that Phillips's service with the WNA pushed him to reflect on his writing accomplishments and use these accomplishments as a springboard to help others.

Phillips, Madison, and Todd articulate how leading the WNA supported their perception of themselves as writers; Phillips points to specific writing techniques that changed; Madison and Todd point to behaviors and dispositions that changed. All three highlight the importance of slowing down and coming together in community, of writing together, of gathering—in-person or virtual—to talk writing. As Todd states, "I fall sometimes into my own bad habits when I'm out of that community." And Madison observed, "I felt more conscious and more aware of my writing process because I had to lead [participants]." The act of slowing down to come into community is at the heart of changes to writerly identity our faculty facilitators could articulate. Both slowing down and building community, we argue in the final section, work against neoliberal imperatives that demand speed and competition.

MAKING MUSIC TOGETHER

Writing groups mean building community through slowing down, coordinating resources, and striving collectively for better prose. Even when the outputs may be single-authored publications and presentations, the nature of a writing group means that any publications that came from the writing group were communally generated and nourished. We see writing groups, particularly the act of leading a writing group, as a move toward community that is counter to neoliberal imperatives that are driving many decisions within U.S. higher education. We use the phrase *neoliberal* with a definition and attributes in mind. The definition comes from legal scholar Voyce (2007) who defined neoliberalism as "policies of competition, deregulation and privatization" (p. 2055). Sociologist Mulya offered three hallmarks of neoliberalism: "marketisation, competitiveness, and standardisation" (2019, p. 87). Both Voyce and Mulya highlighted the central role of competition. The additional traits characterizing neoliberalism, we argue, rotate around the idea of speeding up productivity. Deregulation as a method for speeding up productivity; outsourcing to private companies as a method for speeding up productivity;

standardizing as a method for speeding up productivity. U.S. higher education is witnessing a push toward increased worker productivity and seeing the use of competition (e.g., faculty against faculty) as a vehicle for arriving at this productivity more quickly. In this chapter, we offered a counter to these impulses by hearing stories from faculty who support the publishing of other faculty, who support slowing down and working in community with others.

Here at the close, we extend Mulya's (2019) work to our local context. Like us, Mulya situates himself in the work of faculty development. His article, published in the *International Journal for Academic Development*, specifically considers how faculty might partner with undergraduate students for research projects to contest neoliberalism. Mulya addresses in turn each of the hallmarks of neoliberalism—marketisation, competitiveness, and standardization—and offers the practice of partnering with students on research projects as a method for countering each hallmark. For example, by focusing on "community and belonging" within a partnership, we combat drives toward competition that are inherent in neoliberal forces (p. 88). While we are not engaging with students-as-partners praxis, an exciting approach gaining currency across higher education, we take up his broader arguments and extend them here to our work. Like Mulya we believe, and our qualitative data supports our belief, that "community and belonging" arise in meaningful ways for our faculty facilitators. They quell impulses toward competition by setting aside time for 12 weeks to come together and work and learn and write together. Community and belonging shaped the writerly identity of the three faculty facilitators. Moving forward with the WNA, we will intentionally design opportunities for continued community and belonging by seeking out faculty participants from across varied disciplines and ranks and including university staff who also engage in academic writing—like our colleagues in student affairs. Through encouraging a variety of faculty and staff, we can help faculty build a broad network of communal support.

Community and belonging were central themes we found. So, too, were themes of slowing down. While Mulya does not directly address speed as a hallmark of neoliberalism, we see speed as central to how the free market infringes on higher education. Thus, slowing down is a deliberate act designed to counter neoliberal impulses and an act that profoundly shapes writerly identity. We take seriously theories and practices of slowing down articulated in books like *The Slow Professor* (Seeber & Berg, 2016) and slowing down as a method for assuaging midcareer faculty burnout (Mulholland, 2020). What we learned about slowing down from our three faculty facilitators can help shape how we intentionally embed slowness into future iterations of the WNA.

Ultimately, we will seek methods to emphasize community and slowing down as a method for supporting faculty writing development and countering neoliberal impulses. We encourage readers, especially those working within faculty development, to specifically design and redesign programming to counter neoliberalism. These damaging imperatives play out differently across campuses and contexts and countries. To topple these imperatives, we need to adopt locally specific faculty development programming. Through developing these kinds of programming opportunities, we can ensure that we all are making music together.

REFERENCES

Belcher, W. L. (2009). *Writing your journal article in 12 weeks: A guide to academic publishing success*. Sage.

Boice, R. (1985). The neglected third factor in writing: Productivity. *College Composition and Communication, 36*(4), 472–480. https://doi.org/10.2307/357866.

Brantmeier, E., Molloy, C. & Byrne, J. (2017). Writing renewal retreats: The scholarly writer, contemplative practice, and scholarly productivity. *To Improve the Academy: A Journal of Educational Development, 36*(2). https://doi.org/10.3998/tia.17063888.0036.205.

Cox, M. & Brunjes, A. (2013). Guiding principles for supporting faculty writers at a teaching-mission institution. In A. E. Geller & M. Eodice (Eds.), *Working with faculty writers* (pp. 191–210). Utah State University Press.

Eodice, M. & Cramer, S. (2001). Write on! A model for enhancing faculty publication. *Journal of Faculty Development, 18*(4), 113–121.

Gray, T., Madson, L. & Jackson, M. (2018). Publish & flourish: Helping scholars become better, more prolific writers. *To Improve the Academy: A Journal of Educational Development, 37*, 243–256. https://doi.org/10.3998/tia.17063888.0037.203.

Mulholland, J. (2020). Slow down: On dealing with midcareer burnout. *MLA: Profession*. https://doi.org/10.3998/tia.17063888.0037.203.

Mulya, T. W. (2019). Contesting the neoliberalism of higher education through student-faculty partnership. *International Journal for Academic Development, 24*(1), 86–90.

Patel, L. (2019). Turning away from logarithms to return to story. *Research in the Teaching of English, 53*(3), 270–275.

Seeber, B. K. & Berg, M. (2016). *The slow professor: Countering the culture of speed in the academy*. University of Toronto Press. https://doi.org/10.3138/9781442663091.

Smith, L. T. (2012). *Decolonizing methodologies: Research and indigenous peoples* (2nd ed.). Zed Books. https://doi.org/10.5040/9781350225282.

Stornaiuolo, A., Smith, A. & Philips, N. (2017). Developing a transliteracies framework for a connected world. *Journal of Literacy Research, 49*(1), 68–91. https://doi.org/10.20343/teachlearninqu.9.2.12.

Tuck, E. & Wayne Yang, K. (2014). R-Words: Refusing research. In D. Paris & M. T. Winn (Eds.), *Humanizing research: Decolonizing qualitative inquiry for youth and communities* (pp. 223–247). Sage.

Tulley, C. (2018). *How writing faculty write: Strategies for process, product, and productivity*. Utah State University Press.
Voyce, M. (2007). Shopping malls in India: New social 'dividing practices.' *Economic and Political Weekly, 42*(22), 2055–2062.
Wenger, E., McDermott, R. & Snyder, W. M. (2002). *Cultivating communities of practice*. Harvard Business Review Press.

CHAPTER 11.

FACULTY WHO WRITE WITH THEIR GRADUATE STUDENTS: A STUDY OF NON-PEER WRITING COLLABORATIONS

Kristina Quynn and Carol Wilusz
Colorado State University

Abstract. *We discuss non-peer writing collaborations between faculty and graduate students, exploring the pedagogical implications of co-authorship. Drawing on data from mentorship programs, this chapter argues for a shift in academic perspectives to recognize the value of collaborative writing, underscoring how relational writing processes can better support faculty and student development.*

> Finally, we were led to think most seriously of the pedagogical implications of co-authorship. What do we know as a discipline about the advantages or disadvantages of having students participate in co- or group-writing? If advantages do exist, don't they in some ways contradict our profession's traditional insistence on students working alone? And perhaps most importantly, do we have ways to teach students to adjust readily to co- or group-writing tasks?
>
> – Lisa Ede and Andrea Lunsford, "Why Write . . . Together?" (p. 32)

WRITING TOGETHER: A NEW BEGINNING

Decades ago, Lisa Ede[1] and Andrea Lunsford blazed trails for those in the humanities to explore collaborative writing so that we might better understand the complex and often undervalued processes of co-authorship. As junior faculty, Ede and Lunsford (or Lunsford and Ede as they alternated for publication) started where so many of us do when exploring; they kept journals, asked questions, gathered information, surveyed collaborators, analyzed data, and devised pedagogies.

---

1   This article honors the memory and work of Lisa Ede, a writing studies role model who passed away in 2021.

They co-authored their adventures. They took on an activist mission, advocating for collaborative work so that co-authored texts would *count* in calculations of tenure and promotion in historically single-author fields (i.e., in writing studies). Lunsford and Ede identified key themes and questions that would guide future studies and provide a map for those who followed to pursue collaborative writing research. They pointed the way to *pedagogy*—bringing co-writing projects into the classroom to better support collaborative skill-building—to our *peer processes*, to the impacts of *technology* on our methods, and to the *ethics* of professional responsibility and crediting of work. Long after "Why Write . . . Together?" (1983) and *Singular Texts/Plural Authors* (1990), we still have much to learn about *how* academics write together even as collaborative writing is the norm for science and social science disciplines.

Following in Ede and Lunsford's footsteps, collaborative writing researchers are apt to imagine co-authoring and collaborative peer-to-peer writing relationships: students writing with students, professionals collaborating with professionals, or faculty co-authoring with faculty. The *author* in "co-author" elides differences; the *co* suggests equality, and we naturally imagine *peers*. Current trends in co-authoring across disciplines mean we must reimagine collaborative writing to include non-peer or asymmetric writing relationships if we are to serve faculty writing needs. Most full-time faculty at science, technology, engineering, mathematics, and medicine (STEMM) research universities publish collaboratively with their graduate students or postdoctoral fellows. Often the graduate student—not the faculty member—will take on the duties of the lead writer and the faculty member will contribute variously as an editor, mentor, and supervisor (Kamler, 2008; Bozeman and Youtie, 2017). This widespread mode of writing collaboration among non-peers reveals new territory that we must better understand if we are to facilitate writing relationships, practices, and processes on our campuses. While non-peer writing relationships are often posited as beneficial for graduate student development, we also seek to understand the benefits for faculty writers.

This chapter describes the Collaborative Writing: Mentoring through Writing workshop and the corresponding study of asymmetric co-writing relationships at Colorado State University, Fort Collins (CSU) over three years from 2020 to 2023. This endeavor is itself a collaborative project between two cross-campus program directors to understand how to support faculty and graduate student researchers as they co-write submissible quality (professional quality documents capable of being submitted for publication or funding): abstracts, poster presentations, journal articles, and grant proposals.[2] The workshop's faculty and

---

2   The study is IRB approved and has been funded with monies from CSU's Graduate Center for Inclusive Mentoring, NIH grant #T32GM132057, and CSU Writes.

graduate students come from the interdisciplinary graduate program in Cell and Molecular Biology (CMB) or from other graduate programs in the Colleges of Natural Sciences and Natural Resources.

As collaborating workshop facilitators, we hail from markedly different disciplines, but we share a common desire to support mentoring relationships and the production of high-quality research across the university. Carol Wilusz is the director of CMB, a program of over 100 affiliate faculty and approximately 45 students from 17 departments and six colleges at the university. Kristina Quynn is the founding director of CSU Writes, a program designed to help researchers and scholars across their career-spans build sustainable writing practices.[3]

Our collaboration for the workshop reflects our shared dedication to the campus writing community and interest in facilitating faculty as they write with their graduate students. CMB aims to foster an inclusive learning and research culture among diverse participants in an interdisciplinary research environment. The Graduate Center for Inclusive Mentoring and NIH training grants that fund the workshop are both designed to support students from underrepresented groups. Carol has served as lead or co-lead investigator on training grants from NSF and NIH which support graduate students interested in computational biology and provide support in developing soft skills including writing. Kristina brings a background in transnational, postcolonial, and gendered literary studies to her work in writing studies. The principles of writing sociality that inform much of CSU Writes' curriculum resonate with feminist writing collaboratives and align with models of shared equity leadership (Kezar et al., 2021).

The collaborative writing workshop and study also reflect CSU Writes' career-span writing support approach, which is designed on models of writing containment (Jensen, 2017; Murray, 2014a), writing productivity (Boice, 2000), and writing in social spaces (Murray, 2014b; Murray, 2014c). Carol and I devised a workshop to support collaborative writers and a corresponding study of asymmetric writing relationships and processes. While we designed the workshop for faculty and graduate students in STEMM fields, the facilitative model could easily be adapted to support faculty who co-author with graduate students in social science and humanities disciplines.

---

3   CSU Writes is not the CSU Writing Center, which is a well-respected resource housed in the English Department informed by writing across the curriculum (WAC) and tutorial writing center models. The similarity in names and acronyms does cause some confusion on campus but the differences in approach assure we do not overlap much. Rather than an attunement to pedagogy and curriculum (i.e., WAC), CSU Writes focuses on facilitative approaches to work with writers across their career-span. Subtle but significant. It is housed in the Graduate School and funded, in part, by the Office of the Vice President for Research. CSU Writes works with hundreds of writers each year with over 3000 attendances (2021 CSU Writes Annual Report).

NON-PEER COLLABORATIVE WRITING IN CONTEXT: RELEVANT LITERATURE

The Collaborative Writing: Mentoring through Writing workshop brings together conversations from the fields of writing studies, team science, graduate student mentoring, and higher education to contextualize faculty, postdoctoral fellow, and graduate student voices as they speak about crafting professional documents in asymmetric relationships. We seek to understand the current needs of co-authors in asymmetric, non-peer, academic research contexts so that we can design programming to support faculty and graduate students or postdocs simultaneously as writers. We have avoided the assumption that we know what "collaborative writing" is or how it operates for faculty mentors. One-hundred percent of the CMB faculty participating in this study plan to publish research papers or submit grant proposals as co-authors with their mentees.

The Collaborative Writing: Mentoring through Writing workshop draws on diverse studies of mentoring, team building, and writing pedagogy and advice texts that inform the presentations and workshop guidebook. Not finding a single text that addressed the asymmetric co-writing needs of our participants, we crafted our own guide to help faculty (as well as their mentees). Many studies of and advice about collaborative writing, for instance, tend to focus on peer relationship, classroom instructional modes and industry needs (Ede & Lunsford, 1990; Wolfe, 2010). Studies of research team effectiveness have largely bypassed a direct examination of collaborative writing practices, treating writing as the product or deliverable of a team (Bozeman & Youtie, 2017; Mirel & Spilka, 2002). Similarly, studies and advice about graduate student faculty relationships have either elided writing processes (Allen & Eby, 2007; Shore, 2014) or approached the writing process as shaped by a supervisory or pedagogical relationship (Casanave, 2014, 2020; Kamler & Thomson, 2014). Our programming draws in various ways on these approaches to support faculty and graduate students as they engage in asymmetric co-writing relationships, but not it does not rely on approach or text, exclusively.

The faculty we work with will be listed as co-authors with their graduate students; thus, their investment in the quality of graduate student writing extends beyond the navigation of committee, department, and graduate school criteria for degree completion. The pressures faculty face in helping their mentees write, to turn a phrase from Barbara Kamler and Pat Thompson (2014), intersect with the imperatives to *publish or perish* to career-build in academia. From the graduate student perspective, Kamler and Thomson detail the challenges students face in the growing trend of "PhDs by publication," by which dissertations are compiled out of published articles (p. 138). As the case study by Shvidko and Atkinson

(2019) highlights, increased competition for academic jobs means "Doctoral students are therefore frequently advised, and increasingly required, to publish before graduation" (p. 155). Kamler and Thomson emphasize the challenges dissertators face as they navigate "the journal game," "publication brokering," co-authoring agreements, and other writing for publication processes (p. 144, p. 154). We must recognize that faculty advisors are the principal guides for graduate students as they navigate these processes and that the imperatives of "PhDs by publication" are shared, albeit differently, by faculty whose experiences bring together multiple supervisory roles: field expert, content supervisor, writing instructor, and, in many cases, manuscript editor and contributing author.

To be sure, the writing terrains in which faculty researchers and scholars collaborate are rapidly changing. Research academics now produce articles and proposals at an extraordinary pace, due chiefly to advancements in information technologies that allow large numbers of researchers to collaborate quickly and efficiently across disciplinary, institutional, and international boundaries. New areas of study have emerged to understand the growth of "team science," "collaboration cosmopolitanism," and other features of what Barry Bozeman and Jan Youtie (2017) have coined the "Research Collaboration Revolution" (p. 3). This revolution is characterized by increases in collaborations; team size; diversity on teams; international, multidisciplinary, and/or interdisciplinary collaboration; fair crediting of work; and an interest in how teams operate (p. 3). They share the current outer limits of co-authoring, noting that "a paper (Aad et al., 2015) published in the prestigious journal *Physical Review Letters* included 5,154 authors, such a large number that twenty-four pages of a thirty-three-page article were taken up with the listing of authors" (p. 4).

This transformation in knowledge production has created challenges regarding appropriate crediting and reputation-building among researchers, particularly for team-heavy fields found in the sciences, engineering, and medicine. Research collaboration advice has tended to focus on support for researchers in STEMM fields and more on team building rather than writing, which is generally treated as a *deliverable*. However, writing program administrators would do well to remember that inter- and multi-disciplinary teams increasingly include scholars from the social sciences and humanities. And, with the advent of new digital publishing mediums alongside the development of specialized synchronous/asynchronous writing technology (think Google Docs), co-authorship and coedited projects have become more widely adopted even in such traditionally single-author disciplines as communications, journalism, media, and writing studies.

Professional writing collaborations between faculty mentors and their mentees are crucial to the specialization and career-building success of both parties. While there is a burgeoning body of literature on the solitary academic writer's experience and advice manuals—from Robert Boice's *Professors as Writers* (1990) to Jan Allen's *The Productive Graduate Student Writer* (2019), there are few texts devoted to faculty writing collaboratively or co-authoring with their mentees. Even those that do address faculty, such as *Helping Doctoral Students Write: Pedagogies for Supervision* (2006) and *Doctoral Writing: Practices, Processes and Pleasures* (2020), tend to focus on the supervisory or advisory roles of faculty members—overlooking their concomitant experiences of increasing publication pressures and grant submission imperatives to support their research agendas and build their careers.

THE STUDY: MENTORING THROUGH WRITING WORKSHOP

> [F]or small errors I can just fix them or state the problem (subject-verb agreement), and for problems with organization within a section or across the entire paper it is usually easy to identify what is wrong and explain what needs to be done in a few words. However, within a paragraph I either just rewrite it myself (which is faster, but still takes time, and isn't good for having my students learn to write better themselves), or my explanation of what is wrong and what needs to be fixed is longer than the actual problem and takes a while to think about and write down.
>
> – Faculty Participant, Needs Assessment Survey Response

The workshop calls for a collaborative writing assignment and participation in three distinct information and discussion segments: two workshop-style sessions and a 20-minute facilitated conversation with CSU Writes (Kristina). The workshop runs for three to five weeks and is offered twice per year—fall and spring/summer. We planned to launch the workshops and study in-person spring semester 2020; however, due to COVID-19 pandemic health protocols, 2020–2021 workshops and conversations were held virtually (on Zoom or MS Teams). The Spring 2022 workshop transitioned to hybrid delivery, and by Spring 2023, the workshop shifted to in-person. We have plans for the workshop continuing semesterly as a part of our regular CSU Writes and CMB programming. The workshop study ran from 2020 to 2023.

Each segment of the workshop contains the following:

- Graduate-student-only introductory session covers modes of collaborative writing, types of feedback, and what to expect from the workshop from a student perspective.
- Faculty-only introductory session covers modes of collaborative writing, types of feedback, and what to expect from the workshop from a faculty perspective.

- Faculty and graduate student consultation is a guided conversation with Kristina (workshop facilitator) about their writing assignment and practice of techniques covered in the introductory sessions.
- Combined faculty and graduate student final session provides a review of workshop concepts and techniques as well as an opportunity for participants to share reflections on their collaborative writing and workshop experiences.

The workshop is intensive and requires a month-long participation commitment from the faculty and graduate student dyads or triads. Faculty mentors sign up with one or two of their graduate students. The workshop caps faculty attendance each semester at 10. To accommodate participant writing and facilitator conversations, we build in three to four weeks between the introductory and final sessions. Over that time, faculty and students participate in a collaborative writing feedback assignment which asks them to experiment with strategies covered in the introductory workshop on one of their current writing projects. The assignment, thus, is not to be extra work, but should align with the collaborators' existing writing projects.

The workshop's intake survey allows us to hear what writers at different career stages identify as working well (or not as well) in their individual and partnered writing projects, processes, and practices. Faculty identify a constellation of constraints that impact their feedback decisions and instructional guidance for student writers who also serve as writing partners on manuscripts and proposals: time limitations, project management, and relational dynamics pose some of the greatest concerns. Through the workshop, the oft-experiential knowledge faculty possess of writing in their discipline can be made explicit, shared in conversation and practice, and adjusted by each dyad considering collaborative methods we discuss in the introductory, facilitated, and final sessions.

Research faculty are experienced writers, and most will pass on to their students the writing knowledge and strategies they gleaned from their advisors. We know that few faculty receive formal training in writing or writing pedagogy. Helen Sword's survey of more than 1,300 academic writers found that only 15 percent had received "formal" writing instruction to "learn to write in your field"; 47 percent had received only "informal" instruction, meaning variations of on-the-job or experiential training—as in learning by doing; and 38 percent had some form of "semiformal" instruction such as workshops (2017, pp. 63–64). The faculty in our workshop reflect a similarly varied background in their writing training and experiences, and their participation in the workshop alongside their graduate students reflects the ongoing writing development of faculty to be gained.

As the faculty member's confession above acknowledges, many faculty members struggle with the dual task of providing training and producing submissible-quality writing on a timeline or to meet a deadline. One faculty member who participated in the workshop highlights what seems to be a routinely performed internal calculation that involves work effort, time to task, and efficiency of communication to provide feedback on a student writing: "My explanation of what is wrong and what needs to be fixed is longer than the actual problem and takes a while to think about and write down." Interestingly, the types of writing support this faculty member needs would seem to have little to do with formal or informal writing instruction. In this instance, the learning needs of the student exceed the time and work capacities of the faculty mentor. These non-peer collaborative writing issues will take further study to parse best methods for program and institutional support, for sure. The trend of graduate students taking the lead on writing production has a significant and yet-to-be-studied impact on faculty as writers and defacto instructors of writing. This modest study provides an opening for us to better understand the imbricated collaborative and coauthoring challenges that non-peer research and scholarly writers face and what relational practices will address their needs.

METHODS: NEEDS ASSESSMENT

The methods focused on in this chapter relate to the pre-workshop needs assessment, which we used to identify the collaborative writing interests and desired skill development in advance of our first workshop in 2020 and have been reissued yearly for the duration of our study (2020–2023). In consultation with the CSU STEM Center, we designed a survey to identify faculty and graduate student writing interests and skill development needs.[4] We should note that the intake survey is one of multiple measures included in the broader, three-year mixed methods study. Additional measures outside the scope of this chapter include pre-workshop, post-workshop, and year-out surveys (quantitative/qualitative); faculty and graduate student interviews; facilitator notes (qualitative). This chapter focuses exclusively on data from the pre-workshop surveys of faculty and graduate students in which both classifications of writers identify their current needs and learning expectations. We found the needs assessment data crucial for developing our workshop presentations, activities, and guide (see Appendix C for the workshop guide table of contents).

Needs assessments were emailed to both participating students and faculty mentors before the introductory workshop session. The identity of individual

---

4   We acknowledge and are grateful for the survey design and reporting efforts of Julie Maertens from the CSU STEM Center.

respondents remained anonymous. As workshop co-facilitators, Kristina and Carol reviewed the STEM Center's survey reports in advance of the workshop to clarify participants' collaborative writing interests, challenges, and concerns; we used our review to focus workshop presentations and discussion and to develop a workshop guide.

The pre-workshop needs assessment survey was designed to help us identify both faculty and graduate student learning priorities. Faculty received one version of the assessment; graduate students another; however, the surveys were largely mirrored, with modest differences in phrasing. For instance, faculty were asked to identify their interest in learning about writing "confidence building," whereas graduate students were asked about their interest in writing "confidence." The needs assessment asked about participant backgrounds and interests. It included Likert-scale, open-ended, demographic, and dropdown questions on the following categories of query:

- Demographic data about gender and ethnicity
- Field of study
- Years in program and career interest (student only)
- Prior writing-focused training
- Interests in workshop format (lecture, group discussion, practice session)
- Level of interest in the topics of planning, support, field-specific writing, ELL, writing-focused communication, editing/commenting (faculty), responding to comments (students), confidence building (faculty), confidence (students), co-authoring, resources
- Any additional suggestions (See survey questions in the appendices.)

The survey responses were compiled into a summary report by the CSU STEM Center for facilitator use in the development of workshop materials and discussion topics.

DATA: NEEDS ASSESSMENT

The data in this chapter was drawn from the pre-workshop survey reports, compiled by the CSU STEM Center. The Likert-scale interest and short-answer responses focusing on participants' expressed interests in and described challenges with writing collaboratively. To date, 24 (of an estimated 30–35) faculty and 37 (of an estimated 35–40) graduate students have participated in the workshop. The higher number of graduate students reflects that faculty members may mentor and publish—and thus participate in this workshop—with more than one graduate student. Both faculty and student participants come from such STEMM-focused fields of study as biochemistry, biomedical sciences, chemistry, environmental and radiological health, geosciences, horticulture, immunology, mathematics, microbiology, pathology, psychology, soil and crop sciences, and wildlife biology.

We share the graduate student intake data alongside the faculty intake data because the faculty co-writing experience is in relationship with their graduate students. In general, graduate students expressed lower levels of interest in most workshop topics than faculty did (see Figure 11.1). Expressed interests ranged from 1.33 (English as a second language topics) to 2.83 (field-specific writing—considerations and guidance) on a 1 to 4 scale. Response options ranged from 1) Not interested, 2) Slightly interested, 3) Interested, or 4) Very interested.

Other top areas of interest included information on managing and communicating writing support expectations and the aligned topic of mentor-mentee communications. The top three workshop topic interest categories for graduate students suggest a need for combined field-specific and general writing skill development support among students.

Faculty participants expressed interest at much higher rates across all topics (2.17 to 3.33) than graduate students, and the most highly ranked faculty interests focused on project planning and managing the basic writing needs and expectations of students. The significant difference between the students' interest in learning about "responding to reader comments" (2.17) and faculty's more avid interest in learning about "providing feedback" and in "editing/commenting" (both rated at 3.17) marks a place where faculty and graduate student collaborative writing interests may be relationally misaligned in ways that could cause tensions for faculty as they engage in iterative, time-bound feedback and revision processes with their students.

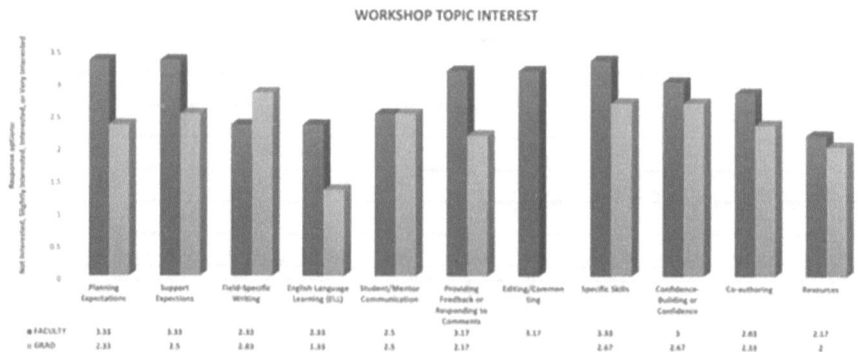

Figure 11.1. Faculty and graduate student interest in workshop topics: From pre-workshop needs survey. Note: This graph represents preliminary data from graduate student responses at the mid-point of our three-year study of collaborative practices for mentoring through writing.

Overall, these findings suggest that faculty have a slightly greater interest in the process of writing and that graduate students have a slightly greater interest in building their confidence in crafting both general and field-specific writing. Excerpts from faculty responses of the open-ended questions have been used as section epigraphs in this chapter so that readers can hear the faculty voices that influenced the workshop focus and materials design.

Putting Data to Work in Workshop

> Students have difficulty drafting manuscripts under time pressure, making it difficult to engage in constructive back and forth writing when we rarely have the luxury of spending months on a manuscript. How can we make the process more efficient such that students will get the most value from the learning experience? In my experience, students learn to write from carefully reading papers, and from studying the edits made by their advisor and others to their own manuscripts. But students don't understand that writing is largely learned through independent-study rather than instruction.
> – Faculty Participant, Needs Assessment Survey Response

We can identify key differences in the expressed developmental needs of graduate students and faculty in the survey data. Graduate student interest, for instance, localizes in field-specific writing skill- and confidence-building, which suggests a newness to the field overall. Comparatively, faculty interest focused on topics of project management and efficient editing, suggesting faculty seek strategies to help move writing projects through to submission. These broad observations make sense, given the asymmetric developmental and career-stages of faculty and students.

More specifically, we can identify key places to integrate advice for graduate students into our workshops about how they can build their reading skills and make best use of feedback. For faculty, we included information in the workshop about what types of feedback and through what medium (for example, as a conversation or as marginal comments) work best and at what stage of a student's project or manuscript. For students, we provided information about how to track the most common types of editorial feedback they receive, to look for patterns, to seek additional writing support resources, and to build confidence in their skills and professional development. Neither of these approaches that we used to address faculty and student developmental needs are innovative; they both are common techniques. Faculty are encouraged to share with other faculty and with their students what does or does not work in their writing processes during the discussion sessions and through guided reflections in the writing assignment with their students. What makes this workshop novel or "work," if you will, is the relational pairing of both faculty- and graduate-student-expressed interests, providing opportunities for writing as professional development and as an inherently collaborative endeavor to be the foci of conversation.

The faculty participant comment above describes *writing* as a practice "largely learned through independent study rather than instruction," which exposes a common desire for writing instruction to happen elsewhere. Our study notes that writing is a key site of relational tensions and expectations. Central to this faculty member's concern are two relational values: (1) the guidance of an independent study and (2) an efficient *iterative* feedback-based training for the student. We interpreted this faculty member's comment to mean that the act of drafting in this collaboration is often a solitary endeavor in which the graduate student takes the lead on the manuscript and through an experiential and iterative "constructive feedback process" learns and becomes a better writer. It is not uncommon for faculty to expect the student to be the lead on drafting a manuscript and reaching out for feedback on a need-be basis or with a complete draft (whatever that may look like). A writer may be writing to learn field-specific content, new genres or styles, and improved quality of expression that serve the purpose of the assigned task or collaborative effort (submissible writing). For our purposes in developing workshop materials, we considered what might help faculty who experience increased pressure from graduate students who seek writing specific support within the discipline, support that a faculty member (an expert in a field of knowledge) may feel ill equipped to provide.

To speak directly to our workshop participants' concerns, we developed a workshop guidebook (https://tinyurl.com/yt4n8wyd), which includes the following:

- The mentor/mentee workshop writing assignment
- Writer's reflection and conversation guide
- Descriptions of collaborative writing
- Recommended feedback practices—types and when
- Strategies for graduate students to track feedback
- Writing reflections and conversation guides for both faculty and graduate students and information on collaborative writing (non-binding) and co-author (legally binding) agreements, including an APA model.

Our goal with this guidebook was to provide writing support related both to their career stage as well as to their skill in writing with others who come to the writing relationship with an aligned interest in the topic but often with a diversity of professional positions, identity backgrounds, and writing experiences. We relied on the responses to the 2020 needs intake survey to develop much of the first workshop's materials: guidebook, slides, and discussion questions.

The intake surveys have revealed that, unlike the collaborative writing relationships among peers, the asymmetry of the faculty-student collaborations means that faculty must juggle the demands of pedagogy and professional writing productivity. In the words of a participant, faculty must "find a balance between maintaining the independence of students who might have limited writing experience and obtaining a high-quality final product (i.e., making sure they retain ownership and don't just have text rewritten by a more senior co-author)." These concerns highlight the intertwined skill- and profession-building quality of the academic collaborative writing relationships of faculty. They also highlight that faculty co-authors often identify their primary duty as one of being an editor for a lead author. On the one hand, for most STEMM faculty who co-author with postdoctoral fellows and graduate students, this observation would seem to state the obvious. On the other hand, for those of us who wish to better understand and support faculty professional development as writers and teachers, it illuminates that faculty would benefit from program or institutional support that emphasizes feedback methods and mentoring techniques to support their own evolving writing practices across the career span.

WRITING IN FACULTY DEVELOPMENT PROGRAMS

> The content and ideas may be present, but the foundational composition/writing skills are very weak. I would like suggestions on how to improve my ability to mentor students in improving their writing in a "back to basics" fashion, and less so focused on "grantsmanship." Grantsmanship is something I am comfortable with, foundational writing skills not so much.
> – Faculty Participant, Needs Assessment Survey Response

We must think outside the curricular box and look to serve the professional development needs of faculty mentors in relation to their writing. When faculty take on graduate students who need more writing support than the faculty member may have the time or skills to provide, both faculty and graduate students can experience stress, leading to challenges in their collaborative writing relationship. We know from both sides of the mentor-mentee co-writing relationship that time constraints and pressure to move students through can impact the feedback students receive on their theses and dissertations (Kumar & Stracke, 2007; Carter & Kumar, 2017). We also know that the "writing a thesis by publication" model is likely to continue as a pedagogical and co-writing practice (Guerin, 2018; Sharmini, 2017). By supporting faculty as collaborative writers, we can maintain the disciplinary contexts for their graduate students as well.

This relational approach can support students who have been selected for graduate studies in competitive fields and who may still be developing basic writing or English language skills. In his argument to situate graduate academic writing as a form of "professional" training, Shyam Sharma (2018) states that approaching writing as professional skill development may be especially helpful for "international students, whose exposure to the society and professions outside can be short and limited" (p. 142). Sharma continues by reminding us that "it is insufficient to teach writing within the narrow limits of 'academic communication,' just focusing on rhetorical and linguistic and genre skills out of context or even disciplinary contexts" (p. 142). For students who will be the lead authors on their theses or dissertations as well as on many co-authored publications, presentations, and other submissions produced during their graduate studies learning to *take the lead*, to develop their unique academic voice, *to wield the field*, as one of Kristina's professors used to say, requires delicate guidance from writing mentors and collaborators.

We recognize that advisors often feel highly competent when guiding their students through the complex knowledge terrains and across the cutting edges of their fields of study. They can also feel correspondingly incompetent or ill equipped to guide students as writers in those fields. If we, as writing program administrators, seek to understand as we walk beside our faculty writing colleagues, we can provide ever higher-quality writing support for asymmetric and increasingly complex and pressured writing relationships. Such understanding and program building will invariably require new studies, new data, fine-tuned methods, and fresh practices. This is a new collaborative writing terrain.

TERRITORIES TO EXPLORE: WRITING ACROSS THE CAREER SPAN

> As long as academic institutions, publishers, disciplines and students themselves require (certain kinds of) writing to help them to develop as knowing scholars, to graduate and/or to disseminate their research, then those institutions who take in doctoral students have a moral and ethical obligation to ensure that students learn these literacies. A successful doctoral candidate needs to make a contribution to knowledge; and that means more than knowing something—it means being able to communicate that knowledge in a way that meets the student's own needs and the needs of the discipline/institution.
>
> – Claire Aitchison and Anthony Paré (2021, p. 23)

We would add to the apt assertion of Claire Aitchison and Anthony Paré that institutions also have an equal responsibility to support faculty mentors and advisors as *writers*. In instances where faculty co-write with their graduate students, we must help faculty develop their collaborative writing literacies. *Literacies*, we propose, that most academic writing facilitators do not yet understand well and that will continue to evolve with the integration of AI and yet-to-be-developed writing tools into our research writing processes and production.

This piece, along with the others in this collection, speaks to our collective desire to understand faculty writers and their writing contexts through data gathered and analyzed. The support needs of many faculty writers require a better understanding of collaborative writing in asymmetric co-authoring relationships. Aitchison and Paré (2021) also noted in their work on "Writing as Craft and Practice in the Doctoral Curriculum," that graduate students have distinctive writing support needs rooted in disciplinary, institutional, and publishing industry standards that oversee knowledge production. We add that facilitators and writing program administrators must remember that the faculty mentors are the behind-the-scenes, powerful, co-writing supervisors, whose duties bring together those of instructor and co-author. We must also better understand faculty's ever-evolving collaborative writing terrains so that we can identify what practices, techniques, and programs can best serve these writing dyads and, in some cases, writing teams.

To address the complex challenges faculty face as we move into ever-changing terrains of research, scholarship, and publishing, we (Kristina and Carol) expand Ede and Lunsford's 1983 map, to provide additional relational-focused questions for studies of the practice and processes of collaborative writing:[5]

1. What distinct features and pressures shape relational writing among academic co-authors (diverse backgrounds and skill levels)?
2. What relational writing practices and collaborative techniques best support writers in partnerships and across teams (which may include hundreds of writers)?
3. How does a co-author's sense of writerly-self change in relationship with others?
4. What writing tools (digital and non-digital) and methods best support writers? At what stages of the writing collaboration are select tools best used?
5. To what extent does collaborative writing reflect or amplify the challenges faced in knowledge production across degree-granting institutions (from support programming to credentialing) and publishing industry (crediting)?
6. What are the impacts or value of co-authorship on individual writer's careers over time, across disciplines, across genres? What counts?

---

5 This conclusion recalls the close of Ede and Lunsford's "Why Write . . . Together" in which they pose eight categories of questions for future study.

What doesn't? How might writing facilitators advise individual writers as co-authors?
7. What types of curricula and programming will best serve co-authors, writing teams, and partners across the collaborative writing spectrum as we continue to write across new terrains of professional research and scholarly writing?

REFERENCES

Aad, G. et al.. 2015. ATLAS Collaboration and CMS Collaboration. "Combined Measurement of the Higgs Boson Mass in pp Collisions at $\sqrt{s}$ = 7 and 8 TeV with the ATLAS and CMS Experiments." *Physical Review Letters* 114, no. 19: 191803. https://doi.org/10.1103/PhysRevLett.114.191803.

Aitchison, C. & Paré, A. (2021). Writing as craft and practice in the doctoral curriculum. In A. Lee & S. Danby (Eds.). *Reshaping doctoral education: International approaches and pedagogies* (pp. 12–23). Routledge. https://doi.org/10.4324/9780203142783-3.

Allen, J. E. (2019). *The productive graduate student writer: How to manage your time, process, and energy to write your research proposal, thesis, and dissertation and get published.* Routledge.

Allen, T. D. & Turner de Tormes Eby, L. (2007). *The Blackwell handbook of mentoring: A multiple perspectives approach.* Blackwell. https://doi.org/10.1111/b.9781405133739.2007.x.

Boice, R. (1990). Professors as Writers. New Forums Press. https://tinyurl.com/2x2ysnhj.

Bozeman, B. & Youtie, J. (2017) *The strength in numbers: The new science of team science.* Princeton University Press. https://doi.org/10.1515/9781400888610.

Carter, S., Guerin, C. & Aitchison, C. (2020). *Doctoral writing: Practices, processes and pleasures.* Springer Nature.

Carter, S. & Kumar, V. (2017). "Ignoring me is part of learning": Supervisory feedback on doctoral writing. *Innovations in Education and Teaching International,* 54(1), 68–75. https://doi.org/10.1080/14703297.2015.1123104.

Casanave, C. P. (2014). *Before the dissertation: A textual mentor for doctoral students at early stages of a research project.* Michigan University Press. https://doi.org/10.3998/mpub.100308.

Casanave, C. P. (2020). *During the dissertation: A textual mentor for doctoral students in the process of writing.* Michigan University Press. https://doi.org/10.3998/mpub.100309.

CSU Writes. (2021). CSU Writes Annual Report. Colorado State University. https://csuwrites.colostate.edu/reports/.

Ede, L. & Lunsford, A. (1983). Why write . . . together? *Writing together: Collaboration in theory and practice.* Bedford/St. Martin's Press.

Ede, L. & Lunsford, A. (1990). *Singular texts/plural authors: Perspectives on collaborative writing.* Southern Illinois University Press.

Guerin, C. (2018). Feedback from journal reviewers: Writing a thesis by publication. In S. Carter & D. Laurs (Eds.), *Developing Research Writing: A Handbook for Supervisors and Advisors* (pp. 137–139). Routledge. https://doi.org/10.4324/9781315541983-25.

Habibie, P. (2022). Writing for scholarly publication in an interconnected disjunctured world. Journal of Second Language Writing, 58, Article 100933. https://doi.org/10.1016/j.jslw.2022.100933.

Jensen, J. (2017). *Write no matter what: Advice for academics*. University of Chicago Press.

Kamler, B. (2008). Rethinking doctoral publication practices: Writing from and beyond the thesis. *Studies in Higher Education, 33*(3), 283–294. https://doi.org/10.1080/03075070802049236.

Kamler, B. & Thomson, P. (2014). *Helping doctoral students write: Pedagogies for supervision*. (2nd Ed.) Routledge. https://doi.org/10.4324/9781315813639.

Kezar, A., Holcombe, E., Vigil, D. & Dizon, J. P. M. (2021). *Shared equity leadership: Making equity everyone's work*. American Council on Education; University of Southern California, Pullias Center for Higher Education.

Kumar, V. & Stracke, E. (2007). An analysis of written feedback on a PhD thesis. *Teaching in Higher Education, 12*(4), 461–470. https://doi.org/10.1080/13562510701415433.

Mirel, B. & Spilka, R. (2002). *Reshaping technical communication: New directions and challenges for the 21st century*. Routledge. https://doi.org/10.4324/9781410603739.

Murray, R. (2014a). *Writing in social spaces: A social processes approach to academic writing*. Routledge. https://doi.org/10.4324/9781315755427.

Murray, R. (2014b). Doctoral students create new spaces to write. *Writing groups for doctoral education and beyond*. Routledge. https://doi.org/10.4324/9781315813639.

Murray, R. (2014c). "It's not a hobby": Reconceptualizing the place of academic work. *Higher Education, 66*(1), 79–91. https://doi.org/10.1007/s10734-012-9591-7.

Sharma, S. (2018). *Writing support for international graduate students*. Routledge. https://doi.org/10.4324/9781351054980.

Sharmini, S. (2017). Supervising a thesis that includes publications In S. Carter & D. Laurs (Eds.), *Developing Research Writing: A Handbook for Supervisors and Advisors*. (pp. 140–143). Routledge. https://doi.org/10.4324/9781315541983-26.

Shvidko, Elena and Dwight Atkinson. 2019. "From Student to Scholar: Making the Leap to Writing for Publication." Novice Writers and Scholarly Publication. edited by Pejman Habibie and Ken Hyland. Cham. 155–175. Switzerland: Palgrave Macmillon. https://doi.org/10.1007/978-3-319-95333-5_1.

Wolfe, J. (2010). *Team writing: A guide to working in groups*. Bedford/St. Martin's Press.

APPENDIX A. MENTORING THROUGH WRITING: GRADUATE STUDENT NEEDS ASSESSMENT SURVEY QUESTIONS

1. What gender category best describes your identity?
2. What ethnicity category best describes your identity?

3. What is your primary field of study?
4. What is your current year in graduate school at CSU?
5. Rate your interest in the following career types: Research and Teaching; Research; Teaching; Private Sector; Non-profit Sector; Business (Likert scale range from "Not interested" to "Very interested").
6. When writing collaboratively, what areas of your writing abilities are most difficult to manage or resolve that you would like to improve, in general? (Open response)
7. What made you pick the areas you listed above (in other words, what aspects of collaborative writing make these areas problematic)? (Open response)
8. With regard to writing, what specific skills would you benefit from learning or reviewing? (Open response)
9. Have you participated in previous writing courses, trainings, or workshops? (Yes/No) Those answered "Yes" to attending trainings in the past were then asked follow-up questions: (Open response)
10. The most effective course, training, or workshop for writing that you have participated in was: (Open response)
11. What made that course/training/workshop effective? (Open response)
12. What, if anything, did you feel was missing from that course/training/workshop? (Open response)
13. Are there specific types of writing you would like the "Collaborative Writing: Mentoring through Writing" workshop to focus on? (Open response)
14. Based on your interest, rate the following topics for the "Collaborative Writing: Mentoring through Writing" workshop: Planning Expectations; Support Expectations Field Specific Writing; English 2nd Language (ELL); Mentor Communication; Responding to Comments; Specific Skills; Confidence Building; Co-Authoring; Resources (Likert scale range from "Not interested" to "Very interested").
15. Which workshop format most interests you?: Lecture; Group Discussions; Practice Sessions. (Likert scale range from "Not interested" to "Very interested").
16. What additional suggestions do you have about "Collaborative Writing: Mentoring through Writing" workshop topics or the workshop in general?

APPENDIX B. MENTORING THROUGH WRITING: FACULTY NEEDS ASSESSMENT SURVEY QUESTIONS

1. What gender category best describes your identity?
2. What ethnicity category best describes your identity?
3. When writing collaboratively, what areas of your writing abilities are most difficult to manage or resolve that you would like to improve, in general? (Open response)
4. What made you list the areas above (in other words, what aspects of collaborative writing make these areas problematic)?
5. With regard to writing, what specific skills would you benefit from learning or reviewing? (Open response)
6. Have you participated in previous writing courses, trainings, or workshops? (Yes/No) Those answered "Yes" to attending trainings in the past were then asked follow-up questions 7, 8, and 9: (Open response)
    a. The most effective course, training, or workshop for writing that you have participated in was: (Open response)
    b. What made that course/training/workshop effective? (Open response)
    c. What, if anything, did you feel was missing from that course/training/workshop? (Open response)
7. Are there specific types of writing you would like the "Collaborative Writing: Mentoring through Writing" workshop to focus on? (Open response)
8. Based on your interest, rate the following topics for the "Collaborative Writing: Mentoring through Writing" workshop: Planning Expectations; Support Expectations Field Specific Writing; English 2nd Language (ELL); Student Communication; Providing Feedback; Editing/Commenting; Specific Skills; Confidence; Co-Authoring; Resources (Likert scale range from "Not interested" to "Very interested").
9. Which workshop format most interests you?: Lecture; Group Discussions; Practice Sessions. (Likert scale range from "Not interested" to "Very interested").
10. What additional suggestions do you have about "Collaborative Writing: Mentoring through Writing" workshop topics or the workshop in general?

APPENDIX C. COLLABORATIVE WRITING: MENTORING THROUGH WRITING WORKSHOP GUIDE TABLE OF CONTENTS (2022 VERSION)

Table of Contents

Letter from Facilitators 3

Acknowledgements 4

Timeline & Process 5

Writing Assignment ✧ 6

Reflecting on Your Professional Writing Experiences ✧ 7-8

Skills Checklist for Competent Scientific Writing (sentence-level) ✧ 9

More about Competency in Scientific Writing 10-11

Feedback Strategies ✧ 12

Communicating About Writing ✧ 13

Collaborative Writing Agreements ✧ 14-16

Tracking Feedback on Your Writing ✧ 17-18

Resources ✧ 19-20

FACULTY MENTOR **GRAD MENTEE**

AFTERWORD.
RESEARCHING AND RESTRUCTURING THE "SCENE(S)" OF FACULTY WRITING

Kristine Blair
Duquesne University

Twenty-five years later, I remember the moment so well. A late Friday afternoon English Department meeting. The manilla envelope I picked up from the mailroom hidden from view under the meeting materials. The anxiety I felt, the rejection I thought was represented with the words "revise and resubmit" in the decision letter from a journal. Though there was a faculty development office on my campus focused on teaching, learning, and technology, there were no faculty writing groups to help me process the editorial commentary. It was an isolating moment for a new faculty member in a new department, not even three years out of graduate school. The panic about the tenure and promotion process clouded my logic to see the potential a revise and resubmit represented, a viewpoint I later encouraged among the doctoral students with whom I worked in a course on scholarly publication I would teach in the years to come. But in that moment, I was isolated and alone, an imposter who didn't belong in the academic club.

The essays within *Faculty Writing Support: Emerging Research from Rhetoric and Composition Studies* document not only the anxieties of academic writing but also the social and material conditions that enable and shape them. Equally important are the contributors' representation of the efforts among faculty developers, academic administrators, and faculty and graduate students to create supportive spaces to develop and sustain scholarly and writerly identities. In an earlier canonical essay, "Modernism and the Scene(s) of Writing" (1987), Linda Brodkey invoked a vision of the "writer" alone in a garret as part of the academic mythos of the solitary toil that contradicts the realities of our social and professional lives as writers and as teachers of writing. Although I was familiar with Brodkey's essay when I sat in that meeting 25 years ago, I had already internalized the institutional pressures to publish. Yet Brodkey wisely "exorcised" the image of the writer as individual genius, a lone literary studies archetype that in no ways aligns with the process-based pedagogical practices of peer response and revision that are the hallmark of the discipline.

DOI: https://doi.org/10.37514/PER-B.2025.2555.3.2

Such an exorcism also extends to how we conduct research about writing, for as Brodkey (1987) asserts:

> Research on composing that isolates individual writers in laboratories and asks them to interact with a text under the observation of a researcher effectively recreates the scene of writing as a thoroughly modern romance: a scientific narrative in which the garret is now a laboratory, the author a subject, the reader a researcher, and reading an analysis of data. (p. 397)

For Brodkey, and for the contributors to this collection, whether we write in a kitchen, a coffeeshop, in a private office, or with a larger group, academic writing is a social process enabled and constrained by material and cultural conditions often ignored by the numerous popular books on the topic. And while literacy technologies have evolved and the writing process has been remediated through digital tools and genres, all too often the culture of the academy is as static and unchanged now as it felt for me then as an early career assistant professor of rhetoric and composition.

The irony within a profession so focused on the socially constituted nature of student writing processes has been the longstanding lack of focus on the presumed to be expert practices of the faculty teaching those students. Just as scholars such as Thomas Kent (1999) advocated a turn from process to post-process, understanding that there is no one way to teach writing, no one set of rules for students' success, and no one context for defining what constitutes good writing, these research-driven essays seek to refocus our attention to faculty processes *in situ*, with methods and methodologies as varied as the spaces in which faculty compose, and with a contemporary understanding of the equally varied positionality and subjectivity of faculty identities. While the academy itself represents a common setting, what diversifies university spaces for these authors is the way in which faculty colleagues, program administrators, and other stakeholders interrogate the working conditions that support faculty writers, understanding the cultural ecologies of academic labor are ones that impact overall research productivity, whether it be a teaching- or research-intensive university. An important model of that space is the writing group, one that dominates numerous chapters in this collection and further attests to the social nature of writing for both novice and expert writers, not to mention the faculty and staff who facilitate these important forums. This model is designed to help writers in impactful, longitudinal ways and counteracts the popular understanding that writing can be mastered and difficulties conquered, evidenced through resources such as *Writing Your Journal Article in 12 Weeks: A Guide to Academic Publishing Success* (Belcher, 2018).

Indeed, for contributors J. Michael Rifenburg and Rebecca Johnston, writing is inherently "a communal art" that fosters reflection about one's own processes and the social influences on both process and product. In their chapter "Leading Faculty Writing Academies: A Case Study of Writerly Identity," they strongly encourage a resistance against neoliberalist structures of marketability and competitiveness to promote "methods to emphasize community and slowing down as a method for supporting faculty writing development but also countering neoliberal impulses that repeatedly shout more, more, more, faster, faster, faster—that seek to pit faculty against faculty." Part of that emphasis on competition, productivity, and speed is tied to extrinsic motivations and anxieties that typically include tenure and promotion for faculty and time to degree and the job search for graduate students. Similarly, research like that found in Jackie Grutsch McKinney's "Faculty as Proximal Writers: Why Faculty Write Near Other Writers" demonstrates the benefits of writing in the presence of others, even when not as formal as a writing group or writing academy. Her findings foreground the sense of motivation, accountability, inspiration, and overall companionship this proximity can foster among writers all too often isolated, an affective response I felt many times throughout my scholarly career. McKinney concludes that "respondents felt insecure about their struggles especially because the struggles of fellow faculty writers were typically invisible to them. Others talked about their mental health and how writing alone activated their anxiety."

Despite these clear challenges, notably for early-career writers, contributors to this collection are careful not to pathologize their participants. Instead, they deploy surveys, interviews, focus groups, and other methods to describe how writerly identities are shaped by factors that impact labor, work-life balance (including child and elder care), privilege, or lack thereof, within academic and cultural structures that are all too often implicitly and explicitly biased on the bases of gender, ethnicity, academic rank, and professional status. Such factors can promote a lack of belonging to that traditional academic club and, as a result, many contributors stress an implicit ethic of care in attending to the needs and differences among writers. To that end, Beth Hewett's "What Professional Writers Want from Writing Coaching" provides a detailed overview of the numerous concerns among the clientele of Defend & Publish, a consulting and coaching company. These go beyond the dissertation, as the company name implies, to include a range of genre transitions and the need for time and project management skills. Hewett concludes that the latter is the largest impediment given the ways work-life balance is a common barrier to maintaining progress. Through these and other chapters, the emphasis on description as opposed to prescription of practices for faculty, faculty developers, and graduate educators is a significant one. Mentors, advisors, peer coaches, and supervisors cannot and should not impose a uniform model of "what works for me will work for you."

Several chapters also focus on the needs of graduate students and the understandable anxiety they face in a far more competitive 21st-century academic job market than past cohorts experienced, tied to the elusive nature of the tenure-track job that those prior cohorts took for granted would be available to them. Citing data on graduate student attrition, Charmian Lam's "Institutional Support for Future Faculty: A Focus on Grant and Professional Materials" connects graduate student success to that sense of belonging to their academic community and the need for mentoring, particularly for historically underrepresented groups. For Lam, knowledge of genre conventions, from grants to articles, doesn't just happen. Instead, it requires a dedicated effort from individual advisors and more structural accountability on the part of institutions to ensure mentoring is consistent within and across programs. Lam's research identifies an important issue related to the static nature of academic genres; while graduate students may develop awareness of article- and book-writing conventions, knowledge of other important genres such as grants or remediation of those genres for external online audiences is far less consistent. Yet securing funding for research through a fellowship proposal or sabbatical application is a standard way to counteract the time constraints that keep faculty at all levels from making progress on their research and resulting writerly identities, which impacts the way they are perceived by disciplinary peers and the way they perceive themselves.

Compounding the genre problem is the reality that with newer technologies of literacy and communication, the modalities in which scholarship is produced, distributed, and consumed have changed (impacting the important role of collaboration), while the definitions of scholarship have remained static in many institutional contexts, reinscribing the privilege of single-authored print books and articles. Just as research processes, including field work and data analysis, often represent invisible labor that impacts the timetable to publication, digital composing contexts are equally invisible. Thus, faculty review committees do not recognize the challenges of creating born-digital texts or migrating existing print content to digital form in ways that move beyond the static *save as .pdf*, as Paul Muhlhauser's and Jenna Sheffield's "Complicating Techno-Afterglow: Pursing Compositional Equity and Making Labor Visible in Digital Scholarly Production" suggests. By documenting the labor of digital composing through interviews with authors, these contributors foreground not only the learning curve and time management challenges but also the difficulties in navigating a culture in which digital, multimodal scholarship is seen as inferior to its print, alphabetic counterpart, often leading to an authorial choice to "resort to print" publishing genres and venues.

Afterword. Researching and Restructuring

When I sat in that meeting with my "revise and resubmit," I couldn't have imagined I would approach the end of my career as a liberal arts dean charged with the ongoing assessment of faculty across the humanities and social sciences. In this role, I can attest to the constant theme of the collection that the academy must acknowledge the impact of workload and work-life balance on the scholarly productivity of its faculty. This is especially true in the aftermath of the COVID-19 pandemic, where course loads have been increased and sabbaticals and other forms of research support are harder to secure. Many chapters consistently make visible the need to provide that support, to use research to assess the success and efficacy of that support, and to acknowledge the intersectionality of the faculty and graduate students with whom they work. As with the research methods we deploy in rhetoric and composition, these efforts must be triangulated at multiple levels through varied types of professional development as we determine the equally varied writing needs of faculty across the disciplines. This process also includes expanding the mission of units such as centers for faculty excellence, which are often more commonly focused on teaching; university writing centers, which can sponsor faculty and graduate student writing groups; and offices of research, which should promote a broader definition of research to move beyond external funding and to provide incentives and rewards for a diverse range of scholarly writing projects.

In addition, graduate schools and university libraries must advocate for multimodal methods and multigenred dissertations that employ the use of audio, video, and other assets so that graduate students, as future faculty, do not "resort to print" as the sole mode of meaning- and knowledge-making in the academy. For faculty across the discipline, this can also include campus digital commons to house and showcase scholarly artifacts. And as academic leaders, our provosts, deans, and chairs must themselves reform incentive and reward structures that enable rather than constrain a more capacious conception of faculty productivity and associated literate practices. These efforts, along with the resources to support them, will undoubtedly benefit the many faculty whose work does not and should not fit into the model Brodkey herself found so limiting in its emphasis on a singular authorial subject known as a writer. For Valerie Lee and Cynthia Selfe (2008), this capaciousness aligns with the compositional equity for which Muhlhauser and Sheffield call. Both administrators and faculty play an important role in revising tenure and promotion guidelines to, as Lee and Selfe advocate, "insist on parity for scholars producing digital media work by removing language that privileged print-based forms over digital forms of scholarship and thus marked digital work unfairly" (p. 57).

Avoiding privilege also mandates recognition that we do not all experience the university in the same way and those concerns about isolation and lack of belonging are heightened for faculty of color, especially as they are expected to mentor students of color in what can easily become an uneven balance of workload that negatively impacts their productivity and retention. Laura Micciche and Batsheva Guy affirm this in their chapter "Writing Support for Faculty of Color," aligning the lack of support to concerns about attrition among diverse faculty, who often persist by going it alone to secure mentoring and other forms of professional support. One way to address these concerns is to involve faculty in this process by not just conducting formalized needs assessments and developing success plans but also viewing them as co-equal creators of the types of programs from which they will benefit, as peer facilitators, mentors, and evaluators of the success of those initiatives. For instance, in stressing the importance of Black women's inclusion in antiracist initiatives, Temptaous Mckoy (2021) argues that "intersectional identity offers the lens to truly see and implement antiracist practices in the humanities and other fields alike." In this way, faculty and administrators are collective agents of change as faculty have more power over the "scene(s) of writing," a process that calls for administrators and faculty to hold themselves accountable for the success and retention of diverse colleagues and create an intersectional scholarly and educational community dedicated to that goal.

Finally, like the researchers in this collection, our larger discipline must develop methods and methodologies for faculty and future faculty needs to be heard and addressed, so that they don't feel as if they must go it alone in what for so many is still an academic club, empowering to some, alienating to others. Overall, the institutional contexts represented in *Faculty Writing Support: Emerging Research from Rhetoric and Composition Studies* powerfully honor Brodkey's call to action for us "to shape and construct and critique their understanding of what it means to write, learn to write, teach writing, and do research on writing" (p. 415). These researchers emphasize, as all good researchers do, those external variables both material and cultural that impact writing processes and products, as well as the overall personal and professional well-being of writers themselves, in the 21st-century academy.

REFERENCES

Belcher, W.L. (2019). *Writing your journal article in 12 weeks: A guide to academic publishing success* (2nd ed.). University of Chicago Press.

Brodkey, L. (1987). Modernism and the scene(s) of writing. *College English, 49*(4), 396–418. https://doi.org/10.2307/377850.

Kent, T. (Ed.) (1999). *Post-process theory: Beyond the writing process paradigm*. Southern Illinois University Press.

Lee, V. & Selfe, C. L. (2008). Our capacious caper: Exposing print-culture bias in departmental tenure documents. *ADE Bulletin, 145*, 51–58. https://doi.org/10.1632/ade.145.51.

Mckoy, T. (2021). Before you check your antiracist practices, check your circle for Black women. In T. Chico (Ed.), *Antiracism in the contemporary university. Los Angeles Review of Books*. https://lareviewofbooks.org/article/antiracism-in-the-contemporary-university-2/#_ftnref6.

CONTRIBUTORS

Rebecca Day Babcock is the William and Ordelle Watts Professor at The University of Texas Permian Basin where she also directs the Office of Undergraduate Research and coordinates first-year writing. Her research focuses on writing centers, disability studies, undergraduate research, and the social nature of writing. Her publications include *Researching the Writing Center*, with Terese Thonus, and *A Synthesis of Qualitative Studies of Writing Center Tutoring, 1983–2006*, with Kellye Manning, Travis Rogers, Amanda McCain, and Courtney Goff. One recent work, *Theories and Methods of Writing Center Studies*, edited with Jo Mackiewicz, won the WAC award for best edited collection.

Kristine Blair is Dean of the McAnulty College and Graduate School of Liberal Arts and Professor of English at Duquesne University. With publications on gender and technology, online learning, graduate education, and electronic portfolios, she completed fourteen years as editor of *Computers and Composition* in 2024. She is a recipient of the Conference on College Composition and Communication's Technology Innovator Award, the Computers and Composition Charles Moran Award for Distinguished Contributions to the Field, and the Lisa Ede Mentoring Award from the Coalition of Feminist Scholars in the History of Rhetoric and Composition.

Dana Lynn Driscoll is Professor at Indiana University of Pennsylvania and the Founding Director of the Center for Scholarly Communication. She specializes in writing transfer, learning theory, expertise studies, and research methodology. Her work has appeared in the *Writing Center Journal, Composition Forum,* and *Written Communication*.

Jackie Grutsch McKinney is Professor of English at Ball State University and currently serves as Director of Immersive Learning and High Impact Practices. She is the author of *Peripheral Visions for Writing Centers, Strategies for Writing Center Research, The Working Lives of New Writing Center Directors*, and co-editor of *Self+Culture+Writing: Autoethnography for/as Writing Studies*.

Batsheva (Sheva) Guy (she/they) is a psychology professor and action researcher specializing in participatory methods, qualitative inquiry, and equity in higher education. She is committed to supporting faculty and students through collaborative scholarship, inclusive pedagogy, and participatory research. She is passionate about writing accountability and cultivates sustainable academic writing practices through mentorship, collective support, and participatory approaches.

Beth L. Hewett is the founder, owner, and past President of Defend & Publish, LLC. She is the author, co-author, or editor of 15 books including *Teaching*

Writing in the 21st Century and *Administering Writing in the 21st Century* (with Tiffany Bourelle and Scott Warnock, MLA, 2022) and the author or co-author of more than 40 articles and book chapters. Her most recent books combine rhetorical principles with grief in faith-based settings (*Grief on the Road to Emmaus*, Liturgical Press, 2023) and with grief for first responders (*Duty, Honor, Hope: Strategies for Understanding and Unpacking First Responder Grief*, ICISF, 2023).

Rebecca Johnston is Associate Director of the Center for Teaching, Learning and Leadership at the University of North Georgia, where she designs and implements faculty development programming and assists in implementing center and institutional initiatives across five regional campuses.

Charmian Lam is Senior Assistant Director of Assessment and Scholarship at University of Chicago's Center for Teaching and Learning. There, she promotes evidence-based teaching practices, supports academic units in program assessment, and engages faculty and instructors in the critical exploration of their pedagogical approaches. Previously, she held administrative positions at Indiana University Bloomington and faculty positions at Virginia Commonwealth University and Brightpoint Community College. Her research interests include equitable assessments, student belonging and inclusion, gamification, writing pedagogy, and how faculty shift their pedagogical practices with evidence of teaching and learning. She earned a PhD in Educational Leadership and Policy Studies from Indiana University Bloomington (IUB).

Kristin Messuri serves as Director of Communication and Language Support at Carnegie Mellon University, where she leads initiatives to enhance academic and professional communication skills and English language learning. Her research examines the intersections of identity and skill development in communication centers and academic writing communities. Her work has appeared in *WPA: Writing Program Administration*; *Gender, Work & Organization*; and the edited collection *Redefining Roles: The Professional, Faculty, and Graduate Consultant's Guide to Writing Centers*.

Laura R. Micciche is Professor of English and area director of the rhetoric and composition graduate program at the University of Cincinnati. She has published over 30 peer-reviewed articles and book chapters, two monographs, and three edited collections on writing-related topics: composing practices, undergraduate and graduate writing pedagogy, and rhetorics of emotion. Most recently, she co-edited *Revising Moves: Writing Stories of (Re)Making* (2024) and is working on a co-authored book project entitled *The Rhetorics of Menopause*.

Paul Muhlhauser is Associate Professor of English at McDaniel College. Zir interdisciplinary research spans digital rhetoric, gender studies, and popular culture, with publications in Humanities, Journal of Popular Culture, and College English. Zir recent work examines posthumanism in food marketing, Gothic elements in media, tenure processes in rhetoric and composition, and digital platform politics.

Kristina Quynn serves as Founding Director of CSU Writes at Colorado State University, where she holds an appointment in the Office of the Vice President for Research. Her research on academic writing support appears in the *Journal of Further and Higher Education* and *About Campus*, where she examines sustainable writing practices for graduate students and faculty. She is also co-author of *Reading and Writing Experimental Texts: Critical Innovations*.

J. Michael Rifenburg serves as Professor of English at the University of North Georgia. He authored *The Embodied Playbook: Writing Practices of Student-Athletes* (Utah State University Press, 2018), *Drilled to Write: Becoming a Cadet Writer at a Senior Military College* (Utah State University Press, 2022), and, with Kristine Johnson, *A Long View of Undergraduate Research: Alumni Perspectives on Inquiry, Belonging, and Vocation* (Routledge/Elon 2024). He is a recipient of the University System of Georgia Regents' Scholarship of Teaching & Learning Award.

Elizabeth Sharp is Professor of Human Development and Family Sciences and former Director of Women's and Gender Studies at Texas Tech University, where she conducts research on gender ideologies and familial relationships. Her work has been featured in *WPA: Writing Program Administration*, *Journal of Family Issues*, and *Journal of Family Theory and Review*.

Jenna Sheffield serves as Interim Associate Vice President for Academic Affairs and Dean of Undergraduate Studies at Salem College. She previously served as Assistant Provost for Curriculum Innovation at the University of New Haven. Her scholarship on digital literacy, networked books, and writing program administration has appeared in *Computers and Composition*, *Computers and Composition Online*, and *Composition Forum*.

Lars Söderlund is a UX Research Analyst and Writer at Baymard Institute, a Denmark-based research company, where he conducts and writes articles about large-scale usability testing of ecommerce sites. Söderlund previously published academic research at Western Oregon University, where his articles on composition and technical writing were published in *College Composition and Commu¬nication*, *IEEE Transactions on Professional Communications*, and the *Journal of Technical Writing and Communication*, informing graduate students, UX profes-sionals, and fellow professors about the mechanics of academic publishing and non-standard models of usability.

Aileen Taft serves in the College of Education and Human Development at the University of Missouri, bringing diverse experience to her educational roles. Specializing in comprehensive literacy, writing, and English studies, she divides her time between consultation work, educator professional growth, and instruction. Beyond the University of Missouri, she also extends her teaching as an adjunct faculty member at the University of Texas Permian Basin.

Christine Tulley is owner of Defend, Publish & Lead, LLC and founder of the Master of Arts in Rhetoric and Writing at The University of Findlay, where she directs faculty writing support initiatives. Her research examines scholarly writing habits, academic time management, and faculty development in *How Writing Faculty Write and Parenting, Professionalism and Productivity*. A frequent *Inside Higher Education* contributor, she provides guidance on academic writ¬ing productivity and career advancement.

Maximillien Vis serves as adjunct faculty at The University of Texas Permian Basin.

Jaclyn Wells is Associate Professor of English and Writing Center Director at the University of Alabama-Birmingham. She has published about writing centers, community literacy, and faculty writing practices in *College Composition and Communication*, the *Writing Center Journal*, and the *Community Literacy Journal*, among other journals and edited collections. With Allen Brizee, she is author of *Partners in Literacy: A Writing Center Model for Civic Engagement* (2016).

Carol Wilusz serves as Professor and Director of the Cell & Molecular Biology Graduate Program at Colorado State University, where she leads a research laboratory.

www.ingramcontent.com/pod-product-compliance
Lightning Source LLC
Chambersburg PA
CBHW060552080526
44585CB00013B/535